my Myanmar years

my Myanmar years

A Diplomat's Account of India's Relations with the Region

Preet Malik

SAGE www.sagepublications.com

Los Angeles • London • New Delhi • Singapore • Washington DC

First published in 2016 by

 SAGE Publications India Pvt Ltd
B1/I-1 Mohan Cooperative Industrial Area
Mathura Road, New Delhi 110 044, India
www.sagepub.in

SAGE Publications Inc
2455 Teller Road
Thousand Oaks, California 91320, USA

SAGE Publications Ltd
1 Oliver's Yard, 55 City Road
London EC1Y 1SP, United Kingdom

SAGE Publications Asia-Pacific Pte Ltd
3 Church Street
#10-04 Samsung Hub
Singapore 049483

Published by Vivek Mehra for SAGE Publications India Pvt Ltd, typeset in 10/13pt Berkeley by Diligent Typesetter, Delhi and printed at Saurabh Printers Pvt Ltd, Greater Noida.

Library of Congress Cataloging-in-Publication Data Available

ISBN: 978-93-515-0627-0 (PB)

The SAGE Team: Rudra Narayan, Guneet Kaur Gulati, Nand Kumar Jha and Vinitha Nair

To my wife and children who have always been supportive and stood by me through times good and difficult.

Thank you for choosing a SAGE product!
If you have any comment, observation or feedback,
I would like to personally hear from you.
Please write to me at **contactceo@sagepub.in**

Vivek Mehra, Managing Director and CEO,
SAGE Publications India Pvt Ltd, New Delhi

Bulk Sales

SAGE India offers special discounts
for purchase of books in bulk.
We also make available special imprints
and excerpts from our books on demand.

For orders and enquiries, write to us at

Marketing Department
SAGE Publications India Pvt Ltd
B1/I-1, Mohan Cooperative Industrial Area
Mathura Road, Post Bag 7
New Delhi 110044, India

E-mail us at **marketing@sagepub.in**

Get to know more about SAGE

Be invited to SAGE events, get on our mailing list.
Write today to **marketing@sagepub.in**

This book is also available as an e-book.

Contents

List of Abbreviations

ACARE	Advance Centre for Agriculture Research and Education
AFPFL	Anti-Fascist People's Freedom League
AIR	All India Radio
ASEAN	Association of Southeast Asian Nations
BBA	British Burman Army
BHEL	Bharat Heavy Electricals Ltd
BIA	Burman Independence Army
BIMSTEC	Bay of Bengal Initiative for Multi-Sectoral, Technical and Economic Cooperation
BSPP	Burma Socialist Programme Party
BTA	Border Trade Agreement
CEP	Cultural Exchange Programme
C-in-C	Commander-in-Chief
COP	Chief of Protocol
CPB	Communist Party of Burma
GCBA	General Council of Burmese Associations
GOB	Government of Burma
GOI	Government of India
GOM	Government of Myanmar
IAI	Initiative for ASEAN Integration
ILO	International Labour Organization
INC	Indian National Congress
IPKF	Indian Peace Keeping Force
ITEC	Indian Technical and Economic Cooperation
JTC	Joint Trading Committee
KIA	Kachin Independence Army
KMT	Kou Min Tang
KNU	Karen National Union

LDC	Least Developed Countries
MEC	Myanmar Economic Corporation
MOU	Memorandum of Understanding
MFO	Myanmar's Foreign Office
MGC	Mekong Ganga Cooperation
MNDAA	Myanmar National Democratic Alliance Army
NCCT	Nationwide Ceasefire Coordination Team
NDSC	National Defence and Security Council
NEC	North-East Command
NLD	National League for Democracy
ONGC	Oil and Natural Gas Corporation Ltd
PIOs	Persons of Indian Origin
PPP	Public Private Partnership
PRC	People's Republic of China
PSU	Public Sector Undertakings
RBI	Reserve Bank of India
RC	Revolutionary Council
SEATO	Southeast Asia Treaty Organization
SLORC	State Law and Order Restoration Council
SNDP	Shan Nationalities Democratic Party
SPDC	State Peace and Development Council
SPV	Special Purpose Vehicle
SSA	Shan State Army
SSA-S	Shan State Army-South
UMEH	Union of Myanmar Economic Holding Ltd
UNFC	United Nationalities Federal Council
UPWC	Union Peacekeeping Work Committee
URN	Uruguay Round Negotiations
USDP	Union Solidarity and Development Party

Foreword

The paucity of writings on our interests in and about relations with Myanmar makes this a timely book, and Ambassador Preet Mohan Singh Malik is eminently qualified to write it by virtue of his knowledge and experience.

He has done justice to the subject.

Myanmar's importance stems from the long land and maritime border it shares with India and the resultant convergence of security interests between neighbours. A relevant backdrop is provided by Myanmar's earlier political ties with British India as also from the deeper cultural affiliations emanating from the spread of Theravada Buddhism.

History records that in recent times the leaders of the freedom movements in our two countries were in close touch with each other. This found an early reflection in the 1951 Treaty of Friendship.

The geographic location of Myanmar makes it an important component of India's Act East Policy. Provision of connectivity to the region is one aspect of it; equally relevant is the enormous potential of mutually beneficial economic co-operation. While Myanmar can be a source of energy and material sources for us, India's burgeoning markets provide an easy outlet for Myanmar's produce, especially agricultural products. We have the capacity, and are increasingly developing to become a provider of industrial wherewithal, technology and investments.

India and Myanmar can thus usher in a new era of co-prosperity in the region. More than ever before, therefore, we need to understand better the dynamics of change now underway in Myanmar.

I am confident that this book will contribute meaningfully to this endeavour.

M. Hamid Ansari
Vice President of India

Preface

This book on Burma/Myanmar has been a long time in the making. It was originally written as a detailed discussion paper, subsequently developed as a monograph and later expanded into a book. On several occasions it had to be updated as it has taken almost four years in coming to its publication. It has been restructured with the hope that its content and reflections on the different periods of Indian influence and involvement shall be of interest to the reading public and experts at large.

The thoughts that lie behind the renderings in the book have been inspired by a number of events that were Burma-centric in design that led to its being written. Early in life it was the stories both positive and negative on the life led by the ordinary Indians who lived in colonial Burma that left a deep impression. There were the writings of Sarat Chandra Chattopadhya that also contributed to this early fascination with Burma. To this were to be added the works of George Orwell and Somerset Maugham that covered their experiences of life in colonial Burma.

The spread of Buddhism and cultural influence from India to Burma and the linkages including architectural systems of the Kalinga period, the maritime and trade linkages with the land known historically as Suvarna Bhoomi were other connections with India that acted as an inspiration.

The other important historical associations arose out of the adoption of the *Manusmriti* and its linkage to the monarchical practices and governance, the adoption of the Pali script and the linguistic influences from India that led to the evolution of common experiences between the people of the two countries. The colonial period savagely interrupted this positive element that had kept the two countries culturally close to each other.

The colonial period created conditions that negated the natural process of kinship that should have prevailed between the people of the two countries. The imposition of Indian migrants and low- to mid-level Indian officials, who were favoured to help administer and govern the country, brought the Indian and the dominant Burman majority into conditions of conflict and distrust. The Indian community in Burma came to be openly discriminated against and the Burmese treated the thousands of Indians fleeing the Japanese occupation, with savage brutality. The return of the Indians after the Japanese defeat and the return of the British colonial authority only came to consolidate the feeling that the Indian migrant community was part and parcel of the colonial domination of the state and the economy of Burma. The fact that the persons of Indian origin (PIOs) had a controlling interest in the commercial, business, real estate and the main areas of the agricultural economy of Burma created rifts between the Burmese and the PIO and helped consolidate this feeling of distrust and enmity of the Burmese. The PIO were seen as not only the beneficiaries of the colonial occupation of Burma, but also as the ones who sought and were provided support and security by the British, this only helped add to the rift, which was also furthered by the fact that the Indians were an important part of the security apparatus of the colonial administration.

In contrast, the Indian National Movement, the Indian Communist Party and leaders like Nehru, M.N. Roy and Gandhi had a positive impact on relations with their counterparts in Burma and there came to exist a degree of co-operation between the two sides that was reflected in their attitude to the Simon Commission.

In the post-independence period, Indo-Myanmar relations began on a note of intimate association particularly at the top leadership levels. Nehru and Aung San developed a close understanding and were on the same page reflecting a commonality of thinking on the defining role that they felt a resurgent Asia would come to play in shaping the new global order in the post-World War II era. The Nehru–U Nu period continued to reflect an understanding furthered by non-alignment, as a foreign policy tool that both countries were comfortable with. The differences of both countries with China intensified this relationship primarily as China continued to interfere in the internal affairs of both countries.

The relations however saw a considerable deterioration with the coming to power, through a coup, by General Ne Win with the isolationist and negative economic policies that he came to adopt leading to the nationalisation of the economy that drove out the Indian business community. These factors acted as barriers to a closer relationship.

However the threat to the sovereignty and security that China posed to both countries did result in a degree of collaborative policy approaches at the top leadership levels of Burma and India reflected in the relations between Ne Win and Indira Gandhi.

A very important area of co-operation, between the two countries, was in the area of security covering the adjoining border areas, of the two countries, to help contain insurgency. What was evident to both sides was that China was seriously involved both against India and Burma providing training and material assistance to Indian insurgents of the North-East and the J&K states of India as well as in exploiting the differences between the ethnic minorities and Rangoon. Till 1988, China was involved directly in supporting the insurgency situation within Burma led by the Communist Party of Burma (CPB) and ethnic groups in the Shan State and Kachin State areas of Burma. China's role in Burma/Myanmar only changed when Beijing came close to Myanmar in the post-1988 period and pulled it into the Chinese sphere of influence.

The book reflects the positives and the negatives of the relations between our two countries. The regional aspects of the relations and the presence and actions of China are part of the analysis. Analysis of the bilateral relations clearly indicates that despite the fact of the two countries sharing a close history of cultural, linguistic, religious, historical perceptions and political experiences, there were major gaps in the relations, largely as no institutional underpinnings were in place that would have granted quantitative and qualitative substance to the relations.

The economic relations that to an extent could have served as the foundation for a close and substantive relationship, however, were negated by the land reforms that U Nu carried out and the socialist economy that Ne Win introduced nationalising the economy. These policy actions effectively drove out the Indian landed and business communities from Burma without compensation and without any compensatory benefits to the relations of the two neighbouring countries.

The post-1988 developments in Myanmar that ensured that the pro-democracy movement would be strangulated and contained created a severe hiatus in the relationship with a break down in contact at all important levels with India. The fact that India itself was undergoing a strong political upheaval with weak coalition governments at the Centre also contributed to this break down. It was only under Prime Minister Narasimha Rao that a review of the relationship took a fresh look at where the relations were headed resulting in the recognition that whatever India's ideological position in favour of democracy, the realities on the ground had to be factored in. This led to the gradual resumption of relations. The book takes a look at the developments during the period 1988–2010 when the military in uniform was in the saddle in Yangon and Myanmar and remained largely isolated from the globalised world. China took full advantage of the opportunities created by the negative position adopted by the USA and the EU against the military regime.

With Myanmar within the Chinese area of influence, an expanding Association of Southeast Asian Nations (ASEAN) became the logical regional arrangement that Myanmar could comfortably join. This way it also kept away from a South Asia dominated by India that adopted a very negative public position critical of the State Law and Order Restoration Council (SLORC) and its nullifying the results of the 1990 elections that were overwhelmingly in favour of the National League for Democracy (NLD), which resulted in the continuation of the authoritarian regime in Burma.

During the period 1988–1991 India adopted a position of support for democracy and the closing down of all contacts covering not only political relations but all bilateral relations including the coverage of India's Indian Technical and Economic Cooperation (ITEC) programme and the banking system that was essential for the continuation of commercial relations.

The book deals with the gradual resumption of a full relationship that followed, also taking into account that Myanmar and the military that governed it should have an alternative shoulder to rest its head on thus assisting the SLORC/State Peace and Development Council (SPDC) to move away, to the extent feasible, from its overwhelming dependence on China. The bilateral relationship got a boost out of commitments made by India at the top leadership levels that brought into play an expanding involvement of India, in the structuring of infrastructural projects backed by financial assistance and grants, covering the vital areas of railways and roads in Myanmar. There was also a grant-backed involvement in institution building that had a socio-economic base to it and furthermore there was a commitment of Indian assistance to the Border Area Development Programme of Myanmar.

The book also deals with the major internal political developments in Myanmar, covering constitution-making in Burma/Myanmar ending in an analysis of the present-day-Constitution of 2008, its controversial nature emanating from the formal space it has granted to the Myanmar armed forces to continue to dominate the governance in that country aimed at preventing any possibility of a civilian leader coming to power. The other issue of great concern revolves around the resolution of the problems afflicting the security and integrity of the country arising out of the long-standing political differences with the ethnic groups. The problem revolves around the demands of the ethnic states that Myanmar as a truly Federal Union should grant full autonomy to the ethnic states and territories, in keeping with the letter and spirit of the Panglong Agreement. To an extent the 1947 Constitution had accepted the basic principles that constituted the essence of the Panglong Agreement, including the right to secede. This was completely negated by the coup carried out by Ne Win and the adoption of the 1974 Constitution that effectively brought about a totalitarian system of one-party-rule and the nationalisation of the economy isolating Burma almost completely from the outside world.

The 2008 Constitution, as presently formulated, pays lip service to the federal system and does not grant the autonomy that has remained a constant demand of the ethnic groups. It shall require a systemic overhaul of the Constitution to grant the ethnic groups and the forces of democracy the rights that would make Myanmar a secure and integrated state that is responsive to the popular demands of the people of the country.

The book while covering the issues arising out of the demands of the ethnic minorities, and the forces of democracy also deals with the current state of play that has arisen out of the political and economic reforms that have been undertaken by President Thein Sein with the backing of the moderate group within the armed forces. It also analyses the relations with China, and the extent to which the current state of play has an impact upon the relations with China. It covers the positive impact of the adoption of political, economic and the attempts at national reconciliation, on the West, with the accompanying return of Myanmar to the global community, resulting in the moderation of the place and influence of China on that country. This constitutes an important aspect of strategic and security aspects of Myanmar to the neighbourhood, the region and the global community that today has to look closely at the direction that China is advancing along and the place that Myanmar occupies in its fulfilment.

Myanmar is of great importance to China in its strategy to establish alternative supply routes to the Malacca and the Sunda Straits for its energy supplies. The establishment of routes through Myanmar will help China access its landlocked and relatively backward states of Szechwan and Yunnan and the outside world. The outlet that Myanmar serves to grant China will help it in its desire to establish a strategic oversight over the Bay of Bengal and as part of the Strings of Pearl strategy to establish Chinese presence in the Indian Ocean.

For India Myanmar is important both in strategic and security terms and the need for India to remain closely involved with Myanmar are analysed in this book covering also the different aspects of the relations between the two countries and Myanmar's vital position in India's Look East or as enunciated now 'The Act East Policy'. Considering the importance of Myanmar to India in major strategic and security areas it is surprising that the dynamism that Prime Minister Modi has brought to the reorientation of Indian Foreign Policy seems so far to have left out Myanmar. The security issue has come to the forefront with the action of insurgents based in the adjoining areas of Myanmar in Manipur and the consequent counter terrorism actions undertaken by India's Special Forces within Myanmar, which only goes to emphasise the importance of that country and the need to have close and co-operative relations with Naypidaw. A substantive bilateral relationship based on a visit by Modi and the undertaking of commitments that are not held hostage to the machinations of the entrenched Finance Ministry bureaucracy is awaiting a Modi initiative.

1
Introduction

Indian foreign policy has, to a large extent, been personality driven and has had an individualistic tone to it. Post-independence, Prime Minister Jawahar Lal Nehru's overwhelming presence determined the direction of the nation's foreign policy. Nehru was understandably influenced by his overall background, including the profound influence that his life and education in England had on him. He had a wide sweeping outlook on what were India's interests and the leadership role that it could play in a world order, which was then being increasingly influenced by the Cold War, as also by the emergence of newly independent countries which, like India, had succeeded in throwing off the colonial yoke. Given this scenario, the ideal of non-alignment was a natural outcome of Nehru's attempt to flesh out the policy approach to safeguard India's national self-interest. In an interview, reported in the *New York Times* on 1 September 1946, Nehru spelt out the direction that Indian foreign policy would take when he said 'that India would develop an active concern in world affairs, pursuing an independent policy compatible with her own national interest'. He initially held out the hope of 'closer ties among Asian countries' with India developing an 'uncommitted and influential stand on international affairs'.

One clear aim of India's foreign policy has been to achieve a strategically secure neighbourhood where peace, stability and the positive aspects of human endeavour would create harmonious and co-operative political and social relations. This has obviously not been achieved, as is evident from the fact that, with a number of India's South Asian neighbours there are differences that often lead to a negative environment of tension and discord. The presence and involvement of China with

India's neighbours has been a contributing factor to the prevailing uneasy relationships that India has had not only with Pakistan which is its 'all weather friend', but also with Nepal and, to a great extent with Sri Lanka and Myanmar.

Nehru was, moreover, a creature of the early twentieth century environment and personality-driven relations were part of his foreign policy make-up. Burma was no exception. He developed a personal relationship with Aung San and subsequently with U Nu, with whom he came to develop a kind of kinship. It was also because of this approach that he did not have any sympathy for Ne Win, whom he considered a dictator upstart.

Indira Gandhi tended to follow her father's approach where Burma was concerned, but with the difference that she was inclined to apply the principals of real politic; she realised that Ne Win could be an ally in India's concerns over the People's Republic of China (PRC). A striking feature of this foreign policy approach was that relations with the neighbouring countries were influenced to a large extent by the depth of the relations with the leaders at the personal level and by the domestic constituencies in India that were emotionally involved with the countries concerned.

What is important in the Burmese context is that it posed no threat to India's domestic political space, unlike the domestic constituencies that governed relations with Nepal and Sri Lanka or the existentialist threat Pakistan posed and continues to pose to India's peaceful existence. The ties with Burma were also guided by the problems of insurgency that afflicted India's North-East exacerbated by China extending material support to the Indian insurgents who were utilising the geographical space of Burma as a safe base of operations. This geographical space within Burma remains of tactical importance for the Indian insurgency groups as it enabled easy logistical and communication linkages, for these groups, with the PRC. It is also a fact that China remains both directly and through its allied ethnic groups in Myanmar, the Wa and the Kokang a major supplier of arms and ammunition to Indian insurgent groups that have found shelter in what are the Naga dominated areas within Myanmar adjacent to the borders with India.

One aspect of Indian foreign policy that needs to be stressed is the individualistic nature of its implementation, which arose from the fact that diplomatic activity in India has 'remained issue-specific and event specific'.[1] Diplomatic practice in India was not an 'institutional and continuous phenomenon',[2] and this continues even today. It accounts to a great extent for the manner in which India's approach to many countries is largely determined by the level of prevailing interest in that country or the issues involved that arise out of a complex of political, strategic, security and historical factors that bear on the relationship and, to an extent, the influence that the individual heads of mission can exercise— all of which in combination determine, to a fair extent, Delhi's approach to the country concerned.

The anecdotal approach that appears to cover the period during which I was directly involved with Myanmar is basically aimed at putting in perspective the nature and direction in which India's relations, particularly with the post-1988 Myanmar were moving.

Keeping in mind that India, as a functioning democracy, would have a natural inclination to support democratic movements and extend support to democratic governments, particularly in its immediate neighbourhood; this factor has played an important role in fashioning India's approach to its neighbouring countries in South and Southeast Asia. Understandably, relations with Burma/Myanmar have been closer in the periods when it has been governed by democratic governments and there has been a time lapse in adjusting to the military takeovers. However, this has not meant that in due course there has not been a course correction in keeping with the compulsions and dynamics that drive relations with a neighbouring country.

Additionally, China's South Asian policies continue to raise strategic concern for India, given that Myanmar forms part of the PRC's strategy for the region which is driven by China's desire to 'contain' India within South Asia; this obviously does influence the manner in which India has conducted its relations with Myanmar. Nevertheless, it would be incorrect to assume that India's strategic concerns do not have content that are natural to the geographic and long-term interests of India which both include and go beyond the China factor.

[1] J.N. Dixit, *Indian Foreign Service: History and Challenge*, Chapter 1, 3.
[2] Dixit, *Indian Foreign Service*, 3.

2
A Rough Landing: 1990

It was towards the end of August 1990 that we (my family and I) were on a Thai Airways flight from Bangkok to Yangon, the renamed capital of a renamed country, Myanmar. We had earlier that morning left Kuala Lumpur after an eventful and fulfilling four-year stint where I had served as India's High Commissioner to Malaysia and Brunei. We had managed to catch the connecting flight to Yangon by the skin of our teeth. Now we were coming in to land through heavy monsoon clouds over Myanmar and had started to see some small white Buddhist chapels among large swathes of water, stream and river courses with extensive stretches of rice paddies. The approach to the runway was clearly visible. The landing gear was down and we were about to touch down when the pilot suddenly pulled the aircraft up into a steep climb. Soon, the landing gear was up and we were making a sharp turn to the right as we continued to climb; finally, the pilot announced that he had been forced into this manoeuvre because of the sudden descent of an electric storm over the airport and, given the lack of sophisticated aviation equipment at the Yangon airport, it would have been dangerous to land.

In the meanwhile those of us occupying the window seats were catching a glimpse of the notorious Insein jail which had amongst its usual criminal inmates a large number of political prisoners, mainly from the NLD, a party which had been incarcerated to negate the possibility of a democratic government outside the control of the military being formed, thereby dealing yet another blow to the desire of the people to restore democracy in Myanmar. It also housed within its walls a large number of Burmese youth who had courageously taken up the mantle of opposing the authoritarian military rule.

Students and student bodies have always played an important role in participative politics of Myanmar, starting from the struggle for freedom from the colonial rule and thereafter the struggle for freedom from the oppressive rule of the military. The military has been equally persistent in trying to curb these uprisings. Whenever the youth of Burma/Myanmar have raised their voices, educational institutions have been shut down in utter disregard of the harm this does to the future of the country. In fact, it has been a part of the military's tactics to ensure that an atmosphere of pervasive fear prevails among the people of Myanmar—an atmosphere of fear furthered by a combination of tactics that comprised kidnappings, forced labour, the dispossession of property/land (to meet the military's requirements or priorities that included the laying of golf courses) and the suppression through ruthless action of any attempt to question or oppose the military regime in power. My readings of doings in Burma in preparation for my posting there as India's ambassador had given me an insight into what had been happening there since the takeover by Ne Win and after the SLORC in 1988.

The aborted landing seemed to portend the difficult and somewhat unrewarding time that lay ahead, reflecting the hiatus that had come to characterise the current state of relations between the two neighbouring countries. In effect, since the events of 1988 and the refusal by the SLORC to handover power to the elected representatives of the people, India had reduced the bilateral relations to one of minimal contact. I had, all the same, managed to secure some leeway in the manner in which I could conduct our affairs, keeping in mind that we had to live with the conditions on the ground. The Vishwanath Pratap Singh government in New Delhi was set in the mode of negative thinking on relations with a country with whom India had extensive land and maritime frontiers and with whom India needed to have co-operative relations to help mitigate the problems created by the insurgent groups from North-East India who were utilising the adjoining areas in Myanmar to take shelter and originate operations against the Indian administration.

I was to take over as India's Ambassador after a gap of one year after the departure, on retirement, of my predecessor, at the end of July 1989, and my arrival at the end of August 1990. The period since the events of 1988 had seen the relations between the two neighbouring countries deteriorate to a point where, for all practical purposes, there was only a nominal relationship between the two countries.

The Indian Parliament had taken a stiff stand in its resolutions condemning the military's brutal actions against public demonstrations, calling for an end to the stifling rule imposed since 1962 by the Myanmar armed forces and the killing spree that was indulged in by the SLORC that had caused the death of innumerable students, monks and civilian demonstrators. Among these demonstrators were some of the braver bureaucrats, including several middle and high ranking officials of the Foreign Office who were subsequently removed from office.

The All India Radio's (AIR) Burmese language broadcasts were carrying out an unrestrained campaign against the SLORC and a largely personalised attack against Ne Win, who continued to be the revered mentor of the army hierarchy. The military was once again under the direct control of the country and continued to brutalise the people, displaying a naked and unrestrained ruthlessness in decimating all opposition. (It was only much later, after General Than Shwe had consolidated his position and Khin Nyunt had been sidelined, that Ne Win was dethroned from the position as the mentor.)

The criticism by the Indian Parliament gained in intensity over the refusal of the SLORC to honour its commitment to handover power to an elected government. The NLD had won the election with an overwhelming majority and a shocked SLORC decided that it would not accept the verdict on the premise that the people of Myanmar were 'stupid' enough not to know what was in their best interests. It was also not lost on the Indian establishment that the SLORC was getting close to the PRC, which was certainly no respecter of democratic norms.

Given these circumstances and the contrast that the policies of India and China represented in their attitude to the events in Myanmar since 1988, the SLORC took the position that India posed a threat to the kind of military controlled stability that it wanted to bring about in post-1988 Myanmar.

The fact that there had been no ambassador for a year was seen by some as a reflection of India's adversarial position on Myanmar. Little did they realise that it was not a position dictated by policy that had stood in the way of appointing an ambassador; it was merely that the Government of India (GOI) had not found itself able to select a person who would not wriggle out of a very uncomfortable position of ambassadorship that Indo-Myanmar relations represented. In fact, the then GOI, particularly the then Minister for External Affairs I.K. Gujral had come to the conclusion that they would have to look at the ranks of politicians (instead of a diplomat) to fill the post. In spite of this somehow, my name had cropped up and, when Gujral had me rung up to seek my confirmation, I said yes and soon I was nominated to take over as India's Ambassador.

A Cold Reception

The drama that had attended our landing seemed to dog us. We were welcomed by the Head of the South Asia desk at Myanmar's Foreign Office (MFO) on arrival at the Yangon International Airport. He seemed genuinely pleased that at last an Indian Ambassador was in place. In fact the impression of goodwill he generated remained with us throughout our stay. He was not overly in awe of his military masters. He mentioned that it had been arranged for me to call on the Chief of Protocol (COP) the very next day. The COP would brief me on the dates for the presentation of my credentials as well as on the ceremony itself. The COP was an army officer and very obviously from the military intelligence. He informed me that I would be presenting my credentials that week on Thursday. This was in keeping with the courtesy normally extended to envoys from neighbouring countries and I got ready to present my credentials and to suggest in the presentation to be made on that occasion that we looked forward to a friendly relationship that reflected the rich historical, civilisational and cultural contact between our two neighbouring countries.

Next was my first call on the Deputy Minister for Foreign Affairs, Ohn Gyaw, himself a veteran diplomat. There was no foreign minister and the effective control over foreign affairs was exercised by Khin Nyunt, who was designated as Secretary I of the SLORC, who was also head of the military intelligence. (Khin Nyunt was the effective number two in the SLORC and was regarded to be close to Ne Win. Despite the knowledge that it was Khin Nyunt who would be calling the shots as far as the relations with India were concerned I was debarred by my instructions to have any direct dealings with him; these were the instructions that were conveyed to me by External Affairs Minister I.K. Gujral and confirmed by Prime Minister V.P. Singh.

Ohn Gyaw was welcoming and confirmed that I would be presenting my credentials on the Thursday of that week. After that, there followed a deep silence and that Thursday went by without any mention of the presentation of credentials.

Incredibly, I was informed by the Ambassador of the Philippines, whom we knew from the time she had been the ambassador to India, that I should not expect to present credentials before China's Ambassador[1] had returned from his consultations-cum-vacation in China a month later. She was right. I was given a date only after he had returned.

I called on the Chinese Ambassador before I had presented my credentials or even provided with a date when that would happen. Just to test the waters, we discussed in detail the issues arising out of the 1990 elections and the refusal of the SLORC to meet its commitment to transfer power, including the Indian and international reaction to that failing. He was polite, but quite firm, making it clear that it was Beijing's decision not to intervene or put any pressure on the SLORC to bring in the promised democratic system of government, adding that there was a continuing threat to the integrity of the country that was posed by the ethnic insurgencies and that his country was involved in strengthening the hands of Yangon to defeat the insurgents.

Obviously, he conveyed the gist of our conversation to Khin Nyunt, whom he met the day after our meeting. Some days went by, but no date had yet been set for the presentation of credentials. It was no surprise that just an hour after the SLORC had heard my telephone conversation with Delhi—pregnant with the suggestion that since the SLORC did not seem interested in the presence of an Indian Ambassador I should be permitted to return to Delhi—that I received a call from the COP saying that I was to present my credentials that very week. Apologising for the delay, he explained the Senior General (Saw Maung) had been very busy.

What this reflected was the state to which the bilateral relations had lapsed, where India was seen by the SLORC as having joined hands with

---

[1] Comment: The Chinese Ambassador interestingly on completion of his posting to Yangon was sent to Delhi as his country's Ambassador and we remained in touch till I retired in February 1995.

the perfidious West and as such a threat to the military imposed stability in Myanmar as India continued to raise its voice for democratic
governance in Yangon recalling the SLORC's commitment in this case—
an assurance that the SLORC had no intentions of fulfilling. Ironically,
China, with whom the Myanmar Government had for long had a difficult relationship, arising out of the fact that China had supported the
CPB, both politically and materially, inclusive of the support that it was
rendering in that connection to the ethnic groups that were allied with
the CPB and the manner in which it had continued to pressurise the Ne
Win government from 1962 to 1988, was now seen as a saviour who
was now extending unquestioning support to the authoritarian SLORC
regime and helping it to meet both international pressure and a solution
to the ethnic insurgencies.

One other element that reflected the degree to which the relations
with India had deteriorated was the close and overt surveillance to which
people from the Indian Embassy including, of course, the ambassador
were subjected. In reality surveillance of Indian embassy personnel in
neighbouring countries is only to be expected but this surveillance is
normally covert except in the case of Pakistan. Burma/Myanmar had in
the past been very circumspect where its surveillance of Indian personnel was concerned but now it considered us as an opponent who posed
a threat and intended to prevent normal functioning including restrict-
ing our visits to parts of the country outside the Yangon–Pegu area. For
instance I never got permission to visit Mandalay. The permission was
never denied but always delayed to ensure that the dates on which I
wanted to travel to the city did not take place. In contrast we could
always get immediate permission to travel to Pagan and other areas of
cultural or civilisational interest. What was worse was the behaviour
towards the few Burmese who came to meet us. They were pulled in
for questioning outside our embassy and subjected to interrogation that
could at times be brutal and there was little restraint shown in this regard
for the entire period of our stay.[2]

It was, perhaps, towards the last few months of our stay in Yangon
that the SLORC softened its attitude to a marginal degree, when it came

---

[2] Comment: As the relations have now progressed, this type of surveillance has disappeared and the jaundiced eye with which all contact was viewed is no longer in evidence,
nor is it difficult for the ambassador and his staff to move around Myanmar.

to realise that my role had been to try and soften India's attitude; this was acknowledged by Ohn Kyaw in one of our last meetings before I informed him that I would be leaving. He mentioned that he and his boss Khin Nyunt understood that I had helped to place the relations in a format where both sides could proceed to rebuild the relations between the two countries. He acknowledged that they had taken time to understand the process that had been set in motion and appreciated that we were now set on a course which, given time, would restore substance to the relations.

Taking all factors into account, I felt that it was essential first of all to understand the status of the bilateral ties and to arrive at an understanding as to what, if any, were the driving triggers of the relations which for all practical purposes appeared not to have any institutional underpinnings (Annexure I which presents extracts from Annual Reports of the Ministry of External Affairs that reflect the official views of the GOI on developments in Myanmar).

Here were two neighbours who had age-old relations that had social, civilisational, cultural, religious, linguistic content, as well as a closely shared colonial past, but still seemed to be lacking in any real bond that would serve as a buffer during the difficult times of their relationship.

3
Let's Go to History First

A shared historical heritage is a strong civilisational link between the two countries, but it has to be acknowledged that this has not always acted as a facilitator to the post-independence relations between the two countries. Myanmar had been a monarchy till the British colonial masters decided to do away with the system. In fact, as a result of British actions Burma for the first and the only time in its history became a part of India and remained so till 1937. This appears to have impacted the Burmese people's attitude towards India and Indians.

Before discussing this aspect further, it would be worth looking at the impact that the Indian approach to kingship had on the monarchical system in old Burma, which were based on the ancient Indian Code of Manu, as also on whether that impact in any sense continues to sub-consciously govern the autocratic nature of the military leadership that prevailed in Myanmar between 1962 and 2010 in an absolute sense and in a more moderate form from the installation of the Thein Sein headed nominally civilian elected government from 2011 onwards. Ne Win and after him Saw Maung and subsequently Than Shwe cast themselves in the role of autocratic rulers whose word was law and could not be questioned.

To clarify matters and to point out the extent of the influence of Indian practices it is worth mentioning that the influence of Indian monarchical practice was evident not only in Burma but, in the form of Hindu and Buddhist practices, widely spread over Southeast Asia. As Heesterman in the chapter 'The "Hindu Frontier"' in the book *India and Indonesia*[1] points out,

[1] J.C. Heesterman, 'The "Hindu Frontier"', in *India and Indonesia*, ed. J.C.Heesterman et al. (University of Leyden, 1989), 1–16.

Hindu Brahmin priests, Buddhist monks, architects, scribes, artisans and perhaps even some warriors from South Asia found outlets for their skills... from Burma to Southern Vietnam. They introduced new ideas and practices which were readily adopted....Various South Asian scripts were adopted for use in Royal Courts; Hindu and Buddhist religious symbolism was used to surround local rulers with more ritual and sanctity...

The trappings of royal power, where the monarch was all powerful and his 'will' irrefutable arose from the belief that the king was a direct descendant of Manu. The *Manusmriti*, as the Code was called, covered all aspects of kingship and the principles of government.[2] The Code had been translated into Burmese and continued to influence the form and manner in which the ruler exercised his powers. What is significant is that the King's authority in old Burma depended also on 'the physical sanctions of political despotism and military predominance'.[3] It was at the same time noted that 'unless a person was prepared to risk being classed as a traitorous rebel, no Burman dared question the theoretical right of the divine monarch to control the lives, the property, and the personal services of his subjects'.[4]

This was the very essence of the attitude that appeared to govern the authoritarian system that was in place since the takeover of the country, by Ne Win, in 1962. However it has to be acknowledged that the Thein Sein government which today rules the country under the cover of the Myanmar Constitution of 2008, has diluted the authoritarian system to an extent and there is a semblance of democratic rule that has a more moderate face that is in form and intent far removed from the Ne Win, the SLORC and the SPDC periods.

It is worth mentioning at this stage itself that scholars have concluded that nationalism after independence was driven by the desire to expunge Myanmar of its colonial heritage. This was also seen as the key motivating factor that lay behind Ne Win's opposition to the re-establishment of participative democracy after his coup, as also his dictum that 'foreign influence must be kept out with force and violence'.[5] Both Ne Win and the SLORC/SPDC 'sought to keep Burmese traditions

[2] Maung Maung, *Burma in the Family of Nations* (Djambatan, 1956), 13–15.
[3] John Cady, *A History of Modern Burma* (Cornel University Press, 1958), 9.
[4] Ma May Sein, *Administration of Burma* (Rangoon, 1938), 18.
[5] Michael Gravers, *Nationalism as Political Paranoia in Burma* (Curzon, 1999).

within what could be called a modern version of the traditional autocratic political structure'.[6]

Before we proceed further, it may be useful to mention that the spread
of India's mores of civilisation were the consequence of the development
of religio-monarchical practices born of the evolution of strong linkages
that grew out of a thriving maritime trade. While Indian ships carried
trade to the West of the Indian subcontinent via the Middle East, particularly the Gulf and the Red Sea into the Mediterranean, it was the region
comprising the eastern half of the Indian Ocean 'centred upon the Bay of
Bengal'[7] that became the 'exclusive domain' of the merchants and mariners
of India, developing linkages to the whole of Southeast Asia. 'The eastward
movements of South Asian merchants and mariners were marked by the
dispersion of South Asian culture and religion into South East Asia.'[8] By
the beginning of the era under discussion, Hindu and Buddhist merchants
were becoming increasingly familiar figures from the 'Irrawaddy valley in
Burma and the Straits of Melaka to the shores of Vietnam'.[9]

The Hindu Period

To better understand the Indian civilisational, religious, linguistic and
cultural influence on Myanmar, it is necessary to refer to the funda-
mentals of the Burmese Buddhist Chronicles, as they continue to have a
strong influence on the thought and behaviour patterns of the Myanmar
(Burman) people even today. The chronicles relate stories that are 'copies
of Indian legends taken from (the) Sanskrit and Pali original'.[10] Burma
in Indian texts was referred to as 'Suvarna Bhumi'[11] or the Golden Land,
where Buddhist scriptures and the Pali script prevailed, endorsing the
omnipresent presence of Indian culture in that land.

Moreover, the Indian influence pre-dates the Buddhist period, given
that the Pyu people, the earliest settlers in Burma, were Vishnu worshippers

---

[6] Gravers, *Nationalism*.
[7] Kenneth McPherson, *The Indian Ocean*, (Oxford, 1998), 17.
[8] McPherson, 'Early Maritime Trade of the Indian Ocean', *Indian Ocean*, 17.
[9] McPherson, *Indian Ocean*, 72.
[10] D.G.E. Hall, *Burma* (Hutchinson University Library, 1950).
[11] Third Buddhist Council at Pataliputra 241 BC.

and the Pyu city of Ksetra (Old Prome) which was the capital city of the Pyu Kingdom showed traces of Vishnu Temples as well as links to the Brahmi script that was linked to the Maurya and Gupta period in India. Interestingly the first major Pyu city was named Beikthano (200 BCE to 100 BCE) that is the oldest site excavated and was named after the Hindu God Vishnu. Ksetra was located on the Irrawaddy River and served as an important entrepot for the trade between Chinese and Indian kingdoms. The links of the Pyu people with India was linked to trade with India and this influenced religion, language and script, culture and architecture that prevailed in the Pyu city states. Further, there is evidence that both forms of Buddhism (Mahayana and Hinayana) were practised here as the successor religions to Hinduism and animism.

The Pyu Kingdom was destroyed in the ninth century CE around 809 CE by the Tai Kingdom of Nanchao, which was in occupation of the west and north-west of Yunnan. The Pyu disappeared as a separate people without a trace, gradually merging with the Burman people and the Pagan Kingdom.[12]

The Mon people, who are to be found both in Myanmar and in Thailand, are generally known as the Taliang people by the Burmans. They were greatly influenced by Indian culture, followed the Hinayana form of Buddhism, and adhered to the Pali language and alphabet, which is the origin of the written form of the Burmese and the Thai languages.

The Pagan Kingdom (originally known as Arimaddanpura-clea)[13] built the striking Pagodas, among which the most famous monument is the Ananda. These monuments were designed and structured by architect monks from India's modern day state of Odisha and reflect the building and design skills of the Kalinga Empire. The skilled workers employed to build the Pagan temples too were Indian Hindus. The civilisational linkages that the Ananda reflects are further fortified by the Shwezigon inscription, where the King, while professing to be a Buddhist, also claims to be a 're-incarnation of Vishnu', clearly

---

[12] According to Professor Than Tun, 'It seems that the Pyu and the Burman mixed freely until the Pyu were absorbed' (24), Third Buddhist Council at Pataliputra 241 BC.

[13] Pagan was also known as Arimaddanapura and Anawrahta, the ruler of Pagan was known as the King of Arimaddanapura as recorded in the records of his conquest of Thaton, G.E. Harvey, *History of Burma-Longmans* (Green and Co., 1925), 27.

indicating the influence of Hindu thought (arising out of the presence of Brahmanism at the Pagan court).

Near the Ananda lies the temple of Shiva and some of the older Pagan monuments host frescos where the image of Brahma holds a central position and presence.[14]

Another evidence of historical ties is the Pagan Myazadi inscription dating back to AD 1113, that indicates clearly that the texts are common to those of the Pyu and the Mon, in Pali and in Burmese languages—a commonality between India and Burma that unfortunately has not led to existence of naturally closer ties of kinship that the historical past and its significant influence on Burmese beliefs should have influenced relations between the two countries, in the post-independence period. This can be largely attributed to the overhang of governance and business practices of the colonial period.

An important aspect of the linkage of the Pyu, the Pagan and the Talaing with India were the links that were developed during the reign of the Chola Kings in the South of India. When Rajaraja Chola consolidated his empire the prevailing Burman kingdoms were Arimaddanapura (Pagan) and the Talaing or Mon Kingdom at what was called Sudhammavati (Thaton). Both the Burmese kingdoms had trading relations with the Chola Kingdom. Subsequently the militarily strong Cholas established a relationship that led to the payment of tribute by these kingdoms to Thanjavur. The trading relationship also influenced the religious, linguistic script and cultural practises among the Pagan and the Tailang kingdoms.

All these historical facts are evidence of the considerable interaction that took place between the kingdoms in India and Burma in those days through literature, religion, language and the form of governance that continued to have relevance in the day-to-day life of the people of Burma.

It is a fact of history that while Indian influence was fundamentally cultural, philosophical and commercial, the influences from the geographical

---

[14] There are also other vestiges of Brahmanic influence at Pagan. The chief icon in the Nanpaya built by Makuta is Brahma. A temple of Vishnu, known today as Nathlaung Kyaung, stands next door to the Pahtothamya. Even in the Burmese inscriptions belonging to the latter half of the dynasty, we find traces of Brahmanic influence. Than Tun, *Essays on the History and Buddhism of Burma*, ed. Paul Strachan (Kisdale Publications, n.d.), 25.

mainland of China were aggressive, often resulting in destruction and conquest of the Burmese kingdoms, as exemplified by the destruction of the Pyu and the Pagan kingdoms. The former by the Tai people of Nanchao and the latter by the Chinese.

Given the nature and extent of Indian influence, it is surprising that post-independence India has played such a relatively minor role in what is today's Myanmar. To a great extent, the responsibility for the change in the nature of the relationship between Myanmar and India could be laid at the doors of the colonial period.

4

The Rice Bowl of the British Empire

The total period of British occupation of 'Modern Burma' lasted 62 years, but, as Smith observes:

> [T]he new Republic of the Union of Burma, which came into being on 4th January 1948 bore little resemblance to any nation or state from the historic past. The power and authority of the Burman Kings and the central courts at Ava and Mandalay had been destroyed…And the institutions of political power bequeathed to the new nation were an ill-fitting suit of clothes modelled on the loose pattern of British parliamentary democracy.[1]

This is a very apt description of what the colonial period had done to the Burma of yore, as also the fact that the integration of the frontier regions with the new nation-state landed the task of administering a diverse group of ethnic minorities straight on the lap of the infant central government. These ethnic groups were reluctant brides to the Burman suitors and this led to a number of insurgencies—a situation begging to be exploited by the PRC and the CPB.

The reality was that the colonial period left behind a number of areas that, in different ways, were to affect the new nation's relationship with India. It was not lost on the new authorities that Myanmar 'was the growing presence along the northern frontier with India that first brought the British into Burma'.[2]

---

[1] Martin Smith, *Burma: Insurgency and the Politics of Ethnic Conflict* (Zed Books, 1991), 27.

[2] Dorothy Woodman, *The Making of Burma* (The Crescent Press, 1962).

Colonisation led to an all pervasive animosity among the Burmese against foreigners. Since the colonial masters chose to use Indians in various ways to administer the Burman people, it was hardly a surprise that anti-Indian feelings were particularly strong, at times erupting into acts of violence. This sense of hostility intensified when the British sent the dethroned and disinherited King Thibaw to Ratnagiri, a town in the then Bombay Presidency.

In sum, the British conquest of Burma, the overthrow of the monarchy and the subsequent merging of Burma with India created a fresh historical anomaly. Though the Burmese had in the past made forays across the border into the north-eastern region of the Indian subcontinent, India had never tried to conquer Burma and certainly never tried to rule that country out of India. The only time aggressive intent was displayed by an Indian kingdom towards Burma was by the Cholas, but unlike in the case of the Malay archipelago they did not occupy any territory in Burma although they did destroy some of the port cities of the Tailang kingdom in Tennasarim. The Cholas, however, established strong trade links with both the Pyu and Mon territories.

A second factor which added to the alienation of the people of Burma from the Indian people was the introduction of an administrative system that inserted a number of persons from Calcutta into the middle and lower levels of the British colonial bureaucracy; that came to play an important part in administering the country and provided a public face to the Indian elements within the colonial administration that focused the resentment of the Burman people against the Indians.

The third factor of alienation was the establishment of a security system that kept out the Burmans and was heavily dependent on recruitment of Indians and the ethnics, in particular the Karens into the security services that came to control the Burman people.

The fourth factor was the coming of Indian businessmen who soon took control of the economy of the country. Then came the development of the Irrawaddy delta as the country's rice bowl with a large export potential, leading to the influx of indentured labour from India, accompanied by money-lenders and the business community, the Chettiars. The latter, over time, came to control a very large chunk of the delta's rich agricultural land.

While the indentured labour for the delta was brought in mainly from the south of India, the development of sugarcane cultivation and the related sugar industry in the central region of the country was spearheaded by the Indian landlord community, such as the Sinhas, originating from the province of Bihar in India.

The final insult that left an indelible imprint on the Burman psyche was the shifting of the capital to Rangoon (now Yangon) that, for all practical purposes, was modelled after Indian cities, where the most commonly spoken language was Hindustani.

A significant aspect of the colonial period was the clear policy adopted by the colonial administration to keep the Burmans out of the country's governance that was reflected in the make-up of the British Burman Army (BBA). At the end of the Second World War, out of the 22,000 men that formed the BBA, 3,000 were Chin, 2,000 Kachin, 2,000 Karen and just 200 were Burmans, the rest being Indians and Gurkhas.[3]

It is hardly surprising that the Burman majority felt a strong sense of discrimination, fully realising that Indians and the ethnic minorities were being used to keep them down and to deny them their legitimate rights. This resentment was clearly reflected in the anti-Indian stance they adopted and in the increasing distrust that they harboured towards the Indian expatriate community that eventually became domiciled in Burma/Myanmar. This was yet another example of the consequences of the typical colonial practice of divide and rule, which pitted one group against the other, leaving behind in its wake permanent scars of resentment and distrust.

The colonial period led to the dominance of the *kala*—outsiders or foreigners—over the country's economy, with business sectors being dominated by the Europeans and the Indians, the latter were seen to ride to prominence on the coat tails of the British. The extent of this dominance was reflected by a number of key factors.

The 'middle class' were dominated by the Indians who held, for instance, a monopoly of the wholesale trade in provisions, pharmaceuticals, money-lending and banking—that is, all the areas where the Burman populace had to interact directly with the Indians on a day to day basis, resulting understandably in further areas of resentment.

In Yangon (then Rangoon), Indians were the largest property owners contributing the largest proportion of municipal taxes. The break up of the municipal taxes paid in the 1930s clearly reflected the extent

---

[3] Robert H. Taylor, *The State in Myanmar* (Foundation Books, 2009).

of the Indians' predominance; they contributed 55 per cent of the taxes collected by the revenue system of the day. The Europeans contributed 15 per cent and the Burmans only 11 per cent. What is more, in the '… larger towns, including Rangoon, much of the property owned by the Burmese was under mortgage to Indian bankers and money lenders'.[4]

These facts clearly illustrated the extent to which the Indians during the colonial period came to dominate the economy, besides depicting a stark picture of unequal class divisions.

A further distortion of the colonial system was reflected in the composition of the student body. The education system in practice 'favoured' the products of the 'Mission Schools' that led to the dominance of the ethnic minorities at the university level; two-thirds of the students in the 1930s were from the ethnic minority communities and Indians. It was hardly surprising that this was one of the areas of intense resentment and that the 'education policy became the fundamental issue of the Burman national movement'.[5]

All these elements in essence are pointers to the attitude that the Burmans came to adopt against both the ethnic minorities and the Indians who were seen as the beneficiaries of the colonial 'divide and rule' approach that disallowed the Burman majority from exercising their legitimate rights, including the dominant role that had been exercised by them during the autocratic monarchical era.

Given the manner in which the colonial authorities followed a deliberate policy of discrimination against the Burman people, it was hardly surprising that the Burman majority chose to reject the foreigner, both from without and within the country, and to refuse to acknowledge the rights to autonomy and exclusivity demanded by the ethnic minorities. In fact, it was only the acceptance by the SLORC to allow a degree of limited autonomy to the ethnic groups that helped secure the agreement of most of the ethnic minorities to refrain from resorting to insurgency. Under the agreement, they were permitted to retain their arms and exercise some economic and administrative control over their own territories. These understandings bought the then military regime time to find a national solution that would bring about a united polity under its control and management.

[4] N.C. Sen, *A Peep Into Burma Politics (1917–1941)* (Kitabistan, 1945).
[5] Mikael Gravers, *Nationalism as Political Paranoia in Burma* (Curzon, [1993] 1999).

The Indian minority, however, continues even today to be regarded as foreigners and are treated as second class residents without any rights. Recently, this thorny issue has seen some movement towards a satisfactory closure, indicative of a more comfortable level of relationship having been achieved between Myanmar and India.

By 1931, the Indian population in Myanmar had 'already passed one million out of an estimated population of 14.65 million'.[6] Over half the population of Rangoon was Indian which during the time of the Japanese invasion was placed at approximately 60 per cent of the capital's total population.

Many government departments were staffed entirely by Indians. 'But it was, in particular, the activities of a caste of landowners and Chettyar money lenders of Indian descent...that were the cause for most resentment.'[7] This resentment has been taken as a contributory, if not the motivating factor, which allegedly fuelled the rise of Burmese nationalism and political consciousness that erupted into anti-Indian riots in 1930 and then again in 1938, leading to the loss of many Indian lives. Again, during the anti-British Saya San rebellion in 1931, it was the Indians who were the target of the Burman people's wrath and violence.

To have an understanding of the attitude towards India it is important to take account of the elements discussed earlier as they have had a bearing on the lack of any commitment on the part of the governments of Myanmar, particularly from the Ne Win period onwards, to attach priority to relations with India. Even when a democratic government was in place, the emphasis was on getting the economy out of Indian hands.

During the period of the Japanese invasion and the exodus of Indians (numbering about half a million) from Burma to India, a strong desire to get rid of these foreigners was all too evident. Little was done to help them survive in the very difficult circumstances they faced, so that the bulk of the Indians died in their attempts to get away from both the Japanese and the militant Burmans. The fact that the Indians did not feel safe in a Burma without a British government reflected their fear of the aggressive Burmans who held them guilty of taking away their jobs and land.

---

[6] J.S. Furnivall, *Colonial Policy and Practice* (New York University Press, 1956).
[7] Smith, *Burma*.

The Nationalist Movement in Burma

India provided a guiding spirit to the Burmese nationalist movement.

This is a factor that does need explanation in the Myanmar context. Unlike the case in India where a cohesive nationalism had linkages to Western concepts and, as such, was in a sense a consequence of the colonial period and the unification of India that it spelt, in the case of Burma it was 'indeed, proto-nationalism in the form of attachment to the crown and the Buddhist (that) predates the modern state'.[8] However, as in India and elsewhere in Asia, the 'emergence of nationalism as a significant political force gained credence and substance as a consequence of the First World War'.

Elements that impacted the people of Myanmar and led to the growth of resistance to the colonial rule were obviously linked to the preferential treatment meted out to the foreign (Indian and European) groups and the sidelining of the Buddhist hierarchy.

Another area was the shift from a benign form of traditional governance to a colonial administration, which intruded into the lives of the people as it was guided by the desire to introduce reforms 'designed to build political support for the colonial order'. This ran parallel to the intrusive colonial system enforced on Indian provinces and princely states that provided the incentive for the nationalists to launch a movement aimed at freeing India as a whole from the colonial yoke.

For Burma, the case was more complex, as the people who benefitted from the economic and career opportunities of the colonial administration were a combination of the ethnic minorities, Indians and the 'wealthier minority'—the urban elite. The Burmans, who were the majority populace, were totally opposed to the stability of the pacification system enforced by the British Administration; there were open revolts to which the administration reacted by putting in place a punitive and suppressive police system.

As the police force was also a combination of ethnics, Indians and Anglo-Indians, this only led to a further estrangement of the majority from the minorities and to the persisting distrust that even today is etched deep in the Burman psyche that looks at the ethnics and the foreigners who are citizens of their country, with a jaundiced eye.

[8] Robert Taylor, 'Introduction', *The State in Myanmar*.

In this context, it is worth pointing out that the Indian expatriates and the common Indian domiciled in Myanmar in the colonial period came to be regarded as people who were favoured by the colonial masters as they were seen as willing participants to further the policy adopted by the colonial administration to relegating the Burman majority to a position of subservience that threatened their culture, religion and economic well-being. Besides the Burmans felt that the British helped by the Indian kalas had also denied them a role in the governance of the country by destroying the monarchy along with the traditional Burman administrative system.

Another bone of contention borne out of the prejudiced attitude that the Burman majority had come to display where the Indians in Burma, whether Hindu, Sikh, Muslim or Christian, were concerned was the belief that they were marrying Burman women with the intention of forcibly converting them away from Buddhism. This led to the adoption of the provision in the Citizenship Law of 1982 that defined citizenship as 'one dimensional' that requires that 'one has to prove that his/her ancestors lived in Burma before colonisation began in 1824, and that they belonged to one of the indigenous ethnic groups. Indians, Chinese and Eurasians can only obtain "associate citizenship" and cannot hold high office'.[9]

Burma's Independence Movement: Influence of India's National Movement

It needs to be recognised that in the Burman majorities' mind,

> [Colonialism] did immense damage to inter-communal relations; the appearance of preferential treatment for different ethnic groups did, without doubt, bring about a widely varying response to British rule...It was largely amongst the Burman majority, resentful of British rule and the subordinate status of Burma to India that the push for independence began.[10]

An interesting consequence of the colonial system was to create an impression in the minds of the Burmans that they had been deprived of all the trappings of power through the abolition of monarchy and the dilution

[9] Gravers, *Nationalism as Political Paranoia.*
[10] Smith, *Burma*

of the central role played by the Buddhist clergy—the two pillars of the traditional Burmese governance system. As Taylor put it, '...had the Viceroy in India not decided to abolish the monarchy' the voice of resistance to the colonial authority would have been considerably muted. 'This action (abolition of the monarchy) made clear to the Royalty, the old nobility and the monkhood that there would be no role for them in the future of the state, and they therefore felt they had little option but to resist.'[11]

For obvious reasons the independence movement in Myanmar found kinship with the national leadership of the movement in India. These covered not only the relations with the leaders of the Indian National Congress (INC) like Gandhi, Nehru, Bose and Azad but also between the leadership of the communist parties of India and Burma. Gandhi, as the undisputed leader of the Indian movement, visited Myanmar in 1929, a visit which was described as reflecting the 'close Indian connection of the Burma boycott leaders'.[12] His visit was looked at with apprehension by the colonial administration in Myanmar, as it was felt that it would add strength to the Burmese boycott move against the Simon Commission in keeping with the position that had been adopted by the Indian national leadership. These relations between the Indian and the Burmese national movements grew closer over time.

It is worth recalling that the national movements in Burma, such as the General Council of Burmese Associations (GCBA), were heavily influenced by the policy of non-co-operation followed by the INC; the instruments of *hartal* and 'boycott' came to be widely used as political tools in the demands for: separation from India; the grant of self-rule with all the major portfolios being given to the elected indigenous leaders and; ultimately, independence modelled somewhat on India's Swaraj demand.[13]

---

[11] Taylor, *The State in Myanmar*.

[12] Report on the Administration of Burma, 1928–1929.

[13] 'The Dobama Asiayone after 1938 regularly sent delegates to the annual meetings of the INC...developed contacts with Pandit Nehru and the socialist Jayprakash Narain and the Indian Communist elements operating within the Congress-socialist ranks.' John F. Cady, *A History of Modern Burma* (Cornel University Press, 1958).
Comment: Cady also records the divisions that followed in the Asiayone caused by the overt communist propaganda and the setting up of the first official communist cell set up at Rangoon which followed the Moscow party-line. Its membership included Thakins Ba, Hein, Soe, Aung Than, Ghoshal and Thein Pe.

It was also a feature of the political developments and the leadership that emerged that those Myanmar leaders who stood for elections or indulged in constitutional political activities tended to be funded by the Indian business community, obviously with an eye on mutual economic benefit. As the people who benefitted from this relationship were the Burman urban elite who were seen at times as part of the colonial exploitative system that worked against the interests of the Burman people, it eventually strengthened the negative attitude towards the foreign, particularly the Indian business community—an attitude which went against the community after Burma achieved independence. When the nationalisation of the economy resulted in depriving the Indian business and property holding community of its assets, there was no expression of any sympathy for their losses and eventual disappearance from the Burman economy.

When it came to the crunch, the fight for freedom in Myanmar took a different turn from that in India. The leadership, called the 'Thirty Comrades' who had adopted the honorific of *Thakins* turned to the Japanese with the expectation that use of force with the assistance of the Japanese would win them independence. The Japanese also extended an assurance to their Burman collaborators that the invasion of colonial Burma that would have the Burman Independence Army (BIA) as the spearhead of the Japanese armed forces into Burma would lead to the return of Burma as an independent country. It was the BIA, commanded by Aung San, that the Japanese had helped create. It was with the full involvement of the Thirty Comrades or Thakins, along with the lead and support provided by the BIA, that eventually shaped the final political push that brought about the independence of Burma.

Despite the problems that arose between the Burmese political leadership and the Japanese occupation forces and administration—that was a direct consequence of the denial by the Japanese of the promised independence to Burma and the eventual alienation of the Aung San-led BIA—the post-Independence relations with Japan have been close. An important aspect of this closeness has been Japan's extension to Burma/Myanmar of generous financial aid and technical assistance. This relationship came to be strengthened when Ne Win took over the country, he had been trained by the Japanese in military intelligence prior to the Japanese occupation of Burma till Japan's defeat at the hands of the

British in Burma towards the end of Second World War. Ne Win had been trained in military intelligence and had spent time in Japan and at that time he had established close relations with the second-rung leaders who became important in Japan after the war.

There was a common feeling among both the Indian and the Burmese leaders (they came mainly from the middle classes, many of them being lawyers and students) who were in touch with each other and exchanged views, that subsequent to the developments linked to the Second World War that had weakened the Imperialist powers, the end of the colonial period was now just a matter of time. However, while there was a degree of understanding between the Indian and Burmese national leaderships, which contributed positively to the bilateral relations and to a closeness borne out of long-standing neighbourly ties, this did not come to the help of the Indian community in Burma when the Government of Burma (GOB) led by U Nu adopted policies that were clearly to the detriment of the community.

One important development where India and its future involvement in colonial Asia was concerned was Mahatma Gandhi spelling out his philosophy on the future of the military forces in India, making it clear that no Indian force would be available for actions aimed at containing movements for freedom from colonial control; he made it a point to refer particularly to Burma in this regard.[14]

This announcement came as a great relief to the nationalist leaders in Burma who were clearly and understandably opposing the assumption of the returning British colonial authorities that they had returned to govern Burma as if it was a continuation of the colonial rule that had been interrupted by the Japanese occupation.

Nehru and Aung San

Once India attained independence in 1947, it was a given fact that Burma would follow. Aung San was in touch with Nehru and visited India to meet with him before proceeding to the UK for the talks with Atlee that finally led to Burma's independence in January 1948.

[14] V. Longer, *The Defence and Foreign Policies of India* (Sterling Publishers, 1988).

In the meetings with Nehru, there was some discussion on the nature of the unified Burma Aung San had in mind. The Panglong Agreement, which gave a degree of autonomy, as also the option of withdrawal from the Union by the ethnic states along Burma's frontiers clearly indicated the direction of Aung San's thinking on the future of a democratic Burma that was bound by a Constitution. He mentioned in the talks that he was ready for a federal or even a confederal arrangement that would be in the mutual interests of the people of the Union of Burma. This plan and liberal approach that was accommodative of the diverse interests that comprised the Union fell through with the assassination of Aung San and the arrival on the scene of a weak, faction-ridden government which inherited a country where the people in general challenged its initial control and where a vast portion of the territory came under rebel control.

After Burma gained its independence, the Burma defence force itself came to be split along political and ideological lines and, were it not for the Karen soldiers, the emergency supply of arms and ammunition by India and the loyalty of the Brigade commanded by Ne Win, nothing could have prevented of the fall of Rangoon.

Before we venture into the post-1948 period to the present relations between Myanmar and India, it would be worth mentioning, at this stage itself, that there were certain given facts that described Myanmar in the past. One was the historical difference between the Indian and Chinese approaches to Myanmar. China's stance was aggressive and all-consuming. The historical past of Myanmar had made this all too clear; the Chinese Mongols conquered and destroyed the Pagan Kingdom that represented the Golden Age of Burma. A further pointer to the nature of the past relations was the tributary system that the Chinese Emperors imposed on Burmese Kings, relegating them to a secondary status within the embrace of China's all powerful 'Middle Kingdom'.

Another aspect of historical interest was the factor that the borders between Yunnan and Myanmar, were porous and enabled the Shans to play a major role including an aggressive one of conquest-and-occupation of mainland Burmese kingdoms. It was the Nanchao Kingdom that destroyed the Pyu city states that contributed to the eventual disappearance of the Pyu as a separate Burmese entity. This was yet another example of aggressive actions taken against historical Burma enacted by interests that operated out of China's geographical space.

Another significant factor has been the manner in which the Chinese have continued to exploit the differences that have existed between the Burman dominated Union Government of Burma/Myanmar to leverage these differences to serve China's interests often to the detriment of the national interests of Myanmar, because of the constant threat these differences have come to project against the integrity and sovereignty of the Union of Myanmar. It is important to recognise that the ethnic minority states and territories are strategically located as a geographical arc that covers the borders of Myanmar with China and Thailand to the east. This arc includes Tibet to the north, India's North-East covering the the north-western and western borders of Myanmar and eventually Bangladesh along the Arakan. The problem is complicated by the fact that the ethnic groups have been dissatisfied with their lot in Myanmar and this has led to insurgencies that have been supported by China with material and political support till 1988. China retains the possibility of utilising Myanmar tribal groups like the Wa and the Kokang to influence decision-making in Naypidaw in favour of its interests and to ensure that Myanmar remains in its area of influence.

In contrast, Myanmar's relations with India have been of a civilisational nature, Buddhism has been one of the most durable factors in the relationship, as witnessed by the presence of Myanmar monks at Bodh Gaya and the scale of religious tourism. A matter of some concern is the apprehension expressed by senior Buddhist monks over the Hinducentric utterances of the then BJP-led NDA government in India. This was a clear indication of the support that the Myanmar Buddhist clergy had for a secular India, the assurance of security it offered to the places of Buddhist pilgrimage/worship, as well as the constitutional guarantees on the freedom of religious practice in India.

The only time that India can be accused of playing an occupational role vis-à-vis Burma occurred during the colonial period and that too when (till 1937) Calcutta was the central point out of which the colonial power controlled the administration and the strategic and security set-up of the whole region, including the peripheries of geographical Burma. It laid the basis for the future pattern of the economic and business practices. Since it was all a part of the pacification process, it tended to neutralise the role of the majority Burman population.

It should be pointed out that the policies followed by the colonial administration led to the alien dominance of the Myanmar economy and since Indians were the most directly visible foreigners at all the places of public interaction, they became the specific targets of animosity both during the colonial period and obviously after independence. The attitude displayed by the BIA and the Burmese political leadership towards the Indians fleeing from the advancing Japanese during the Second World War amply demonstrated the ill-will that was directed at the Indian population.

The racial nature of the attacks on those who were considered the main beneficiaries of the colonial system at the expense of the majority continued to be targeted, besides the Indians, the others being the Chinese (the other commercially dominant community) and the Karens. It is in this context that it becomes important to mention the role played by the *Chettiar* community that had its origins in the present state of Tamil Nadu in India in developing the surplus economy of colonial Burma.

The Chettiars of Burma, became much 'vilified' community known throughout the British holdings in Southeast Asia, but more so in Burma as 'money-lenders'. They were demonised as 'rapacious users, responsible for all manner of vices concomitant with the colonial economy'.[15] They were described by people in that country in very harsh terms. A salient example is the wording in the testimony rendered before the 'Burma Provincial Banking Enquiry', in which they are described as a 'hard hearted lot that will ring out every drop of blood from the victims without compunction for the sake of their own interests…'.[16]

This demonisation was misplaced; the Chettiars were the 'crucial link between Burma and international finance', the suppliers of capital that 'turned the country into the "rice bowl" of the British Empire'. The Chettiars' insistence on land as the collateral for loans led to the alienation of a large amount of the landholdings of the agriculturists, particularly in the Irrawaddy delta, when the global price of rice tumbled. This was a direct consequence of the failure of the landholders to meet their loan repayments or service their debt. The transfer of the landholdings to the Chettiars resulted in the perception that they were a land-grabbing community. In the process what was ignored was the fact that the Chettiars were the primary source of capital and rural credit—filling a major gap that the banking system was unable to cover, and that it was this service

---

[15] Sean Turnell, 'The Chettiars in Burma'.
[16] Burma Provincial Banking Enquiry during the colonial administration.

which had contributed overwhelmingly to Burma gaining the 'rice bowl of the world' status.

All the same, it cannot be denied that all money-lenders in the country were charging very high rates of interest and those charged by the Chettiars 'were high enough to exceed returns [from] the land in all but the best years'. The Chettiars were conscious of the fact that acquiring land against the outstanding amount would make them landlords and that this would antagonise the effected populace which, in turn, could lead to reprisals. 'Their fears were prescient, for in the end the Chettiars were expelled from Burma, in the process losing the land they had acquired and much of their capital.'[17]

It should not also be lost to the pages of history that, just as the nationalist and socialist minded Congress government in Delhi placed 'money-lenders' in the classicist definition 'as predators, and blood suckers of the helpless farming community', there was also little sympathy for the Chettiars at the political level when the U Nu government adopted a landholding policy that was mainly guided by the desire to take the 'ill-gained' land out of that community's hands.

It is ironical that the Chettiars, whose activities had contributed so significantly to the growth of the Burmese economy were seen as almost 'pantomime villains' and treated as such in both official and popular literature. According to Skidmore, the proof that the Chettiars continue to be demonised in Burma 'is surely provided by the constant efforts by the country's ruling military regime to label Aung San Suu Kyi as a Chettiar'.

This is yet another example of the fact that when it comes to assigning the blame for the worst problems that the Burmans faced, the finger of accusation has inevitably been pointed at the domination by the Indian landlords and the business community.

As Martin Smith put it:

> [P]opular cartoons of the time show Burmans squeezed out of their own country by a motley crowd of 'guests' i.e., Europeans, Chinese, Hindus and Muslims. Eventually during the Second World War, an estimated 500,000 Indians [who] fled Burma were chased out by the young nationalists of the Burma Independence Army and untold thousands died in one of the darkest passages of Burma's history.[18]

[17] J.S.Furnivall, Economic Advisor to the GOB.
[18] Smith, 'The Roots of Conflict', Burma, 44.

5

Burma, the Hermit Republic!

With the 'hermit republic', India has had a peculiar relationship—close and cordial, but most unobtrusive and almost unnoticed...[1]

This quotation describes in extenso the nature and quality of India's relations with neighbouring Burma, particularly after the period that commenced from Burma's separation from India in 1937. The unification and then the separation of Burma from India, which was brought about by the colonial masters, common to both the countries, understandably came to influence the nature and course of the bilateral ties that came to exist between the nationalist leaders of both countries. This was particularly so during the leadership of Aung San with whom there was a meeting of minds including on the direction that a resurgent Asia should take to once again become a global driver for peace and understanding. After the assassination of Aung San the close relations between the top leadership of both the countries remained with Nehru and U Nu, Burma's first elected Prime Minister, developing a personal relationship.

Nehru and Aung San had developed a close understanding with Nehru perceiving in Aung San, a strong leader who had a clear-headed approach to the complex situation that he was to inherit on independence. He saw

[1] V.P. Dutt, 'India and Burma: A Peculiar Relationship', in *India's Foreign Policy in a Changing World* (Vikas Publishing, 1984), 336–344.

in Aung San a leader not only of Burma, but one who could play a leadership role in Asia. Nehru expressed these sentiments in his statement condoling the people and the leaders of Burma on the assassination of Aung San (19 July 1947). He said it was an irreparable loss not only to Burma, but to entire Asia, as they had 'lost one of the bravest and most far seeing sons…', adding that India would 'stand by them (the people of Burma) in the difficult days ahead'.

Relations after the coup d'état that led to the fall of U Nu developed a more aloof quality. Initially Nehru refused to have any dealings with General Ne Win till U Nu was released from custody. With Ne Win adopting a policy of isolation, which eventually led to an economic slowdown that reduced a resource-rich country to the ignominy of being placed among the ranks of the least developed countries; the bilateral ties came to be largely confined to the top leadership of the two countries, depriving them of the cultural and economic contacts that had enriched the two civilisations in the past and had ensured areas of permanent respect and influence.

Between 1988 and 1992 the relations almost came to a standstill as public opinion in India openly expressed its opposition to and horror over the brutalities committed by the military leadership against the people of Myanmar with a total lack of respect for the life and welfare of the people of the country. To this was added the harsh position that political and intellectual India adopted when the SLORC leadership refused to implement its promise to handover power to the people's representatives, who had won overwhelming popular support. The imprisonment and uncompromising treatment meted out to Aung San Suu Kyi, whom India accepted as a friend having a close political and philosophical kinship with India, intensified the negative feelings that were openly expressed by Indian public opinion that came to be endorsed by the Parliament.

After 1992, the relations gradually thawed and came to stand on a firmer footing based upon a pragmatic understanding of the strategic and security underpinnings that were expected to guide and govern India's policy directions towards an important neighbouring country, whose co-operation was essential to India's efforts at containing the insurgencies prevalent in its north-eastern region where the Indian insurgents were utilising the ease of operating out of Myanmar to carry out their acts of violence against the Indian establishment and people.

The relationship architecture that has now come to be adopted as part of the bilateral relationship promotes economic diplomacy that would ensure that the Naypidaw government would look at India for assistance in its economic development and place relations on a permanent footing of respect and closer understanding, within the ambit of India's increasing commitment to its 'Look East Policy'.

Relations Covering the Period 1947–1962

The relations between the two countries during this period were warm and close. Nehru's message of greetings at the time of Burma's celebrations on attaining independence, reflected this bond when in a very categorical statement of commitment he stated: 'As in the past, so in the future, the people of India will stand shoulder to shoulder with the people of Burma, and whether we have to share a good fortune or ill-fortune, we shall share it together'.[2]

India looked on Myanmar as a neighbour which was a co-proponent of democracy and a fellow non-aligned country with its leadership professing a similar Fabian socialist bent of mind influencing its socio-economic policies. Relations between the two countries were naturally influenced by the common experiences that both had derived from the negatives and positives of British colonial rule, and a number of common practices that could be built upon to arrive at a stable and close relationship. However, a number of thorny issues limited the scope of the relationship.

The most worrying factor was the weakness of the infant democratic government in Yangon (Rangoon) having to combat the communist forces that, supported by the PRC, were attempting to overthrow the U Nu government. It was also not lost on New Delhi that the army itself had split and that the Karen soldiers in the army were not immune to the Karen leadership's demand for their own independent state. There were also

---

[2] In Nehru's greetings on Burma's independence in January 1948 he mentioned that 'this was a great and solemn day not only for Burma, but for India and *for the whole of Asia*'. The offer to stand shoulder to shoulder with the people of Burma was almost immediately put to the test when the separatist groups and the CPB rebelled and challenged the newly established democratic GOB.

several factions within the Anti-Fascist People's Freedom League (AFPFL) itself that were working to destabilise the government.

Nehru had a good understanding with U Nu, who succeeded Aung San as the head of the AFPFL leading to his becoming the first Prime Minister of independent Burma. Nehru, with his sense of history and an innate understanding of the role that Asia could play in global matters was concerned enough to look at accelerating both the process of the colonial retreat from Asia, as well as to help define a role for Asia as a positive force for peace in a complex world order that was emerging at the end of the Second World War. In this respect he had 'welcomed the idea of an Asian Conference suggested by Aung San'.[3] Nehru as we have mentioned earlier had developed a great respect for Aung San as he saw in him a fellow Asian leader of credibility and in whom he could repose great confidence. To an extent this feeling he also came to repose in U Nu.

The colonial governments in Burma and Indonesia had refused to grant Nehru permission in 1946 to visit the two countries, though on Mountbatten's recommendation he was allowed to visit 'Malaya' and Singapore. Nehru wanted to meet the nationalist leaders of these countries and also the Indian communities living there. It was the weather that helped him fulfil his wish to visit Burma. On his return journey bad weather forced his plane to land in Rangoon and Nehru had to spend the night there. He took this opportunity to meet with Aung San and hold discussions with him on how to tackle a British colonial administration that was still vacillating over granting independence to India and Burma. It was clear to both the leaders that independence for the rest of Asia from the colonial yoke was directly tied to how soon India would gain its independence.

It was also during this visit that Nehru reiterated his assurance to Aung San that he would strenuously oppose the continued use of Indian troops to enforce colonial rule in Burma.

Both Gandhi and Nehru followed through on this principle making it clear to the British Indian administration that India would not permit the use of the Indian Army to perpetuate the rule of the colonial

---

[3] Nehru Archives: Letter from Aung San dated 13 December 1945 and reply to Aung San on 27 December 1945.

administration, which had returned to Burma after the defeat of Japan. This effectively spelt the end of British rule and was a major contributing factor in the liberation of Burma. The Burmese leadership appreciated the importance of the stand taken by Gandhi and Nehru. This act of support by India led to a greater degree of understanding between the countries and continued to underpin the relations after Burma's independence.

After the independence of Myanmar in 1948, the new government in Yangon was confronted with the threat of a communist takeover of the country. The CPB, as the leading opposition, took to the war path, claiming that the British had only granted a false independence and true independence had to be gained by doing away with the U Nu government.

The democrat in Nehru, led to India taking the unequivocal stand of extending moral and political support to U Nu and the democratic polity that had come under great stress soon after independence under the threat to its existence posed by the rebellious forces which had reached Insein on the outskirts of Rangoon. India openly supported the Burmese Government's efforts to repel the rebels. Nehru proposed that the Commonwealth come to the rescue of the Burma Government and at the same time India sent across arms and ammunition to the Burma army on an emergency basis to help push back and contain the rebellious communist forces.

India had acted speedily as Nehru recognised the importance of a democratic and stable government in India's strategic neighbourhood. He was well aware that if the Burmese Communist forces backed by insurgents succeeded in ousting the democratically elected U Nu government and taking over the reins of the government in Rangoon, it would bring China to the north-eastern doorstep of India, creating unacceptable vulnerabilities in that sensitive area.

An important difference between the Indian and Burmese independence movements was the role that the Burman armed forces in the form of the BIA played in gaining independence for Burma. The BIA had been created with the help of the Japanese, before Japan invaded Burma during the Second World War. The Thakin movement had been the force behind the link-up with the Japanese and in the creation of the relationship that had resulted in two clear commitments made to the Thakins. These commitments being that the BIA led by Aung San would head the combined Burmese and Japanese forces that would invade the British occupied Burma and drive the colonial power out of Burma. Thereafter the Japanese were to grant Burma full independence. While the BIA did lead the combined forces that led to the defeat of the British and their retreat from Burma, the Japanese reneged on the issue of full independence for Burma. This led to the defection of the BIA and its co-operation with the British to defeat the Japanese and their eventual move out of Burma. After this it was Aung San who led the independence movement and negotiated the independence of Burma. In contrast in the Indian case where the independence movement was led entirely by the political leadership and there was no role that was played by the armed forces. The situation in Burma/Myanmar was one where the armed forces were part of the nationalists' fight for independence and there was a degree of integration between the military and the political leadership. In the light of this factor it was hardly a surprise that the political leadership found it difficult to ensure that the armed forces stayed neutral in the political affairs of the country.

Another factor that Delhi/Calcutta was aware of was that the national movement in Burma was a fractured one held together only to present a united face before the colonial masters and that it would unravel once independence became a reality. There was a division in the armed forces, with one faction supporting the central authority and the other which was close to the CPB and planned to break away and join the communist rebellion against the Rangoon Government. Further, it became apparent very early on that the strong Karen presence in the armed forces would melt away, leaving the central authority even more vulnerable to the communist-led rebellion.

Though the Constitution of Burma, adopted with inputs from an Indian constitutional advisor[4] on deputation from the GOI, was in essence a federal one where the ethnic minorities would have autonomous rights, in reality it did not play out in that way. This was yet another cause for worry and it was perceived by the Indian leadership as one that would be a major cause for instability. It was not the institutions but the weak and fractured governance that was to blame.

These factors perhaps played a role in determining India's attitude when Ne Win first took over the reins of the country at the behest of

---

[4] B.N. Rau; he had played a very prominent role in the evolution of the Indian Constitution.

U Nu, confirming that the political leadership was too weak to foster the growth of democracy in Myanmar.

The sequence of events following independence made it clear that the GOB intended to follow the social programme advocated by leftists within the ruling party of bringing about land reforms in which land would be returned to the tiller without the landlords being compensated. Though it was purported to be a blanket national policy, it targeted the Chettiars and Indian landlords who lost all their holdings. As it also, in a fashion, followed the Fabian socialist doctrine that had influenced Nehru-led INC's land reform policy, there was no aggressive protest by the GOI.

While the GOB did come up with a compensation package as a result of negotiations with the Indian Government that was to cover the loss suffered by Chettiar and other Indian landlords, the amount was several notches below the real value of the land and the debt instruments were ones that could neither be transferred nor encashed. The aim of the government in Yangon was to ensure that the compensation money was reinvested in Burma, which was hardly an attractive proposition in a country that was progressively becoming politically and commercially unstable. The two legislations that brought about this situation were the 1948 and the 1954 Land Nationalisation Acts.[5] The GOI did not press for a full compensation package, although the then Indian Ambassador M.A. Rauf, who was the Burmese Home Minister M.A. Raschid's brother, fought for a full compensation package, covering 5 million acres of land lost by Indians in the nationalisation.[6]

In fact, the ultimate aim of the whole policy process was to ensure that the despair over the loss they suffered would force the Indians to leave the country.

It was ironical that the GOI followed in principal a policy that on one part encouraged Indian communities who had come to settle in countries like Burma under the aegis of the colonial administrations to adopt those countries as their domicile on those countries attaining independence; did nothing to ensure that these people were granted equality of treatment and were part of the political, social and economic

---

[5] J.C. Furnivall; as mentioned earlier, he was at that time the Economic Advisor to the GOB.

[6] General study of economic development.

fabric of the countries of adoption. In fact the GOI, adopted a laid-back attitude to the policies of discrimination that were adopted by the local administrations against the interests of the PIO who had adopted Burma as their home. Apart from the landholding Chettiars and Bihari landlords there was a major presence of Indians in the overall economy and business sectors of Burma. The lack of interest shown by the GOI to safeguard the business and economic interests of the PIO in Burma only led to the feeling, first to the U Nu administration and subsequently to the Ne Win administration that they could take actions detrimental to the interests of the PIO and there would be no long term negative impact on the bilateral relations. It was hardly surprising under these circumstances that Ne Win could with impunity direct his nationalisation policy to deprive the Indian business community of its business and property holdings. In fact the lack of any real interest shown by the Nehru administration to negotiate a deal that would defend the economic positions of the PIO when Ne Win to impose his concept of socialism and enforce it at bayonet point by the defence forces that he had managed to cast in his own mould were part of the political, social and economic fabric of the country of their adoption.

The Indian Government's approach to the Ne Win and U Nu governments' discriminatory actions against the PIO is mirrored in Nehru's speeches in the 1950s and 1960s. 'In several speeches, Nehru had taken pains to point out the difficulties faced by the newly-independent Burma and that the legislation affected foreigners as a whole and was not aimed against Indians alone.' Addressing Parliament, the then Deputy Minister for External Affairs, Mrs Lakshmi Menon, had the following to say:

> Our nationals do experience a number of hardships as a result of land legislation and various other legislative enactments in Burma which apply to Indian nationals, other non-Burmese nationals and also even to Burmese nationals. Since there is no discrimination at all, there is no point in our taking up this matter with the Government of Burma.[7]

Another result of this soft Indian policy of non-interference was the presumption within the Burman political and military elite that they

---

[7] India Lok Sabha Debates, Vol. 16 (Part I), 26 August 1960.

could ride rough shod over Indian interests and India would merely protest but would not take any hard position which could make the strategically important Myanmar adopt a policy that could work against India's interests.

Ironically, the Burma Socialist Programme Party's (BSPP) nationalisation policy, which was essentially directed at the Indian business and property owning community (and to a lesser extent against the Chinese), effectively brought about the further deterioration of an already beleaguered economy, relegating Myanmar to the ranks of the Least Developed Countries (LDC).

6

From Nehru to Rajiv

In the initial period of U Nu's reign as the leader of the AFPFL and Prime Minister of Burma, the friendly ties between the two governments born out of the parallels between the national movements and the close association of the Burmese political leaders with the Congress movement in India was further bonded by the kinship of mind that developed between Nehru and U Nu. This friendship led to a number of actions which bode well for relations between these two newly independent countries. What had created an atmosphere of co-operation and understanding arose out of the fact that both had adopted as their guiding principles the rule of law, parliamentary democracy, a bureaucratic practice (that had its common origins in what had been put in place by the colonial masters) and a common belief in non-alignment as the governing principle of foreign policy.

The one difference between the two countries was their stand on membership to the Commonwealth. India remained in the Commonwealth once the Commonwealth had modified its rules and accepted a Republican India as a member, but Burma, faced with the Communist Party's strong opposition to any arrangement with the British, decided to opt out of the Commonwealth.[1] Despite this rebuff, the Commonwealth did play a role, at the behest of India, to help the U Nu administration battle the rebellious forces and to extend aid to that country. Ironically it

---

[1] Martin Smith, chapter on the 'Final Seizure of Power' and Tinker refer to the decision having been taken under Communist pressure. Smith, 'Final Seizure of Power', *Burma*; Tinker, *The Union of Burma* (OUP, 1967).

was the Commonwealth ambassadors who intervened and helped bring about the ceasefire at Insein, with the rebel forces, that helped prevent the fall of Rangoon and thus helped preserve the democratic structure that Burma had adopted to govern the country.

Again, India gave unstinted support to Burma's efforts to get the Kou Min Tang (KMT) forces, almost 12,000 strong, off its territory. U Nu wanted them out as their presence in Burma was a sore point with the PRC and was becoming an increasing source of destabilisation. India extended firm support for the UN Resolution which sought the evacuation of the KMT Chinese soldiers and their families out of Burma. The debate on the resolution at the UN once again saw the drama of a vitriolic exchange between India's Krishna Menon and the Americans. Krishna Menon[2] spelled out the nature of the closeness of the India–Myanmar relations, when he categorically stated: '...what hurts Burma hurts us equally. We have no military alliance, but Burma is closely linked to us and it is naturally of great concern to us that she should suffer'.

India's strong support at the UN was greatly appreciated by the U Nu government. Americans in those days supported the KMT to the extent of encouraging opium cultivation as a source of revenue, which resulted in a number of these Chinese settling down along the Myanmar border with China and the entrenchment of the manufacture and trade in heroin out of that region.

One significant fallout of this development was that a number of people in the region today are the descendants of 'unions between Burmese Shan and Wa women and the Chinese who had settled there'.[3] These people are now full citizens, but in contrast the liaisons between Indians and Burman women are looked down upon as being outside the pale of correct social behaviour and the Burmese women are stigmatised with their children losing their rights as citizens.

One famous example of this was the treatment meted out by the SLORC to the wife of K.R. Narayanan, who subsequently became the President of India; she was denied a visa to attend the funeral ceremonies of her

---

[2] Comment: Krishna Menon was looked upon as a saviour of the developing country and the non-aligned cause particularly among those countries that saw the Americans as a nation of bullies.

[3] Renaud Egreteau, *Wooing the Generals: India's New Burma Policy* (Authors Press, 2003).

brother in Burma. She was a Burmese lady who had married Narayanan when he was posted at the Indian Embassy in Burma. Not surprisingly, she was one of the strongest critics of the military regime in Myanmar.

Such behaviour of the Myanmar regime was nothing more than another form of discrimination against the PIO who endured life in Myanmar as second class citizens or non-citizens, having no political rights. For all practical purposes, they were stateless, as they did not have regular papers. It is worth mentioning that in the 1950s the GOB only acknowledged that there were 160,000 PIO in the country. They agreed to the suggestion made by the GOI that the Indians domiciled in Burma should opt for Burmese citizenship. Initially (like elsewhere also in Southeast Asia) most Indians did not exercise this option. The few who did were made Burmese citizens. It is worth mentioning that the GOB figure of Indians in Burma was well below the real figure. Today the figure is close to 2.5 million, most of them stateless.

Nehru continued to be concerned over the increasing problems that insurgency and the PRC's backing of these as well as the material, political and moral support to the CPB as these were creating problems for the unity and integrity of a country that was of immense strategic importance for India. Burma and U Nu were important to Nehru's vision of an Asian Federation, an idea that he had put forward when the 18 nations gathered in Delhi in January 1949 where he projected a leadership role for India. In his inaugural speech to the gathering Nehru spelt out his approach mentioning that,

> [F]rom the point of view of Asia, this conference has been a turning point in history. It means new alignments and a new balance of power, if not now, then in the near future. We do not want to form a new bloc but inevitably the countries of Asia will come together and India will play a leading part in Asia.[4]

Nehru had a comfort level with U Nu where his philosophy of non-alignment and view on the future leadership role for Asia was concerned and he was interested in U Nu strengthening his position as the leader of a unified and peaceful Burma that was democratic and that served as a bulwark against communism in Asia. Nehru accordingly suggested that

---

[4] Inauguration of the conference of 18 nations in Indonesia. Speech made by Nehru in Delhi on 18 January 1949. Nehru's speeches Volume I 1946–1949 from S. Gopal's volumes on Nehru and his papers.

he could play a role in trying to bring about a reconciliation between Rangoon and the Karen who were in open rebellion against the U Nu administration. Nehru felt that the Karen rebellion against Rangoon could further weaken U Nu. He expressed this concern to U Nu reflecting over the differences that had arisen between the GOB and the Karen leadership which had led to the Karen breakaway and a serious and persisting armed struggle. Placing confidence in his personal equations with U Nu, he offered to mediate between the GOB and the Karens. This was not found acceptable and Nehru did not persist with his efforts.

Again, in the thinking on Asia where the countries were emerging out of a colonial past and were faced with various complexities of functioning in a world order that spelled instability, Nehru thought of bringing about an Asian Regional Organisation patterned on the Organisation of American States, in which Burma would be a leading member. This very clearly was indicative of the trust and understanding he had in Burma and U Nu. U Nu too felt comfortable with Nehru and was interested in playing a leadership role at the top table on Asian affairs. This was reflected in his proposal of a defence pact between 'India, Burma, Ceylon and Pakistan', which was rejected by Nehru because, among other reasons, such a pact would have been be seen as an anti-PRC move.[5]

During the U Nu period there were a number of ministerial, official and informal visits exchanged between the two nations. Nehru was impressed by the leadership U Nu had shown by bringing the important ethnic minorities to participate in the task of governance, a step so necessary for the unity and integrity of Myanmar. Nehru encouraged him to take a leadership role on Asian issues (such as in the Delhi Conference on Asian Relations and in support of the NAM). U Nu came to play an important role in both the non-aligned movement and in the Bandung processes. He came to be recognised as a leading Asian policy and decision maker and was accepted as an Asian leader who had a close understanding and a relationship of co-operation with the Indian leadership. His friendship with Nehru developed into family ties.

It was during this period that the Indo-Burma Boundary issues were negotiated and an agreement signed in Imphal when Nehru and U Nu met once again. Another indicator of the closeness of ties during those

---

[5] Nehru to U Nu, 7 January 1950.

days was the signing of the Treaty of Perpetual Peace and Friendship between the two countries on 7 July 1951. This placed the bilateral relations on a firm footing, leading to co-operation covering a plethora of areas such as trade, customs, cultural relations, communications, extradition, immigration or repatriation of nationals and as also other matters of common interest.[6]

On 29 September, a five year Trade Agreement was signed, committing India to the purchase of rice from Burma. Perhaps what was even a more important pointer to the fellow feelings that India had for Burma and its leadership resulted in India, despite being starved of capital and having adopted stringent policies to prevent the flow out of capital, granted Burma two major concessions.

The first was the writing off of '...50% of Burma's outstanding liabilities to India arising out of the separation of Burma from India in 1937'.[7] In 1954, India, which was food deficient in the initial post-independence decades, was granted the supply of much needed rice on exceptionally generous terms by Burma/Myanmar—another example of the remarkable spirit of togetherness the two countries enjoyed.

Another indicator of the close diplomatic underpinnings of the relations was that India, taking into account the economic difficulties that Burma faced, extended a loan of ₹300 million on very favourable terms in 1957, despite her own capital constraints.

It is worth factoring in at this stage the informality that existed in the bilateral relationship in those times, reflected in the fact that the Burmese Prime Minister U Nu and members of his Cabinet and the civil services were welcome to visit as and when they desired to discuss any of the issues and problems confronting them; as Nehru put it 'we are in frequent touch with the GOB on many matters. We are not only friendly in the normal sense of the word, but if I may say so, somewhat more friendly'.[8]

Nehru saw Pakistan turning into 'practically a colony of the United States', and felt that the Great Powers were driving the developing countries to take up positions that would force them into positions of

---

[6] This treaty reflected the closeness of relations even when problems arose on issues of PIO in Burma which could not be resolved. What needs to be noted is that the relations 'remained remarkably relaxed and informal'.

[7] Statement in Indian Parliament by Indian Finance Minister C.D. Deshmukh, May 1952.

[8] Nehru papers—Press Conference 1952.

alignment. Nehru shared the thought with U Nu 'that, with this general attack on the concert of non-aligned countries, it had become all the more incumbent on these countries to hold together'. He stressed the point further, saying this was a matter 'not only [of] practical politics but is the only way to save our real freedom and, if I may say so, our soul'.[9] While Nehru had expressed his views directly to U Nu other friendly countries and the non-aligned were informed of India's views by the Indian heads of mission. This was to be seen as part of Nehru's position that Burma as a leading Asian power with whom India shared common strategic and security interests needed to be kept in the loop at its highest political levels. This relationship of personal briefings on issues of Indian concern that had come to define the relationship between Nehru and U Nu of course disappeared when Ne Win deposed U Nu.

Again on China, Nehru seemed aware of the fact that India's support to that country was being played down by Beijing and that it was maintaining strict neutrality on Kashmir, despite Pakistan being a part of the alliance against it (SEATO). In a letter that Nehru wrote to the Indian Ambassador in Rangoon which was to be shared with U Nu, Nehru stated that 'no country has any deep faith in the policies of another country, more especially in regard to a country which tends to expand. Obviously we cannot be dead sure of what China may do in the future'.[10] Nehru was finally recognising the fact that China was in principal an expansionist power but despite this he did not place emphasis on improving the defence profile of the Indian armed forces to ensure that India could take care of its security interests to counter any aggressive moves by China on the Indo-Tibetan frontiers. Ironically he had failed to take the expansionist history of China in to account by giving up India's rights in Tibet without leveraging this policy to get a commitment from China on the borders.

The U Nu–Nehru relationship once again came into play at the Colombo Conference on Indo-China where U Nu, irritated by the Chinese support for the CPB, was inclined to lean towards the United States (US) position which was vigorously put forward by Pakistan. But he was persuaded by Nehru to support the unanimous resolution that was adopted, urging that 'Indo-China be allowed to settle its own future without

[9] Nehru papers.
[10] Letter to the Indian Ambassador to Burma, 9 May 1954.

intervention by the Great Powers'.[11] Nehru managed to convince U Nu to support his views on the subject by indicating that he would take up Burma's concerns with Beijing and confirming this trust by instructing India's Ambassador to China to request Beijing to extend satisfactory assurances to Burma.

However the problems confronting the relations between the PRC and Burma continued to reach critical moments as U Nu became increasingly incensed over the persistent Chinese support for the CPB and the insurgencies in Burma (which he apprehended were sure signs of China's 'imperialistic designs'), U Nu was even contemplated joining SEATO. He wrote to Nehru: 'I fear to find myself entering the SEATO alliance in spite of myself.'[12] Nehru had to once again intervene with Zhou En Lai in order to prevent such a development which would have come in the way of his design for peace in Asia. He tried his best to reduce the negative impact of the policy that Peking was following. Nehru urged U Nu to go to China and 'talk matters over informally with Zhou' and, to Zhou, his request was that China be more accommodating.

Concerned over the border dispute between China and India, U Nu made the suggestion that he visit China to try and create a suitable political climate for discussions, but Nehru declined the offer, as he felt that China was becoming increasingly obdurate, more given to displaying an 'arrogance of might' rather than showing any desire for genuine negotiations. Nehru pointed out that no Indian Government would ever agree to the 'absurd' Chinese claims, 'and any effort by U Nu might harden the Chinese attitude' as it might suggest that 'India was frightened and anxious to find a way out'.[13] Nehru kept U Nu informed on the progressively widening chasm between India and China, which culminated in the 1962 war. But this healthy understanding between the two top leaders came to an abrupt end when U Nu was ousted from power by Ne Win in a military coup d'état.

In actual fact the cooling off of ties between these two neighbouring countries, which otherwise should have continued on the path of understandings, arising out of the political, economic and cultural co-operation that had hitherto governed their bilateral relationship, was the direct

[11] Archives.
[12] U Nu Letter to Nehru of 4 September 1956.
[13] Letter to U Nu, 29 September 1959.

result of the Ne Win coup and the subsequent actions against the Indian business holdings that followed. It also happened that Ne Win came to follow a policy of balancing the relations with India and China. The relationship further deteriorated because of the differences that arose after the military takeover, particularly over the policies adopted by Ne Win to destroy democracy in Burma, further complicated by Ne Win's fear that India would put pressure on him for the restoration of democratic governance, which led to Ne Win, to an extent, distancing Burma from India. This apprehension was strengthened by Nehru initially insisting that India would recognise the Ne Win regime only once U Nu was released from custody.

The fact that Nehru and later Indira Gandhi continued their support to U Nu was seen clearly in this light by the military dictatorship that Ne Win established and which continued to flourish in Myanmar even in a sense to this day.

A key area where Nehru and U Nu adopted a common approach was their attempt to ensure that both countries co-operated to prevent the exploitation of their ethnic minorities by external powers who wanted to arouse a sense of disaffection in the region, thus threatening the integrity of the two countries. India's Naga problem had direct links with those of Burma just on the other side of the border. There was no doubt in anyone's mind that Communist China was exploiting the situation in India's North-East working out of the adjacent Burmese territory, over which the GOB had very poor if not almost non-existent administrative control. In their keen desire to solve this problem together, the two Prime Ministers met in the Naga areas of India and jointly toured the area, making stops at many places to address the people. The fact that Nehru had confidence in the capacity of such a joint approach only went to integrate the security relations between the two countries as a binding force that lasted on this personal level as long as U Nu retained power in Burma. After his ouster the security relationship became a more formal affair being left largely to the District Officials and the relevant armed forces commanders.

Because of the understanding and warmth that bound relations between U Nu and Nehru, the latter took a softer stance over the signing of the Sino-Burmese Boundary Treaty, that left the issue of the trijunction between China–Burma–India borders in the balance. Nehru took the line in Parliament that it was not 'right to criticise Burma...Burma has been carrying on these negotiations with China since quite a long time ago...We could have no grievance, no objection...' He went on to say, on the subject of the objectionable maps attached to the Agreement by the Chinese, that,

> [T]he Burmese Government made it perfectly clear to us, before the signing of the treaty and after the signing of the treaty, that they were not accepting that interpretation of the maps; that was none of their business, that was a business for India and China to determine and they are bound by the terms of their own treaty and their own boundary.[14]

To sum up, the relations between Burma/Myanmar during the Nehru–U Nu period could be described as very close, bound by a personal warmth and friendship which contributed to an understanding and appreciation of the interests of both countries that covered security and strategic concerns. The leaderships of the two countries kept in close touch with each other on issues that were of common national security and foreign policy interest. These policies were anchored to the ideal of non-alignment and furthering the cause of a united Asia in a complicated, unstable world in the throes of the Cold War.

Nehru described the bilateral position best when he stated:

> Our association with our neighbour country like Burma is a very close one. It may not be signified by a special name, but is much closer in many ways than our association with many of the Commonwealth countries...I just do not understand this, except that I can understand it on the ground of *sentiment*.[15]

The U Nu period came to an end in 1962 with General Ne Win finally taking over the reins of the country by carrying out a coup against the constitutionally elected government, following which,

> Burma gradually took a conscious decision to opt out of the world politics, ignore even regional pulls and groupings...Confronted by the 'awesome power of China' and torn by internal insurgency...sustained with Chinese support...the Burmese leaders...came to believe that 'isolation' was the only way to ensure their (Burma's) sovereignty, integrity and stability.

---

[14] Nehru's reply to the debate on the President's address to Parliament, 23 February 1961.
[15] Nehru Archives.

1962–1988: The Ne Win Period

Initially there was a hiatus in the relations, with Nehru opposing the toppling of a democratically elected government with whom India had a good relationship and, importantly, where Myanmar's strategic stance of maintaining a balance between its two large neighbours, China and India, was now being undermined by an autocratic military leader who was of Chinese ancestry and could be expected to look to China for inspiration. Nehru was reluctant to acknowledge Ne Win and it took a great deal of persuasion to get him to recognise the ground realities.[16] However the relations remained cold and the nationalisation of the economy did not inspire any confidence in what lay ahead for the relations between the two countries. The past exchange of high level visits for the time being came to an end.

This was also the period that saw another exodus of Indians dispossessed of their businesses and properties. The GOB would not even permit the families being evacuated to keep their personal jewellery. The request for due compensation was rejected and the Foreign Office in Yangon protested when the Indian Embassy took charge of personal jewellery that the evacuees tried to leave behind. Obscure reasoning in Delhi led to instructions going out to the Indian Ambassador that the packages should be returned to the owners even though the GOI was in the know that those items would be confiscated by the Burmese authorities.

Once again GOI had abjectly refrained from standing up for its people on the specious grounds that it would not like to interfere in the internal affairs of a friendly neighbouring country. The plight of these hapless Indians is best understood when one looks at the pittance they got as allowance to take out of Burma—Kyat 75 for an adult, 25 for a child and jewellery worth Kyat 250 per family.

Between 1964 and 1968, 150,000 Indians, mainly businessmen who had owned significant assets prior to nationalisation, left Burma; they have never been paid compensation, nor have they been permitted to regain their properties. Most of the properties of the Indian Banks and

---

[16] The then Indian Ambassador had to bring the ground realities to the attention of Nehru and also point out that we could not afford to wholly alienate the Military leadership keeping India's interests in mind.

Insurance Companies, in Rangoon were not taken over by the State because they were taken over by the Indian Embassy.

At this point, what needs to be emphasised is that this policy of accommodation shown by India did not result in any advantage to India and did not give New Delhi any negotiating points in areas of strategic importance. On the other hand, a more aggressive Beijing came to take precedence over the Ne Win regime and it was hardly surprising that the neutrality practised by him in his relations with the two neighbours was tilted in favour of China.

The real issue was that Nehru and the policy establishment had in a sense failed to read the writing on the wall. There were two clear pointers to what the future of democratic polity would be in Myanmar.

The first pointer was the myriad weakness of the U Nu government, which led to U Nu inviting Ne Win to take over as the caretaker head of government and set things right. This was a clear case of disconnect between the people's desire for the continuance of popular government (which had also restored Myanmar's identity as a Buddhist country) and a political class that was driven by ambitions that worked against stability so necessary to meet head on the various threats posed to the integrity of the new nation.

It would be pertinent here to note that Nehru's reaction to the transference of power in Yangon in 1958 was one of apprehension, but he cautiously placed it in its 'best light'. In a press conference, Nehru compared the developments in Burma to those in Pakistan, stating that in Burma,

> [T]here was not that element of going against democratic working as we have seen in Pakistan. The steps taken by Prime Minister U Nu are admitted to be a temporary phase leading to an election...All I can say is that I have high regard for U Nu's person, judgement and opinion.

Nehru was clearly placing credence on U Nu's judgement and felt that U Nu's actions served the cause of stability. However what was not taken into the calculation was the fact that once a military commander had tasted blood it was unlikely that he would ever want to give up his hold on power. Another important element that Nehru perhaps did not foresee was that U Nu was incapable of finding solutions that would reduce factionalism within his political party to manageable levels that would enable him to manage the country effectively, or find a lasting solution within the Constitution that would meet the aspirations of the ethnic minorities including on the two key issues of autonomy and federalism that would help bring peace and establish a united Burma. U Nu unfortunately was a weak leader who clearly showed himself as unable to safeguard democracy in Burma.

The second pointer was the declaration by the then Colonel Ne Win, in 1945, that the Tatmadaw (the army) 'is not only the hope of the country, but it's very life and soul'.[17] Once the weaknesses of the U Nu government came to the fore and there were moves being made by the ethnic minorities to assert their positions the gate opened for the likes of General Ne Win, 'who harboured their own political ambitions under the cloak of military professionalism'.

The authoritarian model adopted by Ne Win and later continued by the SLORC/SPDC only confirmed the 'fundamentally authoritarian nature of the traditional Burmese state'. It also gave credence to the argument that the influence of *Manusmriti* 'continues to drive the manner in which the authoritarian role has cast itself to reflect that the highly personalised concept of power and the role of the central authority stem back to the Indic roots of Burma's royal past'.[18]

India's policy makers could hardly have been unaware of the facts of Myanmar's historical record—its 'long tradition of an army with entrenched political power', which prevailed from the pre-colonial times. Again, there was the politicians' reliance on the BIA/BNA in the 1940s and 1950s, indicating the importance attached to the role of the armed forces in the political process which culminated in the open conversion to authoritarian military rule, in the firm self-belief that it alone could preserve the unity of the state that was under attack from enemies both domestic and external.

The SLORC/SPDC continued to assert Ne Win's familiar commitment to the 'three sacred causes', spelt out as the integrity of the Union, national unity and the preservation of Myanmar's sovereignty. It was a sign of poor assessment on the part of India's foreign policy formulators,

---

[17] Martin Smith and Peter Carey in *Burma Insurgency and the Politics of Insurgency*, 1991.

[18] David Steinberg, *Burma's Road to Development: Growth and Ideology under Military Rule* (Westview Press, 1981).

particularly for Nehru to have failed to understand that Ne Win would become the arbiter of Myanmar's fate for a long period of time and that it was in India's strategic and security interests to keep him close to India. The relationship between India and the Ne Win ruled Burma did reach a certain level of understanding when Indira Gandhi came to power, albeit it was cast in a mould very different from that which had prevailed between U Nu and Nehru.

At this stage it would be apt for to point out the different ways in which India reacted to the two coups in Myanmar, the first carried out by the armed forces under the Command of Ne Win who was also the Defence Minister in U Nu's cabinet in 1962 and the second by the armed forces this time led by Senior General Saw Maung in 1988. Unlike the negative attitude adopted by India in 1988–1989, the GOI in 1962, being preoccupied by the fast deteriorating relations with China (that eventually led to the October war that very year) restrained itself from severely criticising the coup and did not waste any time in recognising the new regime, the aim being to ensure the continuance of the relations. In contrast the 1988 Coup was looked upon in open disfavour and heavily criticised with assistance being provided to those escaping the brutal assault launched against those demonstrating in favour of democracy. All the same there was a qualitative change in the personal relations at the level of the two leaders at the top after the coup of 1962.

Ne Win, under the guise of the ideology that guided the 'Burmese way to socialism', nationalised the economy, without so much as a the fig leaf of compensation and the negative impact this had on the Indian business and property owning community obviously cast a shadow on the relations. Nehru was confirmed in his view that, with Ne Win, it was just not possible to have the kind of understanding he had with Aung San and U Nu.

The fact was that the war with China and the loss in prestige that India suffered at the hands of the Chinese also led to a fall in India's global reputation. It effectively put to an end to Nehru's leading role in the pursuit of his ideal of a united Asia and its role as a global power. Quite obviously, Indo-Myanmar relations could not stay immune to the impact of the changed image of India after its debacle in the Sino-Indian war and, thereby the 'loss of importance in the region'. 'The easy informality and "sentiment" which had been attached to these relations disappeared, and although relations continued to be cordial they were more correct than close.'[19]

Ne Win did try to show that he had goodwill towards India, whatever may have been the attitude he had displayed against the Indians in Myanmar, by trying to show that he had India's interests at heart in its dispute with China. In 1964 he visited Delhi to meet with an ailing Nehru, ostensibly to wish him speedy recovery. Nevertheless he took this opportunity to suggest that he would like to speed up the work of the Colombo Powers[20] to bring about a genuine reconciliation between the two Asian giants that were his country's neighbours. Nehru was not the one to take this suggestion seriously, keeping in mind the disdainful attitude of the Chinese, which he now equated with that country's arrogant refusal to accept the hand of friendship that India had extended, nor was he willing to place any credence in Ne Win's capacity to influence either Chou En Lai or Mao. This attempt by Ne Win to make a breakthrough with Nehru failed.

A Brief Interlude: The Shastri–Ne Win Period

This was the beginning of the period when relations between the two countries slowly moved away from institutional underpinnings towards one that were almost entirely confined to relations at the top political level. This was despite the sentiments expressed in the 1964 communiqué issued at the end of Indian Foreign Minister Swaran Singh's 1964 visit to Rangoon, that made the point that the meeting had in effect raised the relations again on to the platform espousing ties based on 'equality, mutual respect, non-alignment and peaceful co-existence…'. This was in the aftermath of the Indian business community being ousted and the negative impact that had on the relations, as well as the

---

[19] M.S. Rajan, 'Post-1962 Relations', in *India's Foreign Policy and Relations*, ed. A. Appadorai (South Asian Publishers Private Ltd, 1985).

[20] Comment: The Colombo Powers were set up as part of the effort by some leading nonaligned countries to mediate with China and India immediately after the Sino-Indian war of 1962 and the unilateral ceasefire that China announced in November 1962. The countries concerned were Burma, Cambodia, Egypt, Ghana, Indonesia and Sri Lanka. All of whom were acceptable to both China and India. Their efforts however ended in failure.

need to ensure that Ne Win would co-operate with India on mutual security issues.[21]

Lal Bahadur Shastri's period of premiership saw a turn for the better in the ties, but as the September 1964 Swaran Singh visit showed, the element of personal warmth was missing. Shastri visited Yangon in December 1965—a return visit to Ne Win's visit to India in February 1965, during which the two had agreed to maintain frequent contacts at all executive levels as that would contribute to a frequent exchange of views within the ambit of good neighbourly relations. During Shastri's return visit to Yangon in December that year, the problems created for the Indian community by GOB's nationalisation of the economy were discussed, resulting in the 'assurance' contained in the joint communiqué that resident foreigners who 'continued to play a useful role in the new social order that Burma was building would be given facilities to enable them to live and work in Burma, should they so desire'.

This was clearly double tongued statement which very adeptly placed the onus on those who continued to stay and work, in Burma, within the constraints of misconceived policies that were, soon enough, to drag the economy down to the lowest levels of performance. These policies were aligned to Ne Win's unabashed practice of driving the middle class, the professionals and the intellectuals out of the Burmese mainstream, leading to an exodus of all such people out of the country; those who stayed back were forced to lie low in a land where entrepreneurship and 'use or exploitation of opportunity' had disappeared. Ironically discussions on what was argued as the asset base that nationalisation of Burma's economy meant for the Indian business community established that the loss was in the area of anywhere between 2.3 billion in Burmese currency to 1.4 billion depending on what was calculated by the Indian business community or what was acceptable on a rule of thumb basis by the GOI who felt that the claim was inflated and needed to be brought

---

[21] Comment: The Swaran Singh visit was seen in India as one that had overcome the gap in the relationship that had arisen during the Nehru–Ne Win period and was a step in the direction to 'resume meaningful relations, taking into account the various changes in the regional and international contexts'. This was a clear hint at the fact that India did not want a situation where its relations with the PRC and Pakistan were on the boil to result in a further deterioration in its relations with its neighbours among whom Burma was one that had little interest in siding against India when its own borders were facing the threats of insurgency with material and political support from the PRC.

down to what it felt was an acceptable level. In addition the GOI was willing to accept a cash asset claim of 300 million in local currency. These were the figures that were conveyed to the Ne Win dispensation and advanced in the discussions. The claims were however never formalised as part of any official statement that emerged out of the discussions or the exchanges that took place between the two countries. At one stage it appeared that the Burman Administration was willing to peg the claims at 300 million but ultimately nothing came of this also.

The Ne Win–Indira Gandhi Period: Relations Influenced by the China Factor

The Ne Win–Indira Gandhi relationship was one where all interactive decisions were determined by 'mutual necessity'. Both the leaders being autocratic by nature, they came to understand each other and it was this steely understanding that drove the bilateral relationship. It was in this period that security issues and co-operation between the two countries came to the forefront. The then Indian Defence Minister, Y.B. Chavan, informed the Lower House of Parliament that 'the Burmese Government had responded favourably to the proposal for joint patrolling of the India–Burma border to control insurgent activities and prevent the transit of Indian insurgents through Burmese territory to, or from, China or East Pakistan'.[22]

India was in effect acknowledging the geo-political importance of Burma/Myanmar to India and, to date, India continues to deal with Myanmar as a next door neighbour of South Asia with the added advantage of it being a bridge to Southeast Asia, a region which is of economic, security and strategic importance to India. As K.M. Panikkar highlighted in his study, *Future of South-East Asia: An Indian View*, the defence of India and Burma/Myanmar was 'inextricably interlinked and India could not stint on any sacrifice when it came to the question of defending Burma/Myanmar'.[23]

One of the common factors that guided relations between a democratic India and an autocratically ruled Myanmar were the problems that

---

[22] Lok Sabha Records statement by Y.B. Chavan on 21 February 1967.
[23] K.M.Panikkar, *Future of South-East Asia: An Indian View* (Macmillan, 1943).

were being created for both the countries by the PRC. The aggressive show of power displayed by Maoist China during the heydays of the Cultural Revolution and the attempt by the Chinese residents in Myanmar to raise their voice in favour of the doings in China, as also their open opposition to the express wishes of the Myanmar Government led to strong actions against them, which in turn resulted in Beijing's vituperative condemnation of the Ne Win regime.

This led Indira Gandhi to express a greater closeness for Ne Win and his leadership. The problems with China and the support that country was extending to insurgents both in India and Myanmar was also the reason why India reacted with great restraint on the plight of Indians under the Ne Win regime. (Between June 1963 and December 1966, almost 200,000 Indians left Myanmar after being deprived of their livelihood.) As earlier mentioned, the GOI papered over this problem by wording loosely the communiqué that was issued at the end of the Swaran Singh visit.

The two countries were undoubtedly moving closer in the face of the common threat that they felt from China. In 1967 they signed a boundary agreement which only left out the Tri-junction pending the eventual border settlement between China and India. Indira Gandhi, during the 1968 visit by Ne Win to India made it clear to him in unambiguous terms that she saw Burma as a friendly neighbour and that this position was a key factor in her and India's concept of peace and security in 'South Asia'. Stating that the border agreement signed in 1967 between the two countries had paved the way to stability, peace and understanding she suggested that they work together as equals, creating a co-operative arrangement and understanding to check subversive activities by elements hostile to both countries.

The importance of the Indira–Ne Win talks lay in the fact that both the countries were facing insurgencies supported by the PRC. While the challenge to India was exacerbated by Pakistan's nefarious activities carried out from the erstwhile East Pakistan, Myanmar at that time faced a more intense Chinese interference. This brought the two leaders closer together, making them thrash out steps to mutually confront the challenge. This resulted in understandings involving joint patrolling, a degree of hot pursuit (particularly as the Yangon authorities had large areas along their frontiers that were not within their effective control), regular bilateral meetings both at the administrative levels and the local commanders levels, a modified system that took into account the prevailing realities—a system which, after the hiatus in the relationship during the 1988–1992 period, is now once again in operation between the present Myanmar and Indian authorities.

The GOI informed Parliament in 1965 that the Burmese forces had intercepted a 1,000 strong force of Naga hostiles who were attempting to flee to East Pakistan via Burma and had forced them to go back to India.[24] At the same time Parliament was informed that gangs of hostiles were also using Burmese territory, out of the reach of the Burmese forces, for transiting to and from the PRC on missions to acquire arms and training.

Given the compulsions arising out of such a situation, both sides recognised the paramount need to make co-operation on the issue the centrepiece of the relations between the two countries; this was openly confirmed in statements that were made by Ne Win and Indira Gandhi during the several visits they exchanged over those years. The primary goal was to check the acts of insurgency in the border territories of the two countries by hostile elements who were trained, given arms and other supplies and unleashed on to the region by Chinese and the Pakistani agencies.

The clearest statement of intent was made by Ne Win during the March 1969 visit by Indira Gandhi to Myanmar, when he stated that he had taken 'necessary measures against those nationals of India who seek to use our territory for hostile activities against India'. He further clarified this by adding, '...needless to say, such action on our part serves not only our mutual interest but also the larger interest of peace and unity among the neighbours'. The last words are significant, as it did not limit the reference to only India and Myanmar, but extended it to cover other 'neighbours', that is, China which was causing problems by extending material support to Myanmar insurgents and the CPB, that had gone militant against the GOB.

This statement, a strong endorsement of Indo-Burma relations, aroused an equally strong reaction from Beijing, ending in the use of vituperative language against Ne Win, calling his government a 'fascist dictatorship'. This was in keeping with its criticism of what it saw as a relationship that stood in the way of China's attempts at destabilising the two countries. This unabashedly aggressive posture added to the resolve of Indira Gandhi and Ne Win to enter into 'closer political co-operation to meet the common danger posed' by China.

The closer political understanding had its influence on economic ties too, with India continuing to import rice from Myanmar even when it was not really needed because of the supplies it was getting from the US under the PL 480 programme. Further, despite the fact that India was a capital starved country, from time to time it extended assistance in the form of loans for the purchase of Indian goods and commodities at much lower interest rates than those prevailing in India. Of course, India could not match the very low interest rates that Japan and Germany offered on loans to Myanmar. Another factor that came in the way of a more robust trade and economic relationship was the isolationist policy adopted by Ne Win and the fact that his economic policies had in turn made Burma unattractive for investments and its trade potential had also deteriorated reducing its potential as a trade partner.

The aim behind the economic and business co-operation that was being encouraged by the two leaders was to ensure greater regional and bilateral understanding between the two neighbouring countries. However, no attempt was made at this time to expand this relationship by formalising a border trade agreement (BTA), which would have given a more realistic content to the trade relations; such a move would have spurred development activities in the regions adjoining the border trade centres, much to the advantage of people on both sides of the border, besides fortifying the security environment/structure of this strategic region. Ne Win's reluctance to accept India's proposal on the issue was that, if he entered into such an agreement with India, he would have to replicate it with China. This was unacceptable, given the fact that China was supporting insurgency movements in Burma. At the same time Ne Win was also keen to keep a lid on overt relations with India, as any open show of bilateral understanding could further strain his relations with Beijing. In pursuance of his balancing act strategy in his relations with the two neighbouring countries, he made it a point to visit China almost as often as he visited India.

Ne Win tried to keep the contacts confined to the top leaders, which suited Indira Gandhi. The two pushed for the conclusion to the Border (demarcation) Agreement and it was concluded without any glitches as the Tri-junction was kept outside the agreement's purview. They could talk at ease with each other on the problems of South Asia and the problems created by China.

Ne Win showed a close understanding of the problem of East Pakistan and the events of 1971, which ultimately ended in the establishment of the free nation of Bangladesh. His government was among the first to recognise Bangladesh.

He was also in agreement with India's vision of the Indian Ocean as a region of peace and tranquillity, free of foreign bases.

One glitch in the relations was the grant of asylum by Indira Gandhi to U Nu and his family in India. U Nu had shown clearly that he would work for the fall of the Ne Win dictatorship and had taken some infructuous steps in that direction. When these attempts failed, he had sought refuge in India and was given the permission on the understanding that he would not carry out any actions adverse to the relations between the two countries from Indian soil. U Nu was a family friend whose close relations with Nehru had been of such warmth and understanding that India could not turn him away and, despite his concern, Ne Win was satisfied by the manner in which Indira Gandhi handled the situation, especially after U Nu retired to a Buddhist monastery. This action helped keep the asylum issue within the ambit/context of the civilisational and religio-cultural ties that bound the two countries and kept it from becoming an issue of political misunderstanding.

On the other hand, however, what created a lacuna in the GOI–SLORC ties between 1988–1991 was U Nu's daughter Than Than Nu's tendency to attack the SLORC and Ne Win through AIR.

1988–1992: Relations at Their Lowest Level

The 1988 demonstrations and the ruthless manner in which they were dealt with, first by U Sein Lwin and then the SLORC, attracted immediate condemnation from India. The people of Burma had finally risen in anger, forcing Ne Win and his senior party and government leaders to resign from all governmental and Party posts; Ne Win proposed to the BSPP Party Congress that a referendum be held to determine whether the people wanted to revert to multi-party rule and, despite his proposal being rejected by the BSPP Congress, for a brief period there emerged the possibility of the people having their way.

The protests in Myanmar were already winning public and political support in India. The SLORC's suppressive actions aroused strong reaction among all Indians, with the Indian Administration, for all practical purposes, taking the same view as the public, believing that the already critical situation in the relations between the two countries had been exacerbated by the negative impact on them of the ruthless manner in which the demonstrating students, monks and common citizens were killed to crush the uprising.

The Indian Ambassador of the time (1988) took the position that the people's revolt against a system that was blatantly autocratic was substantive in nature and that any government that succeeded the Ne Win regime would be too weak to deal with the sustained pressure that the people were placing on them, inspired as they were by the U Nu era leaders, particularly the dynamic leadership that Aung San Suu Kyi provided to the younger and more aggressive masses. He felt that all of this would ultimately lead to a political compromise in favour of democracy that would meet the wishes of the vast majority of the people of Myanmar.

However, the SLORC came to fill the vacuum created by Ne Win's resignation and, following the failure of both Sein Lwin and then Maung Maung to control the situation. It wasted no time in adopting a policy of taming the demonstrators with deliberate and ruthless acts of suppression. The SLORC, once it had formulated a new economic policy and had made certain that the people understood that it would not tolerate any attempt by them to take over power by force, felt confident enough to permit the holding of multi-party elections; this, in a sense, vindicated the Indian Ambassador's stand. Once again like Ne Win in 1960, the SLORC expected that a stable regime that it had set in place, this time with a positive economic programme, would influence the people to vote in the King's Party (National Unity Party) to power, which would keep the military's exercise of authority intact and entrenched.

During the electioneering period in 1990, the SLORC, apprehending the problem Aung San Suu Kyi and her concept of a free democratic government could pose, placed her under house arrest in the belief that the move would keep the situation under its control. However the people of Myanmar showed once again, in a repeat of what they had done in 1960 that, given the chance, they would vote for democracy and a democratic government. The SLORC immediately nullified the results of the poll that went overwhelmingly in favour of the democratic forces on the premise that the people of the country were not able to judge what was best for them. To counteract the pressure for democracy by the people, principally by the urban populace, the SLORC not only introduced a very extensive curfew system imposing severe penalties on those caught breaking the curfew, but also carried out military exercises in public areas including the streets in the heart of the cities and towns indicative of the ruthless brutality by which curfew violators would be deprived of their lives with their families being incarcerated. The whole idea was to break the will of the people including the students and the monks who had taken the lead in demonstrating against the authoritarian system.

1988: The Rajiv Gandhi Government Reacts Adversely to Events in Myanmar

India reacted very strongly against the ruthless exercise of power displayed by the SLORC and there was a clear call voiced by the Rajiv Gandhi government supporting the movement for the restoration of democracy and the end to the 25 years of authoritarian system of governance that Ne Win had imposed and now his brain child, the SLORC, was imposing on the people of Myanmar. India supported the attempt made by U Nu and Suu Kyi to take over the reins of the country, and condemned the military takeover that soon took the place vacated by the Ne Win regime including its so called civilian face. An uneasy military brass that finally came out in uniform to stage a coup and took over power, immediately abrogated the 1974 Constitution put in place by Ne Win and resorted to the use of force to end the demonstrations.

India's and international condemnation was swift to follow and the support for the movement for democratic rule was loud and clear. The Indian Embassy became a focus of pervasive surveillance as it was seen as co-operating with the various forces including the students, the democratic movement, as also the Kachins and Karens who were battling the Myanmar forces.

Rajiv Gandhi as Prime Minister, had visited Rangoon in 1987 to persuade Ne Win to bring Myanmar into the SAARC and had also presented an economic package, a gesture which showed India's desire for a stronger bilateral relationship. But in 1998, his was a clarion call against the military takeover and its brutal actions.

The Indian authorities openly assisted the students and politicians who fled to India. They were welcomed and the Indian Minister for External Affairs, P.V. Narsimha Rao, in his briefing to the Parliamentary Committee on External Affairs, said India condemned the use of force against the demonstrators, and was doing everything possible in support of the people of that country including providing assistance to those who were seeking the help of India. The SLORC, he added, had been left in no doubt about the support that India would be willing to extend to the democratic forces in Burma. The Parliamentary Committee was also assured that orders had been passed to all concerned that no Burmese seeking refuge in India would be turned back from its borders.

The SLORC was perceived as no better than the continuation of the authoritarian regime that was continuing in a re-modelled fashion the dominance of the armed forces, just as they exercised unlimited power during the Ne Win period. It was this continuation of autocratic rule that the protesters were fighting. Tempers cooled somewhat when the SLORC promised to hold multi-party elections and began the process of adopting economic, business[25] and developmental policies that were set to overturn the BSPP ideology of isolation, which had reduced the country to LDC status.

---

[25] The economic and pro-business policy adopted ironically led to the surfacing of local Indian business persons; these were not part of the mainstream Indian business community who were forced out of Myanmar in the wake of the adoption of nationalisation of all commercial activity under Ne Win; they had remained behind and continued to live subdued business lives, they now emerged out of the background and commenced to provide substance to the new economic policy adopted by the SLORC and given additional support by the SPDC policy pro-business structure. Not surprisingly some of them had continued to remain in touch with the senior military officers and one of them is quite close to General Than Shwe.

7
Of Mistrust, Mutual Discord and Disenchantment

The V.P. Singh government which succeeded the Rajiv Gandhi-led Congress government continued the policy of extending support to the Burmese democratic movement and welcomed the holding of elections, while strongly condemning the house arrest of Suu Kyi.

India lauded NLD for winning the elections with a thumping majority—392 seats in a house with 485 seats, while the National Unity Party (NUP) won only 10 seats. This was an indubitable expression of the people of Myanmar for the return of democratic governance to that country. India and the democratic world were one in voicing their call for the swift installation of a democratic government in Yangon.

India also supported the stand that the newly elected Parliament would in effect act as a Constituent Assembly and set the task of drafting and adopting a new constitution that would also address the concerns of the ethnic minorities. However, the SLORC which had itself given the permission for multi-party elections, now reneged and simply refused to handover power to the elected representatives.

This was the state of affairs when I came to Yangon at the end of August 1990 and took charge of India's relations with Myanmar with a very restrictive mandate from the GOI. The V.P. Singh government and its Minister for External Affairs, I.K. Gujral, were clearly committed to putting pressure on the SLORC to adhere to its commitment and handover of political power to the NLD and its allies.

In the meanwhile, India had put severe constraints on doing business with the SLORC-run Myanmar; even direct trade had been placed on hold with the Reserve Bank of India (RBI) issuing a directive to Indian banks not to open letters of credit. All effective trade was being conducted via Singapore. The co-operative arrangements on the borders that enabled local civilian and military authorities on both sides to check the movement of insurgents broke down and were abandoned for the time being.

The assistance extended under India's ITEC programme had also been suspended. Though this programme had not been of great substantive content, it had become a tool of influence in the bilateral relations. It had covered areas in the economic and social developmental fields and had a semblance of programmatic content that covered the defence area. It thus had a symbolical value that far exceeded the material assistance that was provided under it to Myanmar.

In actual fact, contact between the two sides was minimalised at a time when it was apparent that the SLORC was moving swiftly towards a close relationship with China—a China that had for all practical purposes turned away from supporting the CPB and was willing to co-operate with SLORC in settling its insurgency problems. It was also clear that the PRC was supporting the Yangon regime both militarily and economically while the rest of the world was positing a regime of sanctions, resulting in the SLORC looking upon the PRC as its saviour and quickly moving into China's sphere of influence.

Managing India's relations in the complex situation that had come to prevail in Myanmar was further complicated by the uncertain political climate existing in India along with an economy that was on the skids.

During my stay in Yangon from August 1990 to September 1992, there were three changes of government in India and there was little clarity on how to deal with the prevailing situation that had brought bilateral relations to a dead end. The only possible solution lay in both countries starting a fresh relationship taking the new ground realities into account.

My instructions from the V.P. Singh government were that I was not to establish any kind of relations with the SLORC cabinet. In fact, I was not to meet with or call on any of the ministers, including the powerful Khin Nyunt who had overall control on external relations, security affairs and political settlement with the insurgent groups. New Delhi relented on my insistence that I be permitted to meet with the ministers dealing with economic and developmental policies. I was also able to convince the GOI that we had to remove the RBI directive placing a prohibition on letters of credit, as this would at least send the symbolic message that we were willing to carry out normal trade and economic relations.

What was even more telling was my call on the then Cabinet Secretary in Delhi, who clearly felt that we should support the Western point of view and continue to follow policies that would keep our relations in a limbo until the SLORC gave in and agreed to transfer of power to the NLD and Suu Kyi. This was in keeping with the position that the US administration had adopted, which went to the extent of not replacing the American Ambassador who left soon after I came to Yangon.

It had to be once again pointed out that, while Americans and Europeans were thousands of miles away, we, as next door neighbours, shared extensive land and maritime frontiers and, importantly, we also had insurgency concerns in the North-East that had been exploited by the Chinese and other powers that were inimical to our interests. To mitigate this negative attitude it was essential for India to continue to have the co-operation of Myanmar. In India's own interest, therefore, it was necessary to try and restore a degree of normalcy to our relations.

The PRC Factor

Delhi slowly realised, and accepted this at the political leadership level, essentially only after P.V. Narasimha Rao took over as the Indian Prime Minister, that by not taking ground realities into account we were virtually encouraging China to fill the vacuum in an isolated Myanmar, especially since Beijing had restrained itself from exploiting the post-1988 internal political situation. Beijing had also moved away from the policy of encouraging the ethnic groups to continue the insurgencies against Yangon. There were also clear indications that a closer co-operation was growing between the Beijing and Yangon regimes, while areas of co-operation between Myanmar and India had broken down. A new situation had developed with PRC and SLORC becoming the best of friends, with the former promising to back the latter—all aimed at bringing Yangon under its sphere of influence. This was a price that the SLORC was willing to pay to obtain China's support in resolving many of Myanmar's outstanding domestic insurgency and economic development problems and to help it confront international pressure.

It eventually dawned on the Indian establishment that by developing a close defence and strategic relationship with an entrenched military managed system of governance in Myanmar, China was establishing a relationship that gave leverage to its overall strategy of surrounding India on all three sides of its land frontiers and, gradually developing a strong presence on India's maritime frontier, including the Indian Ocean.

The Overwhelming Negative Impact of the AIR Burmese Language Broadcasts

However, before we move on to the details of what happened in this period, it is worth looking at a few facts that were on my plate in the earlier part of my ambassadorship, as it reflected the state of the existing relations.

The first was the situation that arose at the time of the presentation of my credentials to Senior General Saw Maung. In the briefing, I had been told by the COP that it would be a brief ceremony followed by a cup of tea and a polite exchange of social niceties. There was to be no reading out of speeches, but a written statement could be handed over along with the credentials. It is also worth noting that no one from the Embassy was permitted by the local protocol to accompany me, not even the military attaché. Fair enough. I was not particularly keen to have a major discussion, keeping in mind the limited mandate that I had been given by the GOI.

Soon enough, it was evident that the COP had been wrongly advised; the General was in a mood to have a substantive discussion, starting off with a complaint against the Burmese language service of the AIR which was being handled by two Burmese nationals including U Nu's daughter Than Than Nu. She was using the broadcasting space to air her own views on developments in Myanmar including personalised attacks on Ne Win without adhering to the official Indian position. That morning's edition of news and views, in Burmese, over the AIR mentioned that India did not intend to have diplomatic relations with the SLORC. This was peculiar to say the least, as what was being put across was in direct contradiction to the fact that India had not only not broken off diplomatic relations but, on that very morning, I, as the new Indian Ambassador, was presenting my credentials to the head of state, General Saw Maung.

The point made very elaborately by Saw Maung was that damaging personalised attacks were broadcast by the AIR (which he described as a 'state-controlled media') and that there were attempts being made by it to encourage the people to rise against the government. These were described by him as unfriendly acts that were not in keeping with good neighbourly relations. He also made the point that Ne Win had been close to the Indian prime ministers, that he had dealt with Rajiv Gandhi as a 'nephew' as he was Indira Gandhi's son and he had provided him with avuncular advice on how he could govern India when he condoled with him on his mother's death while extending his hand of friendship. The SLORC considered him (Ne Win) as a father figure and hoped that these broadcasts that were hurtful and subversive in nature would be stopped. He gave me a translated copy of that morning's broadcast.

I had to think out a quick response to try and mitigate the negative impact of the AIR's Burmese service that served no visible purpose; this was soon pointed out in dispatches to the concerned people in Delhi. However, at this stage I felt that damage control was necessary and suggested that the AIR broadcasts should not be seen as having official sanction, as AIR had been granted a fair degree of autonomy. I then pointed out that the very fact that the morning's broadcast had boldly stated that India did not have diplomatic relations with the Myanmar Government of the day which only went to prove that its broadcasts did not have any official validity. In fact, I said, it was contradicting Indian policy.

We then had a fairly extensive exchange on the existing state of relations between the two countries with Saw Maung bearing a somewhat vacuous look touched in some depth on the current state of relations. He suggested that it was India that had resorted to direct attacks on the SLORC's attempts to stabilise the situation that had been created by a misdirected group of Burmese people who had been encouraged to carry out a subversive role by outside agencies that were attempting to destabilise Myanmar. In this difficult period through which their country was passing they expected their neighbours to stand by them and were happy with the current state of relations with China who had stood by them and was providing assistance that was helping them in restoring stability and was enabling them to work towards the economic development of the country.

In response, I clarified that we attached great importance to our ties with a country for which we had always harboured feelings of great goodwill. We had collaborated with each other to meet and address problems along our borders in the past and would hope to see that the collaboration continued, adding that we had always appreciated the policy of a balanced relationship that Myanmar had followed with both its major neighbours, China and India, and we hoped that this balance would continue to be maintained in mutual interest. Saw Maung was quick to suggest that they continued to look on India as a friend, but it was India that had shown reluctance to continue a close relationship.

I made reference to the main point of divergence in the current state of the relations: It was because his government had yet to fulfil its commitment to handover power to the duly elected majority party. I made this point carefully, couching the words within remarks of politely congratulating the SLORC for its having held free and fair elections, adding that, in keeping with that policy and the promises that SLORC had made to the people of Myanmar, it was India's hope that he would transfer power soon. Overall it was apparent that the SLORC at its highest leadership levels was apprehensive of the support that they felt India might extend to the democratic movement, particularly as they had noted the stand that Rajiv Gandhi had taken to support the forces of democracy in Myanmar. They were also worried over the contacts that they felt Indian agencies had developed with the Kachin leadership that was in open rebellion against Yangon.

I was aware that this would be the only opportunity that I would have at the highest level to give the messages that I had to convey, but I also knew that there was little that the SLORC would do to restore democracy in Myanmar. They had come to be deeply entrenched in the belief that the economic opportunities that they were creating would convey the message to the people that the SLORC was committed to improving the quality of life of the people, thus it was in people's interest to support the actions of SLORC. It was apparent that Khin Nyunt had made the assessment that the main reason behind the uprising of 1988 was the lack of economic opportunity and the low quality of life conditions that had come to exist in Myanmar as a result of the national-isation of the economy that had been adopted by Ne Win and the BSPP. The regime believed that the new economic policy framework and the business benefits that these would accrue to the people of Myanmar would gain them the support of the masses. At the same time, their actions sent out the message to the people that they would retaliate with the full force at their disposal to put down any attempts to demonstrate or protest against the refusal to handover power to the people's repre-sentatives.

Khin Nyunt, who was the obvious power behind the throne and, like Saw Maung close to Ne Win, was present at the credentials ceremony. He was the architect of the close relations with China, as a result of which Beijing supplied Tatmadaw with the necessary fire power to secure its frontiers for the first time since Myanmar's independence in 1948.

The co-operative stand that Beijing adopted helped Khin Nyunt to put in place policies that led to a number of agreements with the eth-nic insurgents, making them agree to refrain from the use of force as a trade-off for granting them a degree of autonomy in local administra-tion and allowing them to retain their arms. Beijing backed up its sup-port with a grant of US$1.2 billion worth of defence assistance, which forced the insurgent leadership to come to the negotiating table. The agreements helped bring a degree of stability to most of the Shan State border regions.

The only exception for the time being were the areas held by the Kachins in northern Myanmar and the eastern border with Thailand, where the Karens and the students continued to battle the armed forces. As far as India was concerned the western and northern borders were of immediate concern to it as these were the geographical areas where the insurgent groups from India's north-eastern region continued to find shelter and transit to training areas in Bangladesh and the State of Yunnan in China. Understandably we were interested in the Myanmar authorities establishing a greater degree of administrative control over these border areas and that they would then deny the use of these adjoining areas of Myanmar by Indian insurgent groups. However the policy of reserve that we were exercising in our relations with the SLORC regime had come in the way of our collaborating with them to ensure a greater degree of stability to the common border region which was to our mutual interest.

The V.P. Singh government's instructions were clear that I was not to call on Khin Nyunt. Thus the credentials' presentation occasion provided me with the opportunity to focus on putting across the issue of what India really expected, at the same time maintaining the basic spirit of friendly relations and non-interference in Myanmar's internal affairs. Further, I pointedly reiterated for Khin Nyunt's benefit that, while we were appreciative of the realities of the emerging Sino-Myanmar relations, we expected that India's security interests, of which they were fully aware, would not be compromised. Khin Nyunt maintained silence during the entire discussion, while his deputy (a colonel in the military intelligence) took note of what was being said and I was confident that the SLORC would keep a door open, though it would depend on India when the relations would come out of cold storage.

At a subsequent meeting with Deputy Minister for Foreign Affairs Ohn Kyaw and the COP, I was asked which of the ministers I would like to call on. Kyaw hinted that I may like to call on Khin Nyunt under whose control he was managing foreign policy. I gave them the names of the ministers heading the economic ministries, and told them that I would give them the names of the others later. Both Ohn Kyaw and the COP, who was a serving military intelligence officer, were left with little doubt that I had no intention of calling on Khin Nyunt.

The message that went out was that India was bound by its commitment to support the forces of democracy, which had the endorsement of the people of India as was clearly expressed by India's Parliament and public opinion. Nevertheless, New Delhi gave assurances that the relations with the SLORC would concentrate on economic matters and that there would be no change in India's continuing involvement with the Kachins, an involvement that the SLORC understood was driven by the desire to prevent or contain the insurgencies in India's North-East where the support of the Kachin leadership to deny geographical space to Indian insurgents in the Kachin State was an important factor.

I called on the NLD leadership as it was then constituted, in keeping with our desire to fully underscore the import of our support to the democratic forces and was hardly surprised to see the caution with which I was received. For the record, I was told that they understood that India would do business with the government in power as warranted by India's national interest, but appreciated the fact that India would continue to push for a power transfer in Myanmar. Privately, I was told that they (NLD members) were worried that the relations between the SLORC and China were strengthening the resolve of the former to continue its autocratic rule.

Discussions that I continued to have, at regular intervals at the policy level in Delhi, showed little clarity as to what we needed to do; by our refusal to do substantive business with the SLORC leadership we were giving the Chinese an open field to further draw the Myanmar leadership deeper into the Chinese area of influence, much to the detriment of our strategic and security interests.

It was not lost on me that, for all practical purposes, the area or region east of and up to the Irrawady had come under overt Chinese influence and that their physical presence was rapidly expanding, particularly in and around Mandalay; nor could I ignore the fact that China was increasing its strategic grasp over Myanmar and that Kunming was becoming the nodal point in the Myanmar–China relationship. It was an interesting reflection on the developing situation that SLORC never facilitated my visit to Mandalay. They did not refuse to grant permission, but always delayed the permission to days after dates for the visit were conveyed. More telling was the fact that such delays did not occur when I sought permission for my wife and personal Indian friends who came to visit Mandalay.

Additionally, we were getting indications that the Chinese were still continuing to encourage those who were in conflict with the Indian state and there was some evidence that the Yunnan area was still hosting training centres.

Apart from the China factor, there was the use of Myanmar territory by Indian insurgent groups for transit purposes, particularly by those who were being trained and armed at camps within Bangladesh. The issue, therefore, was one where ultimately the Indian policy makers had to consider in a cold and calculated manner the consequences both in the short and medium term of maintaining a distance from the Government of Myanmar (GOM) that was the government of the day, no matter how offended we were with its complete disregard for human rights and reneging on the promise to handover power to the winning democratic combine.

I spent two years in Myanmar in slowly bringing home to the GOI the consequences of refusing to read the situation on the ground and the need to move in the direction of realpolitik. During the interregnum, there were certain actions that were taken on my advice to try and return some substance to the relations.

Restraint on the Burmese Broadcasts of the AIR

The first step was to rectify the trouble that the AIR Burmese language broadcasts were causing, largely because of the irresponsible reporting and the use of personalised attacks by persons who were patently biased. While one certainly sympathised with their sentiments, these could not be permitted to come in the way of India's interests. Based on the translations and observations on the content of the broadcasts, a decision was taken at the level of the Cabinet Secretary and the Secretary in the Ministry of Information and Broadcasting to reduce the damage these broadcasts were causing by closely monitoring the content. Eventually when the damage continued despite the monitoring, it became clear that the only way to stop it was to remove the two broadcasters including U Nu's daughter.

The incident had its own fall out. The wife of K.R. Narayanan who was of Myanmar origin and was fully engaged with the Myanmar students, politicians and others who had taken refuge in India and was providing support from public platforms in India to the democratic movement, went on to attack me personally on the grounds that I had taken action against the AIR broadcasts because according to her I was afraid of the SLORC and was keen to work with them against the forces of democracy.

Here was a lady whose husband had been a senior colleague in the IFS and had served in Burma where he had met and married his wife and thus knew what Myanmar was all about. He had joined the Congress party following his retirement from the IFS after serving as India's envoy to Washington and he had also served as a Minister of State in the Congress government headed by Indira Gandhi and subsequently by Rajiv Gandhi. He was at this time a Member of Parliament and certainly had a very good idea of what India would eventually face if it did not do something to restore a degree of normalcy to its relations with a strategically important neighbour where China had gained a remarkably large footprint. I met him and explained the situation; he understood, but I had made the mistake of not insisting that Mrs Narayanan also be present so that she would understand too. The result was that her attacks continued and eventually at the insistence of the Ministry I had another meeting with Mr Narayanan, but this time I insisted that his wife be present. Finally, comprehending the damage she was causing, she discontinued her uninformed personalised attacks on me. This did not mean that she did not continue to express herself strongly on the developments in Myanmar.

Border Trade Agreement

The second task we dealt with was to restore the economic and business relations back to a degree of normalcy. I had meetings with Brigadier Abel, who was the Trade Minister and we came to an understanding that we would work towards a better trade relationship. I also met the Minister for Agriculture, who was involved with issues connected with GATT and the Uruguay Round Negotiations (URN). Our discussions evolved in the identification of items that we could work on to promote a substantive content to multilateral trade issues of common interest.

Further, they wanted to know what the implications were of the new regimes that would emerge out of the URN and were given the Indian positions which they found useful in making and finalising their own assessments. The idea behind these discussions was actually to push the envelope on our wish to cast Indo-Myanmar relations in a pragmatic mould and without too much of a fuss find ways and means of carrying out business with the government in power.

The Agriculture Minister became the face of the SLORC that would deal with us. He understood that India was trying to work outside the imperatives of public opinion to shape the relations along the building blocks that the economic side of the relationship provided. However when it came to giving further shape to these relations by reviving the proposals made by Rajiv Gandhi during his visit to Myanmar in 1987, inclusive of an aid-cum-loan package, there was a very limited response. Finally it was the railways sector that was identified for further discussions and the beginnings were made to commence co-operation in this area, which were built upon later.

One thing that became clearer even in the economic areas was that the China factor now impinged on relations with India in an even more pervasive manner. India could only play a secondary role, or rather be the third in consideration, given the priority ASEAN received in SLORC's foreign policy imperatives.

There had been proposals made in the past on the subject of a BTA that would enable both sides to give greater local content to their relations, with the hope that this would to an extent help mitigate grievances that people on both sides of the frontier had against their respective governments. However, Ne Win was not ready for this, as he had his own worries about the conditions on the borders with China and the possibility that a border agreement with India would have to be replicated with China, thereby giving China another tool to exploit the vulnerabilities on the Myanmar borders to its own singular advantage.

In the meanwhile, the traditional border trade that was confined to head loads allegedly through recognised entry and exit points had grown significantly and was certainly larger in value and volume than the official direct trade between India and Myanmar, including the diverted trade via Singapore.

The SLORC had in the meanwhile overcome the Ne Win paranoia over border trade with China and had gone ahead and signed an agreement with the hope that this would also bring in greater revenue. Now an agreement with India was being proposed, which was getting the support at the Commerce and External Affairs Ministerial levels with the Finance Ministry eyeing the financial and administrative advantage that it would accrue.

I argued against this agreement holding out that it would not add anything to India either in revenue or political terms. All the items that were being exported at the border, and this was large in value terms, were retail items that were already taxed in India. From Myanmar there were items of consumer interest that were coming into India from third countries. Additionally, we were getting Myanmar products like rice and timber that were in short supply on the Indian side.

If our goal was really to put in place a progressive system that would allow the free movement of goods, services and people, it would have made sense. Otherwise, we would uselessly be imposing conditions of formal trade that would be difficult to implement in a sensitive and unstable border region without bringing any real increase in revenue. However we eventually gave in and the BTA was signed. In practical terms, the official border trade has yet to reach a dimension of real significance.

SAARC Membership: Proposal Made by Rajiv Gandhi (1987)

An area of discussion with Ohn Kyaw in the regional context was our effort to reintroduce the proposal that Rajiv Gandhi had made to Ne Win on Myanmar joining SAARC. The idea now was that this would bring India, as part of South Asia, to a closer networking relationship with Myanmar. It was also to test the waters, as it would show in which direction China was pushing the SLORC, as far its regional affiliations were concerned. Considering that we were still involved in public denunciations of the treatment being meted out to the opposition—the students and in particular Suu Kyi—we could hardly be seen by the SLORC in a friendly spirit, particularly since they saw India as continuing its push for the re-establishment of a democratic government in Myanmar, an idea for which the SLORC had shown much distaste.

Again, India was not seen as one that could give them real aid and assistance in meeting the economic needs of the kind that they had in mind. China and ASEAN, along with Japan were seen as more beneficial partners and once Beijing showed that it would be happy for Myanmar to become a member of ASEAN within the ASEAN approach of constructive engagement: they went ahead and were taken on board by ASEAN along with the other countries of Indo-China.

Ohn Kyaw took the trouble to inform us that they had decided on ASEAN and would not be interested as such in SAARC but would not be averse to considering a role as a physical bridge between the two regional arrangements. While this might have seemed a diplomatic sop to keep India 'happy', Myanmar acting as a bridge between the two regional arrangements could be seen as a pragmatic fallout of its joining ASEAN while retaining its South Asian links. The comfort level with ASEAN in the face of Western pressure and the pressure being seen as applied by India could not but be an important determinant in Myanmar going the ASEAN way.

The other issue that we tried to place on the map was the possibility of Oil and Natural Gas Corporation Ltd (ONGC) looking at the opportunities for exploring the oil riches of Myanmar. Already the discoveries in the Gulf of Martaban were a matter of fact and evidence was increasing of there being more possibilities within the Myanmar geographical land and maritime region. Meetings with the Minister for Energy proved positive: he suggested that India look at exploring the western offshore and onshore areas that are up for exploration. Thinking that this could be a major factor in bringing relations to a more realistic platform, the Ministry of Petroleum and ONGC were contacted, but the political will to take this proposition seriously was weak. A change in government had taken place in Delhi with the new Prime Minister (Chandrashekar) completely dependent on the Rajiv Gandhi-led Congress party's outside support. There could be no major initiatives that the Chandrashekar government could undertake without the full support of Rajiv Gandhi, who had made it clear that he wanted the pressure on the SLORC to transfer power to Suu Kyi be maintained. Chandrasekhar as PM could not come to any decision without Rajiv Gandhi's approval.

This apart, there was the position taken by ONGC that interstellar surveys conducted by them did not show the occurrence of commercially viable potential in the western areas. ONGC is nothing if not a willing trade horse of the government of the day and is capable of tailoring its technical advice to meet the commands of its political masters. It is ironic that now we have the same ONGC as a partner in the energy scenario in Myanmar, in the very same areas which they had then discarded as of no practical, commercial value.

8

The Security Issue and the Indian Approach: 1992

Another reality that we were faced with surfaced in 1991, when I received an urgent telephone call from the Foreign Secretary on a matter which required immediate implementation; we had received hard intelligence in Delhi that a group of highly trained and armed Indian insurgents were on their way from Bangladesh via the western region of Myanmar to India, with the clear aim of creating havoc in the north-east region of India. He wanted co-operation from the Myanmar authorities to deny them passage and to hold them. There was the implied threat that, if the Myanmar authorities did not take preventive action against the use of their territory, India may be forced to take action in the form of hot pursuit.

It was an interesting stage in the relations, where the lapse of any working political relationship with the SLORC had led to the breakdown in the border arrangements in which the two countries had, albeit fitfully, worked together to deny the use of their territories to insurgents on either side.

Delhi was learning the hard way that sentiment could not be a substitute for practical arrangements which necessitated co-operation, irrespective of the nature of the regime that was wielding power in a neighbouring country.

This was obviously an occasion where Delhi's self-imposed limitations on a meeting with Khin Nyunt were no longer viable. I had been instructed to meet him immediately and take up this matter. I was aware that the Myanmar military intelligence set-up (headed by Khin Nyunt) would have informed Khin Nyunt of the contents of the unsecured tele-conversation (which would have been monitored by them); he would also be aware that I had taken a very moderate tone and advised that there could be a likely positive outcome as the SLORC would in principal want to prevent the use of its land by insurgents.

I was promptly granted a meeting the very next day by Khin Nyunt and we had a long discussion that covered not only the subject at hand but on the whole impasse to which relations had reached and the need for finding ways to deal with each other with respect and understanding.

I could see that it was not lost on him that efforts to restrain the AIR broadcasts had been a positive action on our part and that while there were gaps that needed to be covered, we in India were gradually coming to the conclusion that change in governance in Myanmar was unlikely in the foreseeable future and that India would have to effect a change in its attitude as a part of a pragmatically worked out arrangement that would cater to the imperatives of national self-interest.

Our exchange on the imposing relationship with the PRC and where this left the relations with India was an interesting dance around the need to bring an understandable balance, so that India would feel that there was space in the relationship that would safeguard its strategic and security interests.

However, there were no promises exchanged at this stage except on the subject that had served as the motivation for this exchange. Here Khin Nyunt gave an assurance, albeit it was couched in subtle language, that Myanmar outposts would keep a watch out for any such attempt. Both of us knew that, in the recent past, the authorities on the border had turned their face away from such movements by insurgents and it was a source of satisfaction to the SLORC that India had begun to realise the consequences of the impasse and hoped that steps would gradually be taken to close the gaps in the relations.

In the meantime, we would have to be content with the SLORC's assurance that the closeness of their relations with Beijing were not at the cost of their relations with India. He, in fact, suggested that the responsibility for the gaps in the relations were the consequence of Indian policy positions that failed to understand that the SLORC would never permit a position to develop in Myanmar that would work adversely to the interests of the armed forces, by which he meant that India should recognise that they (the military) would always exercise control over Myanmar's destiny.

This was the only formal meeting that I had with Khin Nyunt, but it left behind the impression that we in India had to have a relook at our relations. It was also apparent to me that I was too closely identified in their minds with the policy of limited relations and the open support for the transfer of power to the Suu Kyi-led NLD.

However, before dwelling on the need for the adoption of a more practical policy, there were other developments that took place that need to be touched upon briefly.

The first was the SLORC's perception of Rajiv Gandhi and the strong position of support that he had adopted on the issue of democracy and Suu Kyi. It was not lost on the SLORC that Rajiv Gandhi was not averse to utilising force to serve India's interests. The Indian actions in Sri Lanka with the deployment of the Indian Army in that country as well as the actions taken in the Maldives to restore the Gayoom government led the SLORC to conclude that India could aggressively support the democratic forces in Myanmar. They were watching closely the re-emergence of the Rajiv Gandhi-led Congress and the obvious possibility that it would form the next government by winning the elections on the fall of the Chandrasekhar government. They had held discussions with the Chinese on what may be the consequences for Myanmar if Rajiv Gandhi returned as Prime Minister. The Chinese assured them that they would assist them to deal with any increase in pressure from a Rajiv Gandhi-led India, but held out the assessment that a physical attack by India was an unlikely possibility.

Despite the Chinese assurance, the SLORC was not able to shed from their mind the apprehension that Rajiv Gandhi would pose a problem. They felt Indian policy would be more aggressive and would prove even more difficult to deal with.

It is an unfortunate expression to use for the tragedy that occurred, but the only way to describe the reaction within the SLORC was that there was a collective sigh of relief when they got the news that Rajiv Gandhi had been assassinated.

Equally, there was a sombre realisation among the Myanmar forces of democracy, within and without Myanmar, that this was bad news for them, as they had the feeling that an India once again under Rajiv Gandhi would have taken firm action to unite international opinion to act against the SLORC. With his death, they felt the loss of a man who had championed their cause.

Whatever may have been the outcome if Rajiv Gandhi had become PM again—it will remain in the realms of speculation—one thing was clear with the coming to power of the Congress party and with former Foreign Minister Narasimha Rao as the new Prime Minister, a change in attitude could be expected because, while his government would no doubt continue to support democracy for Myanmar, there would be a more pragmatic assessment made of what was feasible and realistic in realigning a relationship with a country where India could ill-afford to be a total outsider with little or no influence.

My mandate was changed for the rest of my stay in Myanmar. It was now that we would take positions slowly with the SLORC to restore relations based on pragmatic functioning, keeping the North-East situation in mind and work gradually towards restoring the co-operation that had existed along the borders during the U Nu and the Ne Win periods.

This was an urgent issue and in a meeting with the Prime Minister where the Chief Minister of Assam was present, the issues were discussed in detail. The China issue was the other element that was discussed and a decision was taken that India would have to find means of establishing a relationship with the SLORC to bring about a collaboration that would help bring some balance to the relations—relations that would make Yangon to an extent shift from its singular dependence on China, to a recognition that India too was very much a player in the region and could be the other face that Myanmar could depend on. However, there was still the felt need that we should maintain pressure, though on a reduced scale, for the restoration of democracy and be seen as being one with the international community on that issue, as also for freeing Suu Kyi from incarceration.

The change in policy perceptions required a number of meetings and took some time to be operationalised. In the beginning of his stint as Prime Minister, Narasimha Rao had to show to the party and its conscience keepers, who felt that they were the true inheritors of the Rajiv Gandhi mantle that he was trying to carry the Rajiv–Indira Gandhi tradition forward. It was during this period that the issue of what India should be seen as doing to keep the Suu Kyi image on the forefront became almost an imperative and, with her being awarded the Noble Peace Prize, it was clear that India had to be seen as making a clear and pointed gesture of recognition of the honour that this reflected for Suu Kyi and the people of Myanmar. Even though it would be seen as a slap in the face by the SLORC and any attempt on our part to reach out to Suu Kyi would be seen as yet another sign of enmity to the military way of thinking and functioning, at this stage we had to be seen as acting in the interest of the forces of democracy.

The matter of congratulating Suu Kyi came up during the Common-wealth Summit in Harare. I received a message from the PM enclosing his letter of congratulations with instructions that this be conveyed to Suu Kyi. I was not alone in this. All the Commonwealth Ambassadors in Yangon had been directed by their respective governments to convey congratulatory letters along similar lines to her.

The issue before me was one of carrying out the instructions and at the same time reduce the pain it would cause to the SLORC, so that our action would not stand in the way of the steps that we would be taking to start opening the doors to the SLORC in line with the new pragmatic policy instructions that were in the offing.

I ruled out the suggestion that I try and handover the PM's letter addressed to Suu Kyi by personally calling on the COP, which is what the other Commonwealth ambassadors tried to do and were rebuffed. I merely forwarded a copy of the PM's letter with a verbal note, requesting that the letter be forwarded to its 'august destination'.

At the same time, I sent the letter of congratulations enclosed with a personal letter of congratulations via registered post to Suu Kyi. This obviously became grist to the mill for the gossip-ridden public of Yangon, but at the same time all of us knew that it was a fruitless exercise as nei-ther of the attempts would succeed in the letter ever reaching Suu Kyi.

The matter had an intriguing aside to it; at the reception that Ohn Kyaw hosted for the visiting UN Commissioner for Human Rights, he decided rather foolishly to take up the matter in front of some of the ambassadors, including those from the Commonwealth with whom I was talking. He said:

> Excellency, we have received your note verbal with a letter addressed to Aung San Suu Kyi by the Indian Prime Minister, a copy of which you have very kindly enclosed. Unfortunately, we cannot accept this letter as she has no official position and the Foreign Ministry cannot communicate with her. Accordingly they would be returning the letter to me.

I, in turn mentioned that it would indeed be unfortunate as I had sent the letter to the Foreign Office as she was allegedly the guest of the Myanmar Government, kept under protection for her own security within the confines of her house. If she were in prison I would have sought permission from his government, in keeping with the prison rules in Myanmar, to personally deliver my Prime Minister's letter to her. However as she was a guest of his government I had taken the only route open to me which was to send her the letter through the good offices of his ministry, I then took him aside and suggested that it would be better for him to not take any hasty action to return the Prime Minister's letter, as this would create an unnecessary incident. We were not seeking any confirmation of the delivery of the letter and that it would be best to leave the matter as it was. I also told him that this should be seen in the light of what was a public issue, adding that, since I had not joined the other Commonwealth ambassadors in trying to deliver the letter personally, the Indian action should be placed in its correct perspective.

I left him in no doubt that I was trying to bring some positive content to the relations, now that we had a Congress government in Delhi and there was a reasonable possibility that it would look at things within the potential of long-term relations. The matter finally rested there and Ohn Kyaw was left with the impression that the SLORC could hope to see a gradual change in India's priorities.

9

China in between India and Myanmar: 1991–1992

A final element in the relations between the three countries during the period 1988–1992 was the attempt we made with the GOI at its highest levels to try and draw attention to the strategic factors involved for India where Myanmar was concerned. It was obvious that China had reached a dominant position in Myanmar; this required that we examine the implications of this and what India could do about it. One of the features of China and Myanmar's move from the era of confrontation to one of positive alignment was the influence China could derive from the political, economic and defence relationship that had now become an abiding feature of its bilateral relations with Yangon. This carried implications that could not be ignored. It gave China an immense advantage in its attempt to enter and establish a strategic base at the head of the Bay of Bengal, thereby reaching a goal it had long sought for—making its presence felt in the immediate maritime neighbourhood of India and in the Indian Ocean region. It was apparent that it would set-up listening posts that would give it greater insight into the direction that India was taking both as its defence imperatives and in safeguarding of the maritime trade routes. What furthered its strategy to contain India was that China now had allies on both the western and eastern land and sea frontiers of India which, in conjunction of its presence in Tibet, gave it a surround of strategic depth vis-à-vis India. The, at that time, proposed development of port facilities in southern Sri Lanka only reinforced this advantage.

Another point that needed to be factored in was that the ethnic minorities along the entire northern and eastern arc of Myanmar's border (barring the frontiers with India, Bangladesh and Thailand) have close links with China, particularly since their economic links with that country would continue to be strengthened. This would ultimately become a key factor in influencing whichever government came to power in Myanmar. This ethnogeographic factor was assessed as having long term security and strategic implications both for Yangon and New Delhi. We needed to assess how this could eventually bring Myanmar closer to India, once the reality dawned on Yangon that it faced the possibility of losing control over a vast territory of Myanmar to China. One of the key factors in the internal assessment was the potential for trouble that the Chinese retained on account of the relationships that they had with the ethnic tribes that they shared across the Myanmar–China borders for India. A clear illustration of the threat that China could pose was the relationship that China continued to have with the Kokang Tribes (of Chinese origin who had a very large presence in Yunnan across the border from Myanmar) including the large-scale military support that it had provided to the Kokang. This support continues even today with the PRC providing them with the latest in defence equipment and military training. This is a complex issue as the Kokang have very strong links with the Yunnan State and have been placed in a position from where they can, whenever it suits the Chinese, be utilised to place pressure on the GOM to fall in line with China's interests. However this is a poisoned arrow that could have made the GOM look at other options that would reduce its dependence on China and move Myanmar into the global playing field.

For all practical purposes, the defence collaboration with China succeeded in increasing SLORC's dependence on China. The fact that the international community, led by the USA and the EU was putting pressure on the SLORC/SPDC through sanctions on account of its autocratic rule and human rights violations, left them with little choice but to continue to rely on the support of China; pleading with Beijing to use its domestic and external strengths to mitigate and neutralise the negative impact of the sanctions. On joining the ASEAN the SLORC/SPDC found another partner that helped mitigate, to some extent, the effect of the sanctions on the economic side, but this was secondary to the overwhelming presence that China had secured.

In geographical terms it was clear that for India, it would be opportune to look upon the Irrawady as the dividing line and to seek to develop through its economic presence its influence in the areas west of the Irrawady, while negotiating its way through the minefield created and established by China in the geographical and strategically important areas east of that river. This area was largely if not completely under China's influence, with the Mandalay region being gradually settled by Chinese immigrants making the region almost a Chinese enclave of its Yunnan province.

It was now being suggested that a detailed programme for this purpose, covering infrastructure, business dealings and the establishment of an effective open border which would permit free movement of goods, services and social exchanges while at the same time preserving the security aspects, would have to be formulated by India and be put into operation. The idea was sustained by the need for India to contain and minimise—if not root out the causes of—insurgency by creating a business and trade climate which would treat India's North-East and Myanmar's western geographical space as a single market-cum-development area, which would aim at improving the conditions of life of the local people, giving them a stake in a larger market area, which would be part of a bridge of prosperity linking India via Myanmar to Southeast Asia. This was seen as the most beneficial approach for meeting India's domestic and regional interests. Hopefully, it could also bring the Chinese within the loop of constructive engagement, as it would mean economic benefits, particularly for its relatively backward provinces of Yunnan and Szechwan.

In September 1992, after a two-year stint in Yangon, I left Myanmar for Delhi to join what was to be my final posting in the Ministry of External Affairs. I had a detailed discussion on our relations with Myanmar with the Foreign Secretary Mani Dixit, Prime Minister Narasimha Rao and his Principal Secretary A.N. Varma. It was clearly understood that we could no longer afford to keep the SLORC at arm's length. We had to look closely at what Myanmar meant to India and formulate our policy within the ambit of realisable goals. It was apparent that there was no way the international community, or India for that matter, could force the SLORC (which later transformed itself into the SPDC) to transfer power to Suu Kyi and the NLD. The attempts that it was now making to formulate a new constitution were indicative of its resolve to ensure that

the armed forces would have the controlling authority over the administration of the country, whatever be the circumstances. It was adopting the
direction of converting, through economic and social policies, as also
the approach of exclusivity, to ensure that the armed forces remained
the dominant elite that would ensure the preservation of the unity and
integrity of the country.

Given these factors, it was necessary for India to come up with an
effective strategy to reoccupy the space that it had vacated during the
Ne Win period, mainly because he chose to isolate his country from the
world and limit the bilateral relations to contacts and exchanges largely
among the top leaders of the two countries. Even these reached a total
impasse after the events of 1988–1989.[1]

At our meetings we reached the conclusion that New Delhi had to
give greater depth to our relations with Myanmar to bring them on par
with the dealings we had with the other neighbouring countries. Given
the changed circumstances of the Sino-Myanmar relations, India had to
ensure that over a period of time it would have a relationship with Myanmar that in a realistic sense would help neutralise the possibility of China
using Myanmar as a wedge against India.

In a separate meeting with the Foreign Secretary, I proposed that it
was time to re-establish Foreign Office to Foreign Office level contacts
and see how and to what extent the SLORC would be willing to respond.
Thereafter India should shape its policy to fit into that response and
then to build on it. I warned him that it would take time, but as I saw it,
the SLORC leadership would look on our approach as a positive development and gradually the trust required to move the relations forward
would develop.

---

[1] Comment: In the internal assessment it was finally decided that there would be a two
pronged policy approach: First, continue, but in a more subtle manner, the support for the
evolution of a democratic political structure; and second, to deal with the military on the
basis that it was unlikely for any change in its exercise of authoritarian rule in Myanmar. It
is no surprise that the support for democracy has taken a back seat while the dealing with
the military government has expanded to the exclusion of the forces of democracy. The
last overt attempt to show that India cared for the forces of democracy was the conferring
of the Nehru Award in 1993 to Aung San Suu Kyi. During the NDA government in India
despite the assistance that its Defence Minister George Fernandez was extending to the
pro-democracy forces that were based in India, the move of the GOI to deal exclusively
with the military regime came to be entrenched and this has been the basis that came to
form the policy towards Myanmar.

It was also at this review that we looked at the steps that we needed to take to bring our relations with ASEAN to a higher level—first to the level of a sectoral dialogue that would eventually lead to a full dialogue status and also to India's inclusion in the ARF.

This was the beginning of the thinking that eventually led to the formulation of India's Look East Policy, which was formally announced by Prime Minister Narasimha Rao in Singapore in September 1994 and we had woven our relations with Myanmar also into that policy's fabric. It was an obvious fact that in our efforts to get closer to the ASEAN we had to take into account the strategic placement of Myanmar and that it would be in our own interest to use that country as the philosophical and economic land bridge leading to long term relationships with the ASEAN countries. This would give a focus to the relations that were of long-term interest to India.

An undercurrent to India's perception vis-à-vis Burma/Myanmar, to an extent fed to us by that country itself, is the fond belief that it would like to maintain a balance in its relations with its two big neighbours. During the U Nu era and to an extent while Ne Win was at the helm of affairs, their policy of neutrality would have to be seen also as a policy that aimed at dealing with the dual situation of a comfortable relationship with India on the one hand and a troubled relationship with China on the other.

The reality was that, during the Ne Win period, India was seeking his help to keep a lid on the insurgencies in India's North-Eastern states, while he was seeking a greater understanding with China to restrain them from supporting insurgencies in Myanmar. The practice of neutrality was part and parcel of Myanmar's troubled relations with Beijing and, once the troubling aspects of Beijing's behaviour disappeared, the SLORC showed no hesitation, in accepting the realities of geography and the international isolation to which it had been subjected, to moving quickly into China's sphere of influence.

Thus, when the New Delhi establishment keeps telling itself that Rangoon was not happy with its increasing dependence on China and that they would like to bring the relations with that country down to a lower level, India is indulging in wishful thinking. It is not that there is no duality in the thinking on relations with China. In the first instance Myanmar has historically recognised that a strong China poses a serious threat to Myanmar's integrity as a nation. This had in the past led to aggressive actions by China that were also reflected in the positions that the PRC had adopted in extending material support to the CPB and the insurgent actions that had followed after Burma's independence in 1948. Also in the past in recognition of the strength of China as an influential political and economic power in the region the Burma kingdom had accepted a tributary relationship with China. Significantly the British colonial power in Burma had continued to recognise the tributary relationship with China and maintained a token relationship with China in this regard. The second aspect of the relations with China has been the recognition that China as an opportunity with its burgeoning economy and increasing technological clout encouraged the GOM to expect that the linkages with China would bring in the kind of investments and economic opportunities that would help Myanmar realise its economic potential.

No doubt, the SPDC wanted to have other relationships that would bring greater balance to the overall presence of Myanmar in global affairs. Also, it was not lost on them that circumstances had forced them to grant China a larger place within Myanmar than they would have liked, but the global situation of mistrust and pressure that they faced (where even within the ASEAN there were questions being raised about Burma's internal failures), China had become the only unquestioning friend that they have had since 1988. To believe that their attitude to India and Indians is a parallel to what they really feel about the Chinese and that they are feeling the overwhelming pressure of Chinese presence in the Mandalay region, is understandable but it is also a fact that Myanmar has to have a closer relationship with China in its own interest than it can have with any other global or regional power. History has taught them the lesson that if China is not with them then it works against their interests and has the means to achieve its goals. For China it is important that Myanmar is in their area of regional influence.

The Burman reaction to India and the Indians is steeped in the historical antagonism towards colonialism and the discriminatory treatment that had been meted out, to the Burman majority community, by the kala. Once the way was opened, Rangoon did not hesitate to shape its policies to effectively reduce the economic hold of Indians over land, urban properties, businesses and debts. They continue to treat the people of Indian descent as third class residents with very limited rights, and have never placed their relations with India in any special box, as they have done with China.

They are, of course afraid of the power that China has, but then they have throughout history been aware of that and have bowed to that power; for instance, during the Middle Kingdom era, when they paid tribute to the Chinese emperor. In contrast, they have in the case of some Indian states held the position of victors and conquerors. Burmans with Chinese blood and those who are the products of liaisons with Chinese spouses are not treated any differently from pure blooded Burmans. Both Ne Win and Khin Nyunt bore testimony to this; one became head of state and the other was head of government, as Prime Minister, till he was removed.[2]

It is important for us in India to take into account that, because of our problems in the North-East, the Burmans feel that we come to them seeking their assistance and co-operation in containing the movement and stop Indian insurgents from taking shelter in their territory. They oblige us to the extent they feel it is necessary to keep us happy and also because it helps them to contain the same problem on their side. The gist of the matter here is that for Burma, China comes first and India, though important, stands lower down in their scale of priorities. They certainly do not look on India as a substitute or a replacement for China, but rather as a soft state that would not be able to stand up to China if a situation arose where Burma needed an outside power to help neutralise its dependence on China. We need to keep this factor in front of us to understand our relations with an authoritarian Myanmar regime.

---

[2] Visiting Professor Poon Kim Shee (Ritsumeikan University, Japan), in a paper 'China–Myanmar Relations: Strategic and Economic Dimensions' suggests that China–Myanmar relations since diplomatic recognition since 1950 'can be briefly divided into the following phases: first, 1949–1961 ambivalent peaceful co-existence; second, temporary setback: 1962–1970; third, improving relationship: 1971–1988; fourth, closer entente 1989–2002'.

Comment: This is a clear attempt at fudging the realities that governed the relations between the PRC and the CPB and its ethnic allies. It was only when the CPB-led forces were unable to withstand the onslaughts of the Tatmadaw that the PRC stopped extending the material and military training support that it had been providing to them till then. Ne Win was officially described as a 'fascist dictator'. The events of 1998 in Myanmar and the negotiations carried out by Khin Nyunt to accommodate the Chinese with Myanmar openly moving into China's sphere of influence resulted in the PRC moving away from its past linkages to the CPB and the ethnic insurgents. Professor Poon has in his classification of the four phases been rather generous to the PRC.

10
Thawing of Relations: 1992–2010

L et us first make it clear that the period from 1988–1989 to 1992 was effectively the period of 'mutual disenchantment' *between the two countries*. This was also the era when, barring China, the major powers of the world led by the USA adopted the stand of asserting the promotion of human rights, governance and democracy in Myanmar, fully determined to push for the implementation of their demand. In this context, they decided to make a joint ambassadorial demarche on Yangon and tried to persuade India to join them to strongly protest the failure of the SLORC to handover power to the elected representatives. This was turned down by India, as we did not see any value in joining hands in this manner against a neighbour, even though the SLORC was never in any doubt over where we stood on these issues.

This could be seen as the first significant assertion of the change in policy, which came after the realisation that we needed to work with the government of the day. There were major issues relating to insurgency, the movement into India of Naga and Chin refugees because of the actions of the Myanmar military against insurgents on its side of the border. There was the growing problem arising out of the flow of drugs from Myanmar into our North-Eastern states and the social and health hazards that it posed.

There was also an increasing concern within the foreign policy establishment, in India, over the neglect of our strategic interests and the space that was being taken in this region by China, taking advantage of its ties with Myanmar.

In India, the Prime Minister has had a major role in defining the priorities and in taking major policy initiatives to deal with the relations, in particular with major powers and neighbours, as also in the negotiations on issues of significant concern to India in both the bilateral and multilateral areas. However, this does not mean that he would not let a Foreign Secretary (in whom the Prime Minister sees a professional with political and intellectual acumen that could be depended upon) to take the initiative on key foreign policy issues.

Mani Dixit was one such Foreign Secretary in whose abilities Prime Minister Narasimha Rao had implicit faith, which led him to grant Dixit a fair degree of latitude in the conduct of relations with all major powers, and the neighbouring countries.

Dixit had been in the thick of things in the conduct of India's relations during his postings as the Indian HOM (Head of Mission) in Sri Lanka, Afghanistan and Pakistan. He was also very much the man on the ground during the war that led to the demise of East Pakistan and the creation of Bangladesh.

He had worked closely with both Rajiv Gandhi and Narasimha Rao when the former was Prime Minister and the latter the Minister for External Affairs. Dixit understood the realities of Indian foreign policy. He was well aware of the sheer lack of will, among the Indian political leadership, that was a requisite to back-up strong positions at the intellectual level with hard actions on the ground. Having been involved in the Indian Peace Keeping Force (IPKF) operations in Sri Lanka, he was convinced India did not want to get involved in any similar action again and certainly not in Myanmar. Given this belief, he was able to conclude, after extensive and probing discussions with me and thereafter detailed discussions with the Prime Minister, that the time had come to put our relations with Myanmar on a pragmatic footing, so that we could gradually move towards a relationship that would enable us to take care of our concerns and eventually graduate to the level of good neighbourly relations to mutual benefit.

He then took the first steps to effect a breakthrough in the relations by extending an invitation for a visit to India by U Aye, who had taken over as the Director General of the Department of Political Affairs in the Myanmar Foreign Office while I was still in Yangon. We had got to know each other quite well. He, in fact, was the person who translated the discussion the Senior General Saw Maung had with me when I presented my credentials.

U Aye was close to Khin Nyunt and had managed the relations with the Western powers; he was a trusted diplomat and was in a position to judge how far we were willing to go in taking the first steps towards closer relations. He was accompanied by an eight-member delegation and held extensive discussions on bilateral issues in Delhi. It was made clear to U Aye that, while India would continue with its principled stand of extending support to democracy, it had no intention of getting engaged in the internal affairs of a neighbouring country with whom it wanted to have good and lasting relations. We had been disappointed over the continued detention of Suu Kyi and would keep urging for her release, but this would not in any way be made an excuse for India to support any moves off the shores of India to bring about a change in Myanmar. This, we said, was the task for the people of that country to undertake and our moral support to them would not be permitted to come in the way of managing the relations between the two countries.

Both sides acknowledged that there were issues that were impacting the relations that needed to be corrected, such as the need to address the mutual security issues arising out of insurgencies, as also the need to ensure that Myanmar's relations with China would not come to negatively impact India's strategic interests.

The Myanmar delegation did not shy away from saying that they understood India's position on Suu Kyi and on the issue of democracy, but stressed that the kind of governance and administration that ran a country was the sole concern of that country and should not become a factor that took away from the importance of basing relations between two neighbouring countries on pragmatic considerations of each other's strategic and security interests. They expressed the hope that India would not 'be excessively concerned about internal developments' in Myanmar.[1]

They also accepted that India's concerns on issues relating to drugs and contraband had to be addressed and they were ready to co-operate with India. U Aye drew attention to the fact that his government was committed to taking action on finding alternative agricultural crops and means of livelihood so as to bring about an end to the cultivation of the opium poppy and the manufacture of heroin. In this respect, it was also

[1] J.N. Dixit on relations with Myanmar in Dixit, *My South Block Years.*

pointed out that India had to ensure that, on its part, it would prevent the smuggling of chemicals that went into the manufacture of heroin and the export across the borders of the codeine based Phensedyl.

This visit of U Aye set the framework for a resumption of relations based on a pragmatic approach and the system of exchange of visits was re-established. Foreign Secretary Dixit made the point that India would look at its relations beyond the framework of 1991–1992, which had been a reaction to GOM's non-adherence to what was seen as a clear commitment to transfer power in conjunction with the 1990 election results. However, the delegation was told, India's policy continued to be to deal with governments who were in de facto control of the country concerned and more specifically so when it came to nations in India's neighbourhood.

Dixit made this as the focus of India's policy towards Myanmar when he went to Yangon on a return visit at the end of March 1993. He had meetings with Khin Nyunt, Home Minister Mya Thin, Foreign Minister Ohn Kyaw and with Finance Minister Win Tin. The main meeting was with Khin Nyunt who we now were acknowledging as the person with whom we had to do business. It was also our way of conveying the point that we were willing to deal with all issues with the people in-charge. A concrete step we took to assure Yangon that we were moving forward and would not let the past come in the way of our relations was the formal signing of the first agreement with the SLORC for the control of smuggling and illegal trafficking in drugs. There was now a new emphasis on giving a further thrust to co-operation in trade and commercial dealings.

In his discussions with Khin Nyunt, Dixit took up in detail the issues arising out of his country's defence and strategic relations with China, including the possibility of Myanmar granting naval base facilities to China that would bring it into the Bay of Bengal and the Andaman Sea, pointing out that this would pose an unacceptable challenge to India's strategic and security interests. India was keen for the SLORC to have a clear idea of the sensitivities involved and to make them understand that we expected them to ensure that our interests were not compromised by the actions they were taking to accommodate China's ambitions and moves towards the Bay of Bengal. Khin Nyunt was prepared for this discussion; he came across on expected lines making the point that the defence relationship was largely confined to Myanmar obtaining arms and ammunition as well as training facilities from the Chinese to meet essential defence requirements for the containment of insurgencies. He refuted the contention that any base facilities were being granted to China within the territory of Myanmar and assured Dixit that 'they would never allow any permanent foreign military presence in their territory'.[2]

Space had been made for the first exchange of visits as the talks with the Yangon leadership fructified into a major change in the policy being pursued with Myanmar and it was the beginning of a fairly rapid move towards the normalisation of relations. It commenced with bilateral meetings at the level of senior officials, then among ministers on both sides and finally in the visit by Than Shwe as head of state and the return visit by President Kalam of India. These exchanges have posited the relations into a framework of understanding based on a common programme, which has been set around several factors that take into account:

- issues of security, economic and social co-operation;
- an understanding and appreciation of the fact that, despite India's position on democracy there was no intention to interfere in the internal affairs of Myanmar;
- India's support on issues like human rights, restoration of democracy and release of Suu Kyi would be via the United Nations and bilateral persuasion to meet international expectations;
- India would continue to seek GOM's assurances on issues of strategic importance to India, particularly to ensure that Myanmar's relations with China would not adversely impact upon India's major concerns and;
- As a part of India's Look East policy, there was need for negotiations on the subject of communications, particularly regional co-operation and development of an alternate route for the North-East states of India to facilitate transit and provide a greater opening to these states, since the natural approach via Bangladesh seemed to be largely unavailable.

Signs of the importance that India has come to attach to progressing the relations with Myanmar is reflected in the increase in exchange of visits at

---

[2] Dixit, *My South Block Years*, 169.

both the ministerial levels and at the high leadership levels. An important visit was that by the Vice President of India where, apart from the usual exchange of views there was a stronger emphasis on India's commitment to infuse greater momentum to the economic relationship, including the importance of the projected building of the dams for the export of surplus power to India, while improving the irrigation facilities for Myanmar's dry central region west of the Irrawady. There have been visits exchanged of the foreign ministers of both countries and there have been a greater degree of exchanges at the level of heads of state and government as well as by key ministers in charge of the military and economic ministries.

It is worth drawing attention to the realpolitik that governs India's relations with Myanmar today, in contrast to what prevailed in the 1988 to 1992 period. In 1988 and again in 1990, India was positively hostile to the military regime and there was a complete stagnation of the relations. In contrast, India maintained a muted reaction to the events of 2007, when the Myanmar military regime once again ruthlessly put down public protests led by Buddhist monks against the 'fuel price hike'. India merely suggested that 'Myanmar's process of political reform and national reconciliation should be more inclusive and broad based'.

Facing increased Western pressure, given a concrete shape by even more stringent sanctions and calls for action against the regime for its violation of human rights, Myanmar looked upon its immediate neighbours, the ASEAN countries, China and India to help fend off the actions being taken against it. Post-2007, India's developmental assistance rose to over US$160 million. Indo-Myanmar co-operation in the area of oil and gas increased substantially with India signing up for three exploration blocks. Moreover, India took the route of the UN to influence the SPDC to allow the UN Special Envoy to visit Myanmar and also enable him to meet with Aung San Suu Kyi.

Again as a friendly neighbour, India was welcomed when it swiftly went to the aid of the people of Myanmar and the administration to mitigate to the extent possible the horrors and devastation caused by cyclone Nargis. Where Indian advice to the SPDC leadership to accept the humanitarian aid that the West was offering, particularly the USA, did not raise any adverse reactions.

A significant decision taken by India that is of long-term value was to co-operate with the GOM in the area of Border Area Development.

This would help the adoption of policies that would assist both sides to contain insurgency in adjoining border areas of both countries. This would also become a part of the co-operation between the two countries for combating insurgency and in this regard, apart from co-operating in the area of border diplomacy, the intention is to become partners in strengthening the economic and business sectors that would be result-oriented. The GOM had recognised that a growing young population needed to see a better future for itself and could no longer be forced to live in an era that kept the outside world out which deprived them of the benefits of the visibly expanding global prosperity.

China's economy was one example and the people of Myanmar could also see the changes that had taken place next door in Thailand. They had a good idea of what was happening to the Indian economy through the window provided by the North-Eastern states of India. The military regime, therefore, came to adopt measures to open up the economy to an extent and invited the ASEAN states to help build its infrastructure for tourism and for the establishment of trade and business relations. These were areas which India could look at and see that its involvement would bring about understandings that would permit it to evolve a closer economic relationship that would also ensure that her security and broader strategic interests could be better secured.

Some experts tend to suggest that the change in Indian policy towards the SLORC/SPDC was primarily driven by an effort to 'contain China' in its relations with Myanmar. This kind of thinking is based on the lack of a real understanding of India's intentions. Though India's apprehensions over the growing dependence of Myanmar on China and its repercussions on India's strategic interests is an obvious area of concern, it was well aware of the fact that it could do little about the given situation except by way of providing alternatives that would help Myanmar to restore a degree of balance to its ties with China and India. Yes, China was a key factor, but certainly not the sole factor for the change in India's policy towards the military regime in Myanmar. It was also driven by issues of strategic and security interests.

We in India understand what China intends to achieve by drawing Myanmar into a position of dependence: it is to help Beijing give a greater push to its strategic design of containing India. Containment was China's policy, but India had no such overweening ambitions. Ours is a more realistic approach that is neither guided by any desire to replace China as the guarantor of Myanmar against foreign intervention, nor in adopting sanctions that would force the GOM to bow to the demands of the international community. India is aware of the limitations that govern her capacity to meet the major demands for resources that Myanmar needs. China has the capacity to extend a great deal of support to Myanmar both in the form of aid as well as in the form of investments. The alternative for India is to join hands with the ASEAN, Washington, Brussels and Tokyo to help extend the assistance that would help meet Myanmar's developmental needs.

It was also clear to us that a country that could feed itself and was the beneficiary of China's economic and political support, besides being a member of the ASEAN which guaranteed substantial commercial and developmental benefits, could not be pressurised by the international community into submission. India has held the pragmatic position that a policy of sanctions would not work. It would only drive Myanmar, if there was no other alternative, further into China's sphere of influence; it was therefore in India's interest to remain engaged with Yangon and to be an alternative along with ASEAN as a source of support.

India's Myanmar policy, was guided by the threefold interest: making it a partner in the development of alternative communication routes to the North-East to increase economic and business contacts; to extend financial and material assistance for developing mutually beneficial projects, that included, as with Bhutan, collaborations in Hydel power development, the surplus product of which would be bought by India to meet her growing energy needs and; to exploit Myanmar's potential of becoming a supplier of hydrocarbons and a partner in India's search for external supplies of energy inputs to meet its future and current needs.

Finally, India desired a kind of bilateral trade relationship that is oriented to a development paradigm which would help open India's North-East to the larger market which the area west of the Irrawady and, more particularly, Myanmar's Sagaing Division provides. This would enable India and Myanmar to use economic and commercial growth backed by the establishment of social and economic institutions that would ensure the development and prosperity of the adjoining geographical regions— in the process helping to contain and resolve the issues straining the security of the region because of insurgencies.

This policy promotes the kind of quiet, non-intrusive diplomacy that could help influence a move towards a democratic process, however limited its constitutional reach may be in the beginning. The adoption of a constitution that keeps effective power in the hands of the military is not a new phenomenon for Myanmar; moreover, as the past developments in the region (of which Indonesia is a prime example) portend, in future there could be an increasing participation of the people in the governance of Myanmar. This may take long and require a patient understanding of the fact that time was on the side of the people of that country. Social and economic development would eventually result in a possible change in the attitude of the military forces, making them give greater participative freedom to the people.

There is no doubt the wide gap between the aspirations of the ethnic minorities and the Burman majority will continue, leading to a weakening of the processes set in motion by the GOM. However, it would go against India's interest if the ethnic minorities followed trends of political behaviour that would weaken the central authority in the frontier regions, as this could be to the benefit of China and derogatory to the unity and integrity of Myanmar. Adding considerably to our security concern, it would create yet another frontier in which China would rival India, giving that country an even greater potential to interfere in the affairs of the Indian state of Arunachal, as also in the rest of a vulnerable north-east region of India.

India's position has to be one that encourages participation in the electoral processes under the new constitution. The party or parties in power should use the processes open to the government to move gradually towards understandings that would eventually bring greater flexibility to the decision-making and implementation processes.

One of the positive measures open to an elected government would be to open the economy further, linking it to the extent possible to the global economy; this would facilitate greater exploitation of the country's rich natural resources and help build the necessary manufacturing infrastructure, creating jobs and bringing greater prosperity to the populace at large. In this area, India could put across arrangements and incentives for greater participation by Indian businesses within the Myanmar economy. For this, the route of joint ventures and business partnerships would be the best option to reduce the possibility of adverse Burman reactions, particularly among those that have an elephantine memory of Indian business domination as a consequence of the colonial period.

The GOI could also increase its technical and financial support for the development of the essential infrastructure and to bring about the infrastructural and communication linkages with the ASEAN as a whole, thus also serving India's strategic interests.

The India aid programme should include the development of social infrastructure, including the grant of scholarships for Burmese students to attend technical-cum-vocational courses in India, as also assist Myanmar in establishing institutions of higher learning similar to India's IITs and business schools. This in itself would lead to a greater presence of India at the people–to-people level.

The increasing contact between the armed forces and their leadership on both sides has reached a level where there exists a higher degree of confidence amongst the two nations' chiefs of the three wings of the armed forces, which has led to agreements for the delivery of defence software and some hardware by India to Myanmar. The general impression at the intellectual and command levels of the Indian armed forces is that there is much to be offered in terms of training and operational systems. There is also the feeling that there is a preference for Indian hardware, as it is of better quality than what has been supplied by the Chinese. This may well be true because, in qualitative terms, India has equipment (particularly in the mid-level artillery items) that is better than what is on offer from China. The Myanmar armed forces can also identify more closely with the Indian professionalism and training styles which could bring about a closer sense of 'military kinship'.

That is not to say that India does not have to keep constantly in mind that it must never allow its military to become the key determinant factor in its foreign policy decisions related to the GOM. The military can only be an important instrument in playing one of the two roles in the security system, the second of these being the role to be played by the civilian administration in the states of India that border Myanmar.

While we, in India, can take comfort from the fact that the GOM is co-operating with India on the security aspects and has even in some cases taken physical action against Indian insurgents, this co-operation cuts both ways, as it ensures them a secure relationship with India in which they have the effective upper hand and, as such, it is in their interest to be selective in the actions they undertake. The regional meetings between the Myanmar and Indian authorities carried out annually have as a part of the agenda issues relating to border security, economic co-operation including the coverage to border trade, and trafficking in drugs, which has become a major issue of concern both from the social and security angles and also involves issues of narco-terrorism.

India has extended a considerable amount of aid and assistance to Myanmar, which is related to the development of infrastructure projects including the road development programme, of which the completed Tamu–Kalemyo project is a living example of the actions that India is willing and capable of taking.

The ASEAN aspect of the relationship has also been given a boost with India's involvement with the proposal for the trilateral (India–Myanmar–Thailand) highway, which shall become an important land linkage for India with the ASEAN countries. Also, the BIMSTEC and the MGC (Mekong Ganga Cooperation) proposals would provide a greater future for regional economic development, bringing down to a realistic level the dependence of Myanmar on China. India has seen a fair increase in trade between the two countries which would register a significant increase once the projects like the Tamanthi Hydroelectric project and co-operation under the MOU on energy co-operation come to be implemented. Myanmar could also see a greater degree of revenue earning when projects like the Kaladan Multi-modal Project come into effect.

One negative factor of India's economic policy has been the tardiness in decision-making and implementation. It needs to be realised that it is in India's own interest to make the economic relationship the cornerstone of India's presence in Myanmar (and the need to factor this in as part of institution building) so as to put India's relations with that country on a firm footing, unaffected by any change of regime in Yangon. It is essential that we have a mechanism that speeds up the decision-making and implementation process for all projects and business dealings. Such a mechanism should be handled by the PMO under the direct charge of the Principal Secretary to the Prime Minister. The Foreign Secretary should be the principal interlocutor, as the MEA has to be the keeper of the policy. It should have the secretaries of the sanctioning and the implementation ministries concerned as members, in particular the finance and revenue secretaries who would ensure that the decisions taken are implemented on time. This mechanism would have to work in a businesslike manner and must have the capacity to take innovative steps to ensure that actions are in keeping with the need to realise on time the development, completion of planned projects and business objectives. It should also have a relevant business group associated to it, as that would be an essential driver for substantive growth.

As has been mentioned earlier, what is needed is to create a market link within a planned programme to bring India's North-East and Myanmar's Sagaing Division, the Chin State and the Arakan Region into an investment-friendly market hub that would open job opportunities for the people of this entire region west of the Irrawady. When I was in Yangon, I had sent a detailed proposal on this subject to the GOI and many of my successors have followed with similar proposals in intent, as all of us have recognised that this was an area that would bring the seal of permanence to the relations while serving the common security and strategic interests of the two countries. This would also become an effective part of India's Look East Policy which cannot but place Myanmar at its centre. It would also help bring prosperity that in itself would act as the guarantor of peace, security and tranquillity to the region and help place Chinese presence within manageable limits.

To sum up it is important to point out that the Indian establishment had in the post-1992 period till the 2010 elections that were held under the provisions of the constitution of 2008 had already ensured a movement towards a relationship of understanding. It is worth at this stage before we get into the post-2010 period recalling that India and Myanmar have had a history of a rather muddled relationship. Ironically, it is with an authoritarian regime—the kind with which we would normally find it difficult to deal—that we finally ended up doing serious business. The relations that developed with General Maung Aye, who at that time, before the elections, was seen as the probable successor to Tan Shwe, were reflective of growing trust between the leadership of the two countries. India for all practical purposes had accepted the reality that democracy could only come to Myanmar on the basis of understandings developing between the political leadership and the military leadership. Till such a moment came about in the future in Myanmar India had to deal with the powers that were on the ground and establish understandings with a military that had been ruling Burma/Myanmar since 1962.

On the issue of democracy, India took shelter behind the credo of non-interference in the internal affairs of an important neighbouring country and hoped that whatever pressure the ASEAN can put on a member country to effect political change and deliver on human rights would be acceptable to India. India had come to accept that for practical reasons China was the security blanket that the SPDC needed and was dependent on to help it meet global pressure and to neutralise the multilateral actions that the western countries were promoting against it. The strongest actions were undertaken by the International Labour Organization (ILO), particularly on issues like abuse of workers' rights, the use of prison labour and child labour. Myanmar showed itself as quite capable of resisting such international pressure, making cosmetic changes from time to time to level off such pressure.

In the case of Suu Kyi, the SPDC adopted all measures to not only to isolate her but also to neutralise her public popularity. They permitted the UN representatives to meet with her as a means to let the international steam to disipate, but did nothing to comply with the express desire of the international community to see her released from house arrest. The UN efforts have also had the quiet support of India and, at the Foreign Secretary/Vice Minister exchanges; the Indian side has made an effort to persuade the Myanmar side to be more positive in its response to the UN's efforts.

India made allotments of aid and technical assistance that gave greater substance to the Indian relations with Myanmar. India hopes that these actions determined by the conduct of economic diplomacy shall encourage the GOM to adopt a policy that would bring a greater balance to Myanmar's relations with its two big neighbouring countries China and India. In this effort, the defence relationship has also been factored in, as also a heavier emphasis on institution building by India in Myanmar to strengthen socio-economic developmental process, health services, education and IT services. However during its interactions at the bilateral level with the SPDC a bit of tight rope walking was carried by the GOI that while carrying out bilateral interactions are with the SPDC as the government of the day, care was taken to ensure that these efforts did not convey the impression that there was in any way an endorsement of Yangon's policies—a view that could have lowered India's status as a democratic country of international substance.

A fundamental concern that underlies the conduct of Indian diplomacy in Myanmar has been driven by the desire to try and ensure that the relations between Myanmar and China are not at the cost of India's strategic interests. It was no secret from India's policy makers that during the period that Khin Nyunt was a power centre within the SPDC, there was always a twist in the tongue where his affiliations with China coloured his view of what he was willing to do with India. Thankfully, at least with Maung Aye things changed and the relationship achieved a degree of comfort. In the post-1988 period the relations between China and Myanmar had reached a point where China's maritime ambitions and interests in the Bay of Bengal, the Andaman Seas and its projection on to the Indian Ocean region were being served by the arrangements that the GOM was willing to permit China. India has however taken some comfort from the statements of the GOM to the effect that China has not established any bases in the territories of Myanmar and that they shall not permit hostile actions against India from their soil. The fact that there is a relationship building up between the navies of India and Myanmar is also seen as a hopeful sign, but we certainly cannot let down our guard and must make our own assessments on what needs to be done to strengthen our own defence arrangements in the area. Defence preparedness is equally necessary where the China and Sri Lanka developments are concerned.

India can be said to have determined a more down-to-earth and level headed approach to its relations with Myanmar, which has now to be carried forward by bringing about greater relevance and content to the economic relationship, as also to put in place an implementation and decision making mechanism to ensure that collaborative projects are launched in time. The trade relationship has to work towards larger market capabilities and to more effective containment of extortion and narco smuggling. It is equally important that we show greater pragmatism to speed up decisions on energy collaborations and joint ventures.

Indian businesses have to be extended appropriate security and financial incentives to invest in setting up business entities that, while bringing economic returns, have an inclusive element built into the effort that would bring the North-East states into the business mainstream with the extended market in Myanmar, covering the market space to the region west of the Irrawady becoming an additional economic and business incentive. Further, the social and economic infrastructure linking

India's North-East to Myanmar and the port of Sitwe needs to be looked upon as a holistic development model which also permits a Public Private Partnership (PPP) approach, thus making it more attractive as an investment destination for the private sector. This should factor in a joint venture approach with the involvement of entrepreneurs from Myanmar and from other countries with whom we may have a common interest in strengthening Myanmar's economy and its moving to a more rational position by thus reducing the overwhelming presence of China in Myanmar.

To the extent possible, an agreement should be worked out for extending the business model to also open up job opportunities for the Indian population in Myanmar so as to improve their conditions of life. The stabilising effect of such economic growth may one day enable India to build the case for granting these people full citizenship in that country. Bilateral negotiations on the tricky subject of awarding greater rights to the people of Indian descent have been underway and some progress has been made which is a reflection of the greater comfort that is governing the relations.

Co-operation in education, help in building institutes of excellence with linkage to job creation and the extension of technical co-operation would provide the kind of underpinnings that India would like to have with such an important neighbouring country. This has to be part of the economic diplomacy that India has come to place its trust in for the development of its influence in Myanmar.

To this has to be added the role of Buddhism, which is central to any political system in Myanmar given its empowerment and its hold on the majority of the people. India, as the pre-eminent host nation for Buddhist religious tourism—with the presence of Buddhist monks from Myanmar at the seat of the holy of holies at Bodh Gaya—needs to build on this advantage and launch programmes with the backing of the government and the spiritual leadership in Myanmar to make this yet another thread in the web adding to the durability of the relationship. The women of Myanmar exercise great influence and should be the targets of such religious tourism efforts, as this would be a method that shall help bring the people of the two countries closer and weave a tapestry of relations that would be in India's long term interests.

India in the period prior to the elections of 2010 had rightly taken the position that sanctions cannot serve any purpose and would certainly not bring the military to heel or to a mood of submission. What the international community had to understand was that its efforts were not only alienating the very source of power in Myanmar, a source that has had an integral role in the politics of that country right from the era of the battle for independence, but that it was also pushing them into greater dependence on China, that was likely to do great damage to the regional balances by helping China to gain the strategic means to dominate the Indian Ocean region. It was, therefore, in India's interests to suggest to the US administration and the European Powers to look at the overall strategic architecture of this region and recognise that it had to find a comfortable way of doing business with the armed forces-dominated governance in Myanmar.

Strategic factors should also become a part of India's overall dialogue with the USA, the EU countries as well as Japan and Russia on the development of not only political but also socio-economic developmental issues that would assist in reducing the overwhelming influence that China had come to wield over a SPDC-ruled Myanmar. There is no question that India's relations with China would remain a mix of increasing pressure on our security and strategic interests while at the same time there would be an increasing role for the economic relations between the two countries. Myanmar, which today stands at the crossroads, needs to be persuaded by India to adopt a more balanced relationship with both China and India. At the same time, India has to encourage the GOM to increase its economic presence in the ethnic areas to the north and east of Myanmar that abuts on China and Thailand in the interest of preserving the security of its vulnerable border areas.

To sum up this period, it would be best to make the point that the relations with Burma during the U Nu–Nehru period were guided by 'sentiment', the Ne Win–Indira Gandhi period by 'mutual necessity' and finally, the relations with the SPDC were driven by 'real politik' which, ironically, recognised with greater substance the role of Myanmar in the common security and strategic interests of the two countries. They are not primarily driven by the motive to 'contain China' in Myanmar, but by Myanmar's relevance as a meaningful partner in India's espousal of regional understanding for peace, development and close neighbourly relations, despite Nay Pyi Taw's closeness to Beijing as China remains the largest investor and economic partner for Myanmar.

11

Getting Closer, but not Claustrophobic

In the post-2010 period, the relations between the two countries have developed a closeness that is in keeping with the political and economic changes that have taken place in Myanmar. Exchanges at the highest political levels have expanded with a greater emphasis being attached by both sides for a greater engagement by India with Myanmar. This relationship has gained in relevance with India agreeing to engage itself not only in the economic and business prospects thrown up by Myanmar becoming a part of the globalisation process, but also because of the strategic and security considerations driving it to participate extensively in Myanmar's border areas development plans. The unfortunate part has however been that India has not been able to put aside a larger dose of financial resources that are warranted by the involvement in the infrastructure projects in Myanmar that promote connectivity between the two countries and are in keeping with India's strategic interests linked to Southeast Asia.

One of the areas of co-operation keeping the immense needs of Myanmar in mind has to be institution building. The Indian Prime Minister during his visit at the end of May 2012 kept this factor in mind and offered assistance and expertise in a wide range of areas that Myanmar could take advantage of in the strengthening of its institutions and in institution building. The areas include border areas development, human resources development, connectivity, 'assistance in developing capacity of democratic institutions such as the Parliament, National

Human Rights Commission and the Media'.[1] This kind of approach has to be reciprocated by the international community to meet Myanmar's requirements in areas vital to its future prospects.

Dr Manmohan Singh's three day visit to Myanmar was a visit by an Indian Prime Minister after a gap of 25 years. The immediate previous visit was by Rajiv Gandhi in 1987, a visit that despite his good intentions did not achieve much, being seen by Ne Win as merely a goodwill gesture by Indira Gandhi's son rather than a serious attempt by the Prime Minister of India to provide substance to the relations between two neighbouring countries. Ne Win had by that time convinced himself that even small openings to the world were not in Burma's interest. Subsequently during Vajpayee's Prime Ministership steps were undertaken to further India's relations with Myanmar. The concrete shape to these steps was provided by the Indian-funded road project that connected Moreh to Tamu, Kalewa and onto Kalemyo, eventually to be linked up to Manadalay. The road was built by the Border Road Organisation of India and was inaugurated on 13 February 2001 by Foreign Minister Jaswant Singh. Singh was the first Foreign Minister of India to visit Myanmar after a gap of 20 years thus furthering relations with that country in keeping with the vision first projected by Narasimha Rao in 1994 of the Look East Policy of which Myanmar was an important part as well a linkage to the south-east emphasis in that policy. Jaswant Singh then made a second official visit to Myanmar at the invitation of his Myanmar counterpart U Win Aung in May 2002. This visit covered many aspects that would help India gain further traction in Myanmar. The Foreign Ministers of India, Myanmar and Thailand also on this occasion gave shape to the trilateral highway that would connect India's North-East to Myanmar and onwards to Thailand. It was also on this visit that the Kaladan Multi-modal Transport Project was identified as a key project that would help link Kolkata port via Sitwe port in Myanmar—to be developed by an Indian entity—Mizoram through Myanmar's Chin State.

Manmohan Singh's visit in May 2012 took place in an entirely changed atmosphere, an atmosphere built up by a reforms process that showed Myanmar as having adopted a totally different and meaningful framework

---

[1] The joint statement issued 'on the occasion of Prime Minister of India Dr Manmohan Singh to Myanmar'. 27–29 May, Strategy 2012 extracts from paras 8 and 9 of the joint statement. The full text of the joint statement is at Annexure VII.

that had economic reforms and national reconciliation as its drivers
and the wide range of areas of co-operation that the two countries could
undertake within the broad framework of friendship and co-operation
in keeping with their 'vision for the future in the pursuit of the common
good—bilaterally, regionally and globally'. This very clearly placed the
relationship in the context of a new and wider ranging strategic partnership within a framework that recognised the positive actions that
Thein Sein's Myanmar has undertaken to liberalise both the polity and
the economic framework that would enable the countries to co-operate
towards growth and a more practical security partnership; which while
denying space to insurgency on both sides of their common frontiers
would within a new co-operative format for socio-economic development provide new grounds for restoring peace and stability to the
region secured by bringing jobs and prosperity to the ethnic people on
both sides of the border.

The May 2012 visit helped in recognising that Myanmar could
become a very effective partner in helping establish a more practical and
people-oriented security structure that would comprise of the promotion of border area management with an 'assurance that territories of
either country would not be allowed to be used for activities inimical to
the other', identifying the need for special focus 'on the development and
prosperity of the people in the bordering areas…to co-operate to bring
about overall socio-economic development in the border areas by undertaking both infrastructure development and micro-economic projects'.

The Indian Prime Minister's visit helped project India as a serious
partner for the Myanmar Government, a partner whose proposals were
acceptable and doable in all the areas that Myanmar is concentrating on
in policy terms. India's endorsement of the policies adopted by Thein
Sein including those helping it integrate with the international community, helped restore India as part of the balanced relationship that
Myanmar favours for its relations with its neighbours where it can leverage its relationship with one to gain preferences for itself from the other.
It has also ensured that both countries can function together to establish
a secure environment on their respective borders where denial of space
to insurgents can be successfully coupled with the schemes adopted
as part of the border area development arrangements where India is
extending, both technical and financial assistance. The fact that there is

already in place a developmental arrangement that revolves around the Kaladan Multimodal Project that would benefit also the Chin State—one of Myanmar's most underdeveloped states—while benefitting not only Mizoram on the Indian side but also other North-Eastern Indian States illustrates what can be successfully achieved in a spirit of mutual benefit.

The Modi Dispensation and Myanmar–India Relations

With a change in the government in India after the May 2014 elections and the establishment of Narendra Modi as the Prime Minister heading a government that was voted in with an absolute majority, the decision-making on greater involvement in Myanmar keeping the vision of increased connectivity with the whole of Southeast Asia and the Far East by utilising the advantages that Myanmar's geographical position places it in, should gain greater focus. However the initial steps taken by the Modi government do not reflect such a focus.

Prime Minister Modi has shown a dramatic flair for the execution of foreign policy. He has used his entire repertoire of communication skills to promote himself as a formulator and executor of the key areas for the promotion of Indian interests and has in the process come to establish a role for India as an emerging power set on the road to a global power status. The initiative that he undertook to promote and project what he and India wanted was to extend priority to the relations with India's South Asian neighbours by inviting the SAARC heads of state or government to his swearing-in ceremony was a master stroke and set an agenda that the world powers had to take notice of and commend.

He has also shown a deft touch in promoting relations with his counterparts at a personal level that bodes well for India's gaining its rightful seat at the high table of global politics. In the process he has established a personal relationship with America's Obama, Japan's Abe, Australia's Abbot and with China's Xi. Making Bhutan and subsequently Nepal as the first neighbouring countries to visit and to establish a personal equation with the leadership in both nations is yet another milestone that he has crossed with success where these important neighbours are concerned.

However one error of judgement that emerged among the rapid strides that he has taken in the realm of foreign policy is the failure to include a strategically important Myanmar among the invitees to his swearing-in ceremony. This was either a failure on the part of whoever was advising him or an error of judgement on Modi's part. Myanmar is of immense importance and value to India in both strategic and security terms. It has a long land and maritime frontier with India. It is also geographically located on the crossroads that connect India to the rest of Southeast Asia and forms an overland connection to Mainland China. It was the latter factor that played an extremely important role during the Second World War when it provided the logistical connectivity for the supply of military support to China as part of the Allied War effort.

What makes Myanmar of singular importance is the fact that it not only is strategically placed providing connectivity to the rest of Southeast Asia, but significantly Myanmar is connected by both its land and its maritime frontiers with South Asia being thus connected to both India and Bangladesh.

Another element in India's relations with Myanmar, that Modi should have taken into account, is the imposing presence of China in that country that has implications also for India's relations with Myanmar particularly as we have to keep in mind the overall strategy that China is employing to contain India's influence even in its own neighbourhood and backyard. The recently concluded SAARC Summit was indicative of China's increasing interest in developing a larger and more expanded role for itself in South Asia. In this context, it has sought to gain entrance as a member of SAARC obviously trying to suggest that it is a part of South Asia having land frontiers that are common for instance with India, Bhutan, Nepal and Pakistan because of its presence in Tibet. It is a different matter that Tibet is an evidence of aggressive behaviour on the part of China who for all practical purposes is in illegal occupation of Tibet. Tibet was never historically part of China. China's South Asian adventures are and should be seen by India as part of China's policy of trying to contain India and reduce its potential as a possible alternative to China in the overall Asian and Indian Ocean region contexts.

Further China's approach is of import to India's strategic and security interests covering relations with the entirety of Southeast Asia. Illustrative of China's aggressive intent is the challenge that it has offered to India's relations with Vietnam. This is particularly aimed at India's involvement within the maritime territory and economic zone of Vietnam in the South China Sea. This is part of the aggressive intent that China is putting across to favour its expansionist claims in its disputes over the regional maritime claims of several of the Southeast Asian nations in the area of the South China Sea and East China Sea. One obvious fallout of the Chinese position is on India's relations for instance with Vietnam where China has attempted to contain India's maritime presence in what Vietnam claims are its maritime waters. Another case in point is the attempts made by China through its proxies among Indian and Myanmar insurgents of using the Myanmar space to materially support Indian insurgency movements in the north-east region of India.

Given all these factors it is in India's interest to have a very effective and expanding relationship with Myanmar. It was a matter of pure ill-judgement on the part of Modi that he failed to appreciate this aspect when he was inviting the SAARC neighbours and Mauritius to his swearing-in ceremony to which he also invited the head of the Tibetan government-in-exile but failed to include the President of Myanmar in his invitation.

Again when he decided to make visits to Bhutan and Nepal thus giving greater content to relations with these extremely important neighbours he failed to extend the same attention to the relations with Myanmar. In this respect Modi failed to appreciate the importance of Myanmar to India as a neighbour who occupied a geographical position that provided it with strategic and security importance to India and the gravitas that this provides to relations between the two countries.

Modi's first visit to Myanmar in November this year was multilateral in nature as it was connected to the ASEAN and East Asia Summits that Myanmar was hosting as the current head of ASEAN. The bilateral with President Thein Sein was thus part of the bilateral meetings that are carried out on the sidelines of multilateral summits and conferences. It certainly cannot be given the status of a regular bilateral visit that was exclusive to the relations with Myanmar. What were of even greater significance were the messages that India was sending to China. The invite to the Prime Minister of the Central Tibetan Administration Lobsang Sangay was an obvious message to China that India could play the same game that China continues to play on Arunachal Pradesh by theoretically extending support to the Tibetan government–in-exile. It amounted to the fact that India was willing to up the ante if China failed to take India's strategic interests into account. If this was correct then how could India not also include Myanmar as a vital factor in India's strategic and security space that would help negate China's efforts of containing India. The very nature of the geographical space that Myanmar occupies on India and China's frontiers requires that India has to grant a very special status to Myanmar granting significant content to both the socio-economic and political aspects of the relations with Myanmar.

There is little doubt that India has shown since 1992 that it has come to attach value to the relations with Myanmar and that it would not permit the type of regime in power in that country to determine the course of India's relations with it, instead it would be the importance attached to the obvious and extremely significant geostrategic aspects that would drive the relations between the two countries. In this context, it is understandable that it is in India's interest to ensure that Myanmar comes to rely on India as both an economic and political partner that would enable it to reduce the overwhelming presence that China has come to enjoy that was working against Myanmar's overall global interests and imposing negatives on the logical direction that Myanmar had to take to promote its national interests.

When the previous Indian Prime Minister Dr Manmohan Singh had made a bilateral visit to Myanmar the joint statement issued on that occasion had made a very significant commitment to the border area development, apart from extending financial assistance that was subsequently added to during the East Asia Summit hosted by India in 2013. The border area development commitment has both strategic and security angles to it. Strategically, it places the Indian involvement in the socio-economic development of Myanmar's border areas that would bring India into direct contact with the ethnic groups that not only border areas along India's frontiers with Myanmar but also that border Myanmar with China. This would make India an important player within the areas dominated by ethnic groups like the Myanmar Naga's in the Eastern Naga Region of the North Sagaing Division of Myanmar, the Kachins and the Shan groups that would also help reduce the mischief that China has played encouraging Indian insurgency groups from India's north-east region. The involvement would also assist Myanmar to establish greater control over these extremely important geographical areas by encouraging development as well as the social indicators covering health services, education, skills development, agricultural practices and economic development; by establishing small and medium sized industrial enterprises, including in the IT and Communication services areas that would create jobs; by bringing growth oriented stability to the area to reduce the insurgency-related foot print of these Myanmar areas that have been and continue to be utilised by Indian insurgents. This would contribute also by encouraging the relevant socio-economic developmental activities on a cross-border basis that would safeguard India's security interests in the region.

The main issue confronting India is the fact that the follow-up in terms of implementation has been extremely tardy, reflecting poorly on India's ability to deliver on its commitments. This covers not only the border area development programmes, but also the areas of project identification and a timely implementation of the Indian projects. India has laid emphasis on the area of connectivity not only centred on bilateral road and possibly rail connectivity but also on the a multi-country roadway that would connect India's north-east region, through Myanmar, to Thailand and beyond, covering in this manner India's connectivity with the whole of land based Southeast Asia. The first such project was the Tamu–Moreh road construction and upgradation that helped connect India through its National Highway network to Western Myanmar. However, the basic problem of building on this initial road connection has remained a very slow implementation process. To this has to be added the additional and in many ways the more serious impediment that is the result of the prevailing unrest on the Indian side due to insurgency with the consequent disruption of the movement of traffic on the national highways within and through the north-east region. Not surprisingly also is the element of poor maintenance of these highways on the Indian side.

Another major hurdle, which has contributed to the problems of implementation covering both delivery and quality has been the impossibly complex regulatory system that India's Finance Ministry imposes on the release of committed budgetary funds for the implementation of the projects. It is a reflection of the Indian mindset that wants to control not to ensure efficiency but to impose its will, a consequence of this being a disconnect between project time frames and delivery resulting in the recipient country, in this case Myanmar, coming to question India's ability to live up to its commitments. In other words India is gaining the reputation of a country that fails to deliver on its promises and the seriousness of its intent as possible important economic partner is constantly under question.

There are certain facts that need to be taken into consideration and to be acted upon to ensure that India becomes a serious player in the global economic scene including areas where India has made commitments under bilateral understandings serving the purpose of expanding India's sphere of influence within the ambit of India's Look East Policy and in particular among India's neighbouring countries which include Myanmar. As already put across, Myanmar is particularly important to India and close relations with it help progress its infrastructure, overall socio-economic development and ensures that Myanmar's overdependence on China is reduced to comfort levels that it finds acceptable would also serve strategic and security interests that arise out of the geo-strategic importance that Myanmar carries for India.

To this has to be added the fact that Myanmar is taking steps that would bring about, perhaps in a graduated manner, a true democratic rule in that country. This is what the people of Myanmar want; they have consistently displayed their commitment to a democratic Myanmar whenever they have been given the chance to express their wishes. Not only the people but also the monks who hold a very important position in a Buddhist country have demonstrated that that is what they want for their country.

What India has to do to gain more than a foothold for its influence in Myanmar is to ensure that the past inefficiencies in delivery on India's commitments are replaced urgently by a new regime that adheres strictly to time frames and cost-competitive approaches that are in keeping with the goals of real time socio-economic development as set out in the joint statement that was arrived at during the bilateral visit by former Prime Minister Dr Manmohan Singh and President Thein Sein of Myanmar. To achieve these parameters that should form the imperative for the success of India's presence in Myanmar, the first reform has to take place in the role of the Indian Ministry of Finance relating to the manner in which financial aid committed by India is disbursed. At present, and this has been the practice followed by the Ministry of Finance is one of negative interventions of an overly bureaucratic nature that creates delayed release of funds ensuring project delays for Indian-aided projects thus creating questions over time frames and cost overruns that effectively raise questions of credibility as well reducing the sustainability of many of these projects. The approach to aided projects should be one that ensures that all the rules are followed in determining and awarding the concerned projects including the determination of the financial commitments that have to be budgeted for. Once the project and the financial overlay has been established the only role of the Finance Ministry should be one that gets it regular reports from the implementing department of the Ministry of External Affairs that would cover all expenditure incurred based on the progress being achieved in the implementation of the project. The auditing of the accounts maintained in the project would be the basis for scrutinising the issues of rules relating to expenditure having been adhered to by the implementing agency.

Another weakness of the system has been the overdependence on utilising the public sector to cover issues of determining the viability and the parameters of the proposed projects. The other issue has been the tendency to favour the involvement of the Public Sector Undertakings (PSU) for taking on the projects even when it has been established by experience that even the best performing PSUs like the Bharat Heavy Electricals Ltd (BHEL) suffer from inefficiencies in carrying out their project implementation commitments that very often lead to delays as well as the use of outdated technologies. The correct approach has to be one where the most efficient entities from India involving both the private and the public sectors to bid for the projects and there is also preference attached not only to the cost competitiveness but also to the utilisation of best technologies and provide the best delivery and adherence to international standards.

Nothing that the Modi government has so far indicated of its intentions where deliverables on bilateral commitments are concerned have conveyed any improvement in the area of procedures or by ensuring that a more efficient system to ensure adherence to time frames and cost competitiveness is effectively under consideration. So far the bureaucratic over hang that has ensured that India continues to fail on its commitments is still in place and there is no attempt to monitor progress at the political levels. The Finance Ministry that has shown itself as the main stumbling block to efficient management and conduct that would help place India as a major economic partner for countries of importance to India, as Myanmar, is being changed because the political decision-making machinery is aware that change is necessary. In fact there has to be a mechanism in place in the Prime Minister's Office that monitors progress in the implementation of the financial aid projects and programmes that are part of India's bilateral commitments to Myanmar and Southeast Asia.

It is also necessary that Prime Minister Modi takes early steps in the coming year to make a bilateral visit to Myanmar and to review the current status of the projects and programmes that India has put in place where Myanmar is concerned. All the important projects that India has already undertaken such as the connectivity projects that include the Trilateral Highway, and the Kaladan Multi-modal Project are completed without further delay. There has to be additional emphasis employed to further and provide serious content to the Border Area Development process. This has to ensure that in the areas of social and economic development including cross border economic and commercial developments there is innovative thinking, institution building and the ease of connectivity and communication that covers both Myanmar's border regions and the adjoining areas of India's North-Eastern states.

Another factor that needs urgent attention is the promotion of business interest in investing and developing an industrial base that would be in the mutual interests of Myanmar and India. This requires a degree of financial engineering that extends assurance to Indian business interests that they have a secure base from which to operate from where the risk aspects have been reduced to acceptable levels. The present approach to link the commercial and business interests that would help industrialise and create job opportunities in India's North-East should be directly linked to what can be gained by creating a single market area that covers Myanmar and India. This area is again one that has so far not shown that there is any improvement in the approach by the Modi *sarkar*. It is imperative that Modi's visit to Myanmar—he has already received a direct invitation from President Thein Sein during the bilateral meeting between the two on the sidelines of the ASEAN and East Asia Summits that took place in Myanmar in November 2014—should be in 2015–2016. It should have substantive content to it including a freshly drawn-out agenda of bilateral commitments and implementation timelines as well as programmatic and funding clarity with assurances that from then onwards there would be no slippages and India shall ensure that the implementation is on schedule and adheres fully to agreed parameters.

As already argued earlier, Modi has to show that he means business slogans are good as a means to ensure that there is content that shall be provided and adhered to in the form of acceptable deliverables otherwise time shall throw the harsh light of failure and further disillusionment over India being a serious partner for Myanmar. It is in India's interest to not only be perceived as a reliable partner to actually be taken as one that permits no slippages between promise and performance.

Strategy for Successful Relations with Myanmar

To take advantage of the opportunity base that the new policies that Myanmar has now put in place has created, India has to ensure that the stakeholder arrangements that have been brokered by both sides do achieve the ambitious programme that the various MOUs and the Indo-Myanmar Joint Statement resulting out of the Indian Prime Minister's visit in May 2014 imply. It is imperative that India carries out the requisite implementational actions within a time-bound approach. The following actions could be some of the important steps that it could undertake:

- Set up a co-ordination group at a very senior level chaired and located within the PMO that ensures the timely implementation of projects including coordination of efforts that fall under the purview of different ministries and departments particularly for obtaining the necessary clearances covering technical and financial requirements.
- Ensure that the establishment of border area economic zones are given the priority and attention that they deserve in order to locate industry and services within them that serve not only the commercial aspects but bring to the area developmental investments that help the security of the people by granting them jobs,

entrepreneurial opportunities, developing the essential and necessary skills and managerial requirements, granting to the people a long-term stake in the prosperity that the schemes are intended to bring about as part of a regional arrangement.

- Major projects that are to be undertaken, like the dams on the Chindwin River for instance, do not suffer from the lack of co-ordination among different public sector agencies that by their unco-ordinated actions have slowed down the progress of the Kaladan Multi-modal Project. It is essential that the implementation of such projects is time bound and not a pre-determined responsibility of the PSUs but is subject to a competitive approach that involves all Indian parties that are capable and have the capacity to compete and adhere to time frames. If the PPP approach is now the norm for infrastructural projects in India then it should also be the approach that can be adopted for the successful implementation of the Indian-aided projects. The need is to prove to Myanmar that India is a reliable partner who is willing and able to deliver on its commitments on time.

- Put in place a programme that grants priority to the implementation of all arrangements and commitments on the social development side. The approach should have components that are sensitive to meeting the needs of Myanmar in its urban areas and in a more appropriate manner along the border regions that have been neglected even during the colonial period and certainly since Myanmar's independence. The areas to be covered under this part should be in the areas of skills development, education and research, public health and sanitation, water and water management, extension schemes and agro-industry, timber and other natural resourcesbased industrial entities that would bring prosperity to the border regions as much of these natural resources are located in the Frontier Areas of Myanmar with India.

- Assist in the setting up of irrigation systems particularly in the Sagaing Division of Myanmar that borders India and has a rich agricultural potential. It could be encouraged to produce agricultural products that have a ready and expanding demand in India such as pulses.

- Encourage and support investments by Indian industry in Myanmar. One area that would be mutually beneficial could be the establishment of a paper pulp industry that could make use of Myanmar's vast bamboo reserves. Among the incentives to drive the thrust by Indian industry could be a guarantee of low cost funding and the establishment of a bilateral framework that grants protection to the investments for which a BIPA and an invest agreement should be part of such a framework.

• India should take more steps to encourage investment by Indian companies in the oil and gas sector as well as in the power sector for which there should be a strategic approach that envelops this sector in a projected energy security arrangement that benefits both countries and stakeholders.

• India should involve itself in large scale infrastructure projects such as transportation corridors that help India link up with Southeast Asia, in ports developments, and in this regard seek a definite place, as offered by Myanmar at the highest level, in the Dawei port and industrial development in that area.

Politically it is important for India to keep encouraging the 'moderates' to take further steps towards the democratisation of Myanmar and its integration within the international community. Its steps towards national reconciliation that would help bring stability and security to the frontier regions requires support and it would be useful to make a distinct financial and technical provision that support the developmental arrangements that Naypidaw is trying to put in place in this regard.

India should also not shy away from encouraging an increased presence of the USA in Myanmar as it should help contain some of the more Indian Ocean centric policies of China where Myanmar is central to their achievement. It is certainly in India's interest to help reduce Myanmar's dependence on China to meet its military needs. This would involve a much closer Indian involvement in the supply of military equipment and an expanded training regime. It is obvious that India needs the cooperation and involvement of Myanmar in actions against Indian insurgents who continue to utilise the unstable frontier areas bordering India, particularly for actions by the Myanmar military to deny such forces space in that country. The mechanisms are already in place they need to be more efficiently managed and projected to reduce the activity areas for the Indian insurgents. It is also necessary, in this regard, that India ensures that Myanmar has its full support in preventing insurgents and disaffected people on the Myanmar side from utilising the porous borders to contravene Myanmar laws.

It is also evident that any transportation corridor arrangements that India's North-Eastern states gain to the ASEAN Region through Myanmar would require India to ensure that movements along the requisite connecting highways on the Indian side permit safe and secure passage. It is a curious reflection of the state of affairs on the Indian side that while movement of Indian cargo through states like Manipur is a difficult proposition because of the controls that are exercised by the Indian militants there is no barrier in the way of largescale movements of Chinese goods that make their way across the Myanmar side of the border. Hopefully the developments envisaged under the bilateral actions under the Border Area Management shall bring about a change that shall remove the incentives to insurgency once the economic and social benefits are seen to flow from developmental activities.

The Kachin insurgency is a factor that India can take lightly only to its own peril. The Kachins have shown themselves as close to China's overall regional designs at the same time whenever they have not been able to leverage their geographical importance to China they have resorted to actions against Chinese projects as has happened in the case of the Myitsone Dam and Hydropower project that the Kachins see as mainly extending economic benefit to south-western China and thus would increase the Chinese stake in bringing about a settlement for the Kachins with the GOM, a settlement that would be more favourable to the Kachin demands that practically are seeking independence from Myanmar while willing to settle for a wide ranging autonomy that so far has been opposed by the Myanmar armed forces. It is also ironical that while in the past the Kachins had shown themselves as questioning the Chinese bonafides at a time when the Chinese were supporting the CPB related insurgent movement against Rangoon, and had shown an affinity and trust in Indian support. They had also on many occasions permitted their territory to be utilised by China to gain secure passage for Indian insurgent groups who were trained and provided material support to cause disruption in India's north-eastern region. Interestingly in the present situation where they are involved in armed action against the Myanmar armed forces they have sought and obtained the good offices of China to arrive at an acceptable agreement with the Myanmar Government.

For India the turmoil in the Kachin State provides space for their activities to the Indian insurgents. There is also the issue of a Chinese involvement with the Indian insurgents, it is therefore in India's interests to keep in touch with Kachin Independence Army (KIA) to reduce—if not contain—the activities of the Indian insurgents and also to keep a watch on the motivations that are driving Chinese actions with them. At the same time it is in India's interest that the Kachin state is stabilised and remains a part of Myanmar. The very nature of the problem makes it imperative for India to help the GOM to restore peace in the area and for this purpose it could define a development strategy that could benefit the Kachins specifically and thus provide an incentive towards peace. However there is no doubt that the GOM has to arrive at an arrangement with all the ethnic groups that grants them a stake in the governance of the country on a federal basis that would bring peace and prosperity to a united Myanmar. Failure to retain the Kachin State could reopen the Pandora's box and a continuing instability in which foreign entities could play mischief to attain their own goals.

The first steps taken by the Modi government in India do not reflect a focus on greater involvement with Myanmar despite the emphasis on the conversion of the Look East Policy to Act East Policy. The fact of the matter is that Modi has announced that he is setting up a Special Purpose Vehicle (SPV) that would look into the implementational aspects of the Indian projects in Myanmar. Despite this the trilateral highway has fallen further behind because of the lack of funding by the Indian side and the Kaladan Multi-modal Transport Project has also fallen behind because the road connection that would link the boat head on the Kaladan River at Paletwa has still to be brought into the implementation process. Again the problem is budgetary in nature. It only goes to show that Modi has still to put in place a policy where the delay factor is robustly dealt with and adherence to timelines becomes the rule rather than an accidental exception.

12

Developments after the 2008 Constitution

This part deals with the developments that have taken place after the adoption of the 2008 Constitution and the elections that followed the retirement of Senior General Than Shwe held in November 2010 that brought about the installation of President Thein Sein and his government in early 2011. Thein Sein and his party, the Union Solidarity and Development Party (USDP) came to power having secured an overwhelming electoral victory in elections that were denounced as heavily skewed in favour of the Myanmar military. Once having secured power there was a remarkable turnaround in the behaviour and approach of this government. The President took steps to grant Suu Kyi and her party (NLD) the opportunity to become part of the governance process by permitting the registration of Suu Kyi's political party and permitting her personally to stand for election to the central legislature. This in itself was a departure from the position hitherto held by the military authorities that having married a foreigner she was no longer eligible for elections. There was understandably a considerable amount of speculation on what brought about this sea change in attitude and what it portends for the future of Myanmar?

The ruling party, USDP, is effectively the civilian projection of the military. President Thein Sein spent most of his adult life in the army and though seen as a low key media shy personality, he was fully engaged in the internal intrigues that were part and parcel of the period when the SPDC was in control of the Myanmar administration. The fact that he continued to grow in stature eventually securing the post of President of the Republic of the Union of Myanmar after having served as the Prime Minister of the SPDC under General Than Shwe is clearly indicative of the fact that he has the ability and the hard headedness to survive the intrigues within the Tatmadaw and to retain the support and endorsement of the now retired General Than Shwe. It is still alleged that the latter continues to wield a strong influence over major decisions. It was clearly apparent that Thein Sein was seen by the older generals headed by Than Shwe as a person who could be trusted to safeguard their interests. While Thein Sein secured a fair amount of authority to enable him to adopt reforms to bring a degree of liberal functioning and putting forward the more moderate face to the continuing dominance of military control he could do so only in consultation with and having the support of the National Defence and Security Council (NDSC). The NDSC derives its constitutional authority from the 2008 Constitution and dominates the executive decision making. It is headed by Thein Sein as President, has the Speaker of the Lower House of Parliament, the two Vice Presidents, the Foreign Minister, Than Shwe's replacement Min Aung Hlaing and all six of the regional military commanders who form the Bureau of Special Operations as members on it. The NDSC is obviously the real centre of executive authority.

Thein Sein set in motion several policy options that went some way to suggest that Myanmar was slowly moving in the direction of a managed multi-party democracy in contrast to the authoritarian rule that had been placed under the SLORC/SPDC governance of the country. The fact that Suu Kyi and her political party the NLD were permitted to stand for bye-elections and were elected to become Members of Parliament could come to serve as the opposition, with the eventual possibility of Suu Kyi being taken directly into the government was a major reversal of the military control that had been exercised by the Tatmadaw since the Ne Win takeover of 1962. The official stance taken by the Myanmar Government that the country is a 'young Democracy' as put out by Foreign Minister Lwin, was suggestive of an acknowledgement that the armed forces were willing to support a degree of participative involvement of the people in the governance of the country. This move that had come about much earlier than anticipated reflects that the military had realised that it needed to permit key reforms that would make Myanmar acceptable not only to the international community at large but more importantly to the ASEAN.

The steps taken by the Thein Sein government, in the areas of people's participation in governance (albeit this was a limited opening up), labour reforms to meet some of the provisions of the ILO, the setting up of a national Human Rights Commission, a substantial release of political prisoners, the new economic policy that favoured investments in the industrial and services economy by offering tax and other incentives, with a move towards quality of life improvements driven by social and economic development, and the settlement with the Karen ethnic minority that had been perhaps the longest prevailing insurgency, with the attempt to arrive at an understanding with the Kachins, met with a positive domestic and external response. The 14th ASEAN Summit was eventually hosted by Myanmar, which was again a positive development. These are an important part of the moves by Thein Sein to patch a moderate and liberal face on the present system of governance.

The reforms put in motion created a favourable climate that received a positive response from the USA, the UK and France that lead to visits by the US Secretary of State Hilary Clinton, the British Foreign Secretary William Hague and the French Foreign Minister Alain Juppe including the visits by US Senators and Congressmen all of which amounted to the first significant steps suggestive of an acceptance of the Myanmar regime with a consequential partial lifting of sanctions. The leadership of the USA and the EU obviously took Suu Kyi's views into consideration before the sanctions were modified, suggestive of the intent of the international community that the Thein Sein government ensure that the pace and the content of the reforms would proceed further and expand to become more representative of the will of the people. The final stamp of approval was of course provided by the game changing visit made by President Obama of the US and the encouragement provided to the Western business community to look more favourably on the economic opportunities that Myanmar's economic reforms and monetary policy were creating. The other important development was the involvement of the international financial institutions in providing developmental funding to Myanmar.

In conclusion the more balanced approach being adopted by Thein Sein and his colleagues including the attempt to reduce the overwhelming presence of the PRC to a more acceptable level should encourage the greater and more intense involvement of ASEAN, India, Japan and the Western democracies in the socio-economic development of Myanmar. India's efforts so far have remained more in the realm of promise than performance with many of the projects remaining in the pipeline rather than achieving implementational progress; the need is to make an effort to ensure the adoption of a time bound approach. India should also expand the nature of its involvement covering apart from infrastructure projects the funding of socio-economic developmental projects that affect the lives of the people directly by providing extension services, water and sanitation, public health and educational inputs along with an encouragement to invest in the setting up of small and medium enterprises at the village and small town levels. The efforts should ensure to a large extent the linking of these works, projects and investments to bring about a greater market area comprising of the North-Eastern states of India with the regions of Myanmar lying to the west of the Irrawaddy.

13

Myanmar in the Post-2010 Election Period

Taking account of the trends that have emerged in Myanmar and the direction in which the country appears to be moving rapidly it is worth taking a closer look at the developments that have taken place since the adoption of the 2008 Constitution and the subsequent elections that took place, under its provisions, in 2010. It is also necessary to take a call on the sustainability of the reforms and the steps that have been taken to make the political scene where a degree of participative governance has come to be established, more in keeping with the desires of the people who have in every free and fair election shown their preference for a democratic polity to govern the country. Any analysis has to take into account the possible deepening of the democratic process and the role that the domestic and external factors have played in the emerging political and economic scene and to what extent this momentum can be maintained. The constitution-making involves the assumption that the armed forces now feel that they would retain their dominance over the administration of the country backed by a constitutional sanction, the moves toward national reconciliation where the hope lies in the expectation that the prevailing internal conflicts, particularly with the ethnic community at large would stand resolved, the moves towards a more inclusive economic policy that has realigned the currency to its real market value and the encouragement to both domestic and external investment, where the impact of these changes and reforms, it is hoped, would help integrate Myanmar into the global economy. The analysis has to take account of the impact of the new policy on Myanmar's foreign policy and in particular the direction that the policy would take where the PRC, ASEAN, India and the Western powers are concerned.

Constitution Making and the Dominance of the Defence Services in the Governance of Myanmar

Before entering into an examination of the Constitution-making in Myanmar it is necessary to explain the importance of this instrument within the context of the internal conflict which even today continues to adversely impact the unity of the country and continues to create conditions of insecurity that could be exploited, as has happened in the past, by forces that are inimical to the sovereignty of the Republic of the Union of Myanmar. The Burma that the colonial masters had created had brought in the geographical areas that were dominated by the ethnic peoples who were not comfortable with the Burman people. Further though the major ethnic forces like the Shans and the Kachins and the Chins had clearly demarcated areas that were identified with them. The Karens who constituted a very large ethnic community were widely spread over the eastern and southern parts of Myanmar but did not have a clearly demarcated area that they could call their own. Recognising this anomaly the Panglong Agreement had made provision for the establishment of a separate Karen State that would comprise the Karenni State and the Salween District in eastern Burma and such other adjoining areas that a special commission would determine could form part of the Karen State.

The fact that the colonial masters utilised the services of the ethnic minority, particularly the Karens, the Chins and the Kachins for the security of colonial Burma from the Burman majority contributed to the suspicions that the Burman and the ethnic groups harboured against each other. In the lead up to the independence of the country and the negotiations that took place between the colonial authority and the nationalists led by General Aung San the latter accepted the need to hold separate talks and negotiate an agreement that would take care of the concerns of the ethnic community. These discussions at Panglong eventually led to the Panglong Agreement whose provisions came to be broadly reflected in the first constitution of independent Burma. Keeping in mind the implications of the Myanmar constitutions on the internal conflict situation that still persists it is important to look at the three constitutions that the country adopted under differing circumstances as essential to any analysis of the direction in which governance in Myanmar is headed.

Given the circumstances under which the constitution-making in Burma/Myanmar has taken place it is hardly surprising that Myanmar has so far had a rather chequered history where its Constitutions are concerned. Aung San and his colleagues, particularly U Tin Tut,[1] developed the first draft of the Constitution that was to be adopted in 1947 to give shape to the democratic form of governance that would be adopted to govern the country. That draft reflected in full the promises made to the ethnic community by incorporating in extenso the provisions of the Panglong Conference and the Panglong Agreement. The draft was motivated towards allaying the fears of the ethnic minorities implying that their interests would not be ignored and trampled over by the Burman community that enjoyed a clear demographic majority within a United Burma. It was, however, clear from the very beginning that there were differences between what Aung San and his followers were prepared to grant to the ethnic groups and what the more nationalistic Burman majority was willing to accede.

The first draft prepared by the committee of 110 under the Chairmanship of Aung San clearly adhered to the provisions of the Panglong Agreement in spirit and deed ensuring that there was a real federal arrangement that included the provision that each 'unit' (state) to have its own government to perform, safeguard, promote and protect the interests and benefits of their own states.[2] This draft entitled the 'Constitution of Burma Union

---

[1] A result of the 2nd Panglong Conference (7 February 1947) was the 'Unanimous Agreement that the political freedom of all peoples (Frontier People) there represented would be hastened by immediate co-operation with the interim government,' Cady, *History of Modern Burma.* The other agreements at Panglong provided for the enjoyment of democratic rights by all citizens, development aid to the Frontier Areas, Local autonomy, and the demarcation of the Kachin State. 'The personality of Thakin Aung San and the skillful negotiations of U Tin Tut were reflected in these arrangements.' Cady, *History of Modern Burma.*

[2] Salai Ngun Cung Lian, a former Chin freedom fighter who now heads a law firm Herzfeld, Rubin, Meyer & Rose in Yangon and is a part time but key peace negotiator. He is a key member of the of the Nationwide Ceasefire Coordination Team (NCCT). The line is from the comment that he had offered during the peace process stressing the need to keep the Panglong commitments as central to the Constitutional process and making it inclusive of the interests of the ethnic minorities.

and its Territories', was approved by the AFPFL National Convention and unanimously endorsed on 27 May 1947. This draft was changed in the amended draft that was adopted under the Chairmanship of U Nu after the assassination of Aung San and the provisions for a real federal structure were overtaken by the desire of the majority community to have a largely unitary administration of the country. This failure by U Nu and the majority community to adhere to the promise of federalism contributed to the unease with which the ethnic groups looked at their future in a United Burma.

The unease of the ethnic communities is best represented by what the Karenni representatives at Panglong made clear that they would only be a part of 'federated Burma until it had been demonstrated to their satisfaction that the Burmans would live up to their promises'. Another aspect of this process enjoined by the Panglong Agreement that was subsequently endorsed by other ethnic groups was the feeling or rather assumption by the ethnic groups that their inclusion in a United Burma/Myanmar was a voluntary expression and as such they were in a position to renounce being an integral part of the Union of Burma/Myanmar if their interests were compromised by the actions of the majority community that worked against both the physical commitment to the Panglong Agreement and the imperatives deriving out of the Panglong spirit. The 1947 Constitution thus contained the assurances that U Nu and company felt would help settle the fears of the ethnic groups.

The Panglong Agreement enabled the establishment of the Constituent Assembly of a United Burma and the adoption of the 1947 Constitution by it. *This Constitution, under its Chapter X, section 201, granted the right to every state to secede from the Union according to the appropriate provisions of Chapter X.*[3] This was incorporated to meet the promises of the Panglong Conference, to help ameliorate/counter the distrust that the ethnic communities harboured over the intentions of the Burman

---

[3] While this provision had provided a degree of satisfaction to the Shan and Karenni States, it came into question once the ten year period after independence had been reached and the Shan State decided to exercise the option to breakaway which was denied to them and this led to the breakout of insurgency in that State. The same was true of the Karenni State. The failure on the part of the Burman dominated political system to adhere to the main provisions of the Panglong Agreement and the understanding that had been arrived at with the Late General Aung San in 1947 only granted the ethnic groups a clear confirmation that they were right to distrust the ethnic Burmans. This distrust was eventually further strengthened by the intent and content of the 1974 Constitution.

majority. This right was considered questionable, particularly by the conservative Burmans and the armed forces led by Ne Win who set out to overturn this right in the name of maintaining the sovereignty and integrity of the Union; which in any case was under great stress due to the insurgencies led by the CPB with the material support of the PRC. One important aspect of the 1947 Constitution was the abbreviated federal structure that had provisions that reflected the interests of the states but did not grant the specifics of autonomy that the ethnic groups had expected in keeping with the discussions at Panglong. However constitutional provisions that granted the right to secede, the establishment of a bicameral parliament that had the Chamber of Nationalities, which had 125 seats held in the majority by the representatives of the states, gave the ethnic community sufficient scope to derive some comfort from the democratic nature of governance that it ensured. However the Karens began their fight for a separate and independent Karen State in 1948 itself and it is only now that the present government has been able to work out a ceasefire with the Karen National Union (KNU).

The other aspect of the 1947 Constitution that the U Nu government violated was the clause assuring religious freedom. U Nu, a staunch Buddhist, tried through various means to grant Buddhism a central and official position which sowed suspicion and caused the ethnic and religious minorities to question the intent of the majority Burman community. His final contribution was to make Buddhisim the official state religion in 1961, an action that intensified the opposition of the ethnic groups, which provided the excuse to the mainly Burman armed forces to take the position that the integrity of the nation was in danger and that this threat could only be prevented by the takeover of the country by the Tatmadaw.

The 1947 Constitution was overturned by Ne Win when he carried out his coup in 1962. It was eventually replaced by the 1974 Constitution that effectively endorsed totalitarian rule to be conducted by the adoption of the principle that, 'The State shall adopt a single-party system. The BSPP is the sole political party and it shall lead the State.'[4] One of the key aspects was the removal of any reference to the Right to Secede that was an important safeguard within the Constitution of 1947.

---

[4] Article 11 of the 1974 Constitution. The Constitution also changed the name of the country from the Union of Burma to the Socialist Republic of the Union of Burma.

Under Article 170 of the Constitution it was categorically stipulated that 'every citizen shall be under a duty to protect and safeguard the independence, sovereignty and territorial integrity of the Socialist Republic of the Union of Burma. This is a noble duty'. This Constitution ensured that every breakaway attempt would come to be categorised as an insurgency against the State and be put down by force. The ethnic community was reinforced in its belief that it could not trust the Burman majority to safeguard its rights and autonomy within a federal political system which in the past had recognised their right to secede if they were dissatisfied with the way in which the country was being governed. Another aspect which raised their apprehensions was the reversal of the multi-party democratic system that the 1947 Constitution had enshrined within it. One factor that needs to be reiterated relates to the events of 1988 which resulted in Ne Win retiring from the political scene, while having stated from the podium of the Party that the possibility of restoring a multi-party system be considered and a referendum to establish what the people wanted should be undertaken.[5] This was at that time turned down, however the SLORC led by Saw Maung, having overturned the 1974 Constitution, did permit the restoration of a multi-party system under which the elections of 1990 took place. The results of that election were overturned and the SLORC/SPDC rule continued till early 2011.

The SPDC continued the process of constitution-making where the NLD and Suu Kyi were not enabled to participate. This constitution-making process came to be highly criticised as it was considered a process by which the armed forces would perpetuate their power to govern the country. At the end they succeeded in putting in place the Constitution of 2008 which was endorsed by a contrived referendum. What the SPDC under Than Shwe succeeded in ensuring was that while this

---

[5] Extract from the July 1988 speech by Ne Win as head of the BSPP:

> It is necessary to assess whether among the people of the entire country, a majority is behind those lacking confidence or a minority. As I believe that holding a national referendum on what they wish—a one-party system or a multi-party system—would bring out the answer, I am asking the Party Congress to hold a referendum. If the majority wants a multi-party system, the present Constitution's provision under Chapter II, Paragraph 11 for the sole political party leading the State will have to be substituted with wording in consonance with a multi-party system. A suitable lapse of time would of course be needed for convenient movement of the people, production of ballot cards and other requirements.

constitution prevailed no civilian authority that came to power under it could overturn the primacy of the armed forces. Than Shwe clearly did not want to repeat the mistakes that had been made in the past where a free expression of the will of the people, both in 1960 and in 1990, had clearly expressed itself in favour of democratic governance where the armed forces could be expected to remain under civilian control.

The 2008 Constitution[6] restored the multi-party system within a controlled democratic model which granted the armed forces a major role in safeguarding their interests and ensured that the constitution could not be amended without their consent. The right to secede was specifically addressed and denied under Article 10 of the Constitution that states that '*no part of the territory constituted in the Union such as Regions, States, Union Territories and Self-Administrated Areas shall ever secede from the Union*'. Further under Article 20 the armed forces have been granted the responsibility for the preservation of the sovereignty and integrity of the nation and 'is mainly responsible for safeguarding the Constitution'. This is in keeping with the Basic Principles defined under Article 6 (f) of the Constitution that states, 'enabling the Defence Services to be able to participate in the National political leadership role of the State'. Again in order to preserve the primacy of the Defence Services, Article 17 states that 'in the executive, of the Union, Regions, States, Union Territory, Administrated Areas and districts, Defence Services personnel, nominated, by the Commander-in Chief of the Defence Services to undertake responsibilities of the defence, security, border administration, so forth, shall be included'. It is significant that the role of the Defence Services, within the Executive at all levels is to be played by nominees of the Commander-in-Chief (C-in-C) and not the President and his counterparts at the state and other administrative levels. This is further spelt out in the provision that grants the C-in-C the right to take over and exercise sovereign power in case a state of emergency arises.[7] In other words the Constitution grants sweeping powers to the C-in-C

---

[6] In a joint statement of National Reconciliation which was made after the adoption of the 2008 Constitution the opposition asked for the restoration of the spirit of Panglong which it addressed to the armed forces regime also at the same time seeking that the Tatmadaw seek a path to national reconciliation aimed at long lasting peace and development, this was in a document issued by the NGUB in 2009.

[7] Article 40 of the 2008 Constitution.

of the Defence Services which in times of emergency and when there is a threat to the security and integrity of the country appear to override the role of the President and the executive.

It is significant that the President who is the head executive of the nation is elected by an electoral college that comprises of elected representatives of the Parliament, inclusive of an equal number of representatives elected from the states and regions, and finally the group of nominated defence services personnel by the C-in-C to the two Houses of Parliament.[8] The President and his executive are electable to Parliament but on taking up their positions have to resign from the Houses of Parliament. However their functions and terms of office are controlled by the relevant provisions of the Constitution.

---

[8] The Constitution of 2008 specifies that the Pyithu Hluttaw shall comprise of 330 elected representatives and 110 (namely 30 per cent of the House) nominated Defence Services nominees of the C-in-C. Similarly the Amyotha Hluttaw or the upper house shall have 224 members of whom the Region, State or Territory would elect 168 while 56 shall be nominated by the C-in-C of the Defence services. The nomination of a third of the members of the Regions, States etc. would again be nominees of the C-in-C.

14

The Position of the Ethnic Minorities

For an understanding of this extremely complex issue it is important that the background to the Frontier Areas and their inclusion within the geographical confines of Burma/Myanmar took place under the force of circumstances arising out of the outgoing British Burman administration's anxiety to quit Burma after the signing of the Aung San–Atlee Accord without any overhang as a responsibility for the Frontier Areas or the implementation of promises made by Mountbatten and Auchenlik to the Karens. The Aung San headed AFPFL spelt out the following demands on 10 November 1946 with the aim of pressuring the British government on the issue of the independence of Burma:

1. On or before April 1947, elections were to be held for a constituent assembly.
2. The elections were to embrace the Frontier Areas as well as Burma Proper.
3. On or before 31 January the British government would pledge to give Burma full independence within a year.
4. There would be a review of the project's scheme (reserving to British firms the contracts for rehabilitating Burma's economy).[1]

---

[1] Taken from *Burma: The Curse of Independence* by Shelby Tucker quoting from F.S.V. Donnison's book *Burma*.

These elements came to be reflected in the Accord and it had as a congruent development of the Atlee–Aung San Agreement that was signed on 27 January 1947 that set out in Article 8 the relations to be brought about for the establishment of a unified Burma; it sets out and reflects the approach that was to be adopted leaving it to the ethnic groups to determine the nature and extent of their presence in an independent Burma. It was however clear that the colonial masters were intent on ensuring that the Frontier Areas were part of independent Burma and would not be left behind as a separate entity where Britain would have to retain a security and a financial presence. More to the point they reneged on their commitments to the Karen who had remained loyal to them throughout the Japanese occupation of Burma, which led to the Karen group placing themselves against the unification of Burma, a clear case of pushing the ethnic groups to arrive at a compromise that would see them joining hands with Burma Proper to gain a jointly worked out independence and a constitution that would safeguard their primary and fundamental interests. It should also be noted that the Karens formed the KNU a day after the full text of the Atlee–Aung San Agreement was made available in the local media and the ball was set in motion for the insurgency that they initiated immediately after the independence of Burma. An extract from the agreement setting out the understanding over the Frontier Areas is as follows.

Article 8 Frontier Areas (extracted from the Atlee–Aung San Agreement of January 1947):

It is agreed objective of both His Majesty's Government and the Burmese Delegates to achieve the early unification of the Frontier Areas and Ministerial Burma with the free consent of the inhabitants of those areas. In the meantime, it is agreed that the people of the Frontier Areas should, in respect of subjects of common interest, be closely associated with the Government of Burma in a manner acceptable to both parties. For these purposes it has been agreed:

(a) There shall be free intercourse between the peoples of the Frontier Areas and the people of Ministerial Burma without hindrance.
(b) The leaders and representatives of the peoples of the Frontier Areas shall be asked, either at the Panglong Conference to be held at the beginning of next month or at a special Conference to be convened for the purpose, to express their views upon the form of association with

the Government of Burma which they consider acceptable during the transition period whether—

    (I) by the appointment of a small group of Frontier representatives to advise the Governor on Frontier affairs and to have close liaison with the Executive Council; or

    (II) by the appointment of the Frontier Area representative as Executive Councillor in charge of Frontier affairs; or

    (III) by some other method.

(c) After the Panglong meeting, or the special conference, His Majesty's Government and the Government of Burma will agree upon the best method of advancing their common aims in accordance with the expressed views of the peoples of the Frontier Areas.

(d) A Committee of Enquiry shall be set up forthwith as to the best method of associating the Frontier peoples with the working out of the new Constitution for Burma. Such Committee will consist of equal numbers of person from Ministerial Burma, nominated by the Executive Council, and persons from the Frontier Areas, nominated by the Governor after consultation with the leaders of those areas, with a neutral Chairman from outside of Burma selected by agreement. Such Committee shall be asked to report to the Government of Burma and His Majesty's Government before the summoning of the Constituent Assembly.

Article 8 formed the basis for the setting in motion the process that led to the Panglong Conference and the Panglong Agreement (February 1947) where the representatives of the Shan, the Kachin and the Chin were able to negotiate with the AFPFL delegation the provisions that would safeguard the interests of the ethnic groups being included within the constitution that was to be drafted under the Chairmanship of Aung San. That draft and its subsequent adoption by the Constituent Assembly would bring about a United Burma comprising of Burma Proper and the Frontier Areas within one single geographical area. The draft clearly made a commitment on the Union adopting a multiparty democratic system of governance within a federal arrangement that would guarantee the 'full autonomy' that the ethnic groups desired and would permit a ten-year period of functioning at the end of which if the ethnic groups were not happy with the functioning of the Union then the concerned ethnic state could leave the Union. The KNU representing the Karens remained aloof from the Panglong process and made it clear that they were seeking an independent state for themselves.

The ethnic groups barring the Karens had reposed their trust in Aung San and this trust appeared to have been fully reciprocated by Aung San who ensured the draft worked out under his leadership and guaranteed the full autonomy that a federal system would assure to the ethnic groups that their interests would be fully safeguarded. Unfortunately before the approved draft could be brought into implementation forming the content of the 1947 Constitution, Aung San and most of his cabinet colleagues were assassinated. U Nu who succeeded Aung San and carried forward the process for the adoption of the constitution did not stick to the Aung San draft and the eventual constitution adopted considerably reduced the extent and scope of the federal arrangement. The ethnic groups however showed a willingness to go ahead with the constitution as they appeared to be content with the provision that they could secede from the Union after a ten-year period under Chapter X Section 201 of the Constitution.

The improved relations between Myanmar and China in the post-1988 period, enabled the SLORC to arrive at understandings with most of the ethnic groups with assurances of localised but limited autonomy including a limited but undefined control over local governance. This was undoubtedly the result of the close relations that came to be developed by the Myanmar military junta and the PRC where Myanmar was placed by the SLORC within China's sphere of influence. This relationship resulted in the upgradation of the armed forces with the flows of approximately US$2.2 billion worth of arms and military equipment from China. Part of the positive trend from the Burman point of view was the shrinkage of the space within which the ethnic insurgencies had operated, in the period 1948–1988 within the support that was being provided to the CPB and the ethnic groups allied with them that came to a stop after the developments of 1988 and the takeover of Burma/Myanmar by the SLORC and the alliance that it secured with Beijing. In the final analysis the persistence of the internal conflict came to be largely confined to the Southern Shans, the Karens and the Kachins[2] who continued to resist the SLORC/

---

[2] With the Kachins after a string of battle victories a ceasefire agreement was put in place in 1994 which lasted for 17 years of peace but hardly resulted in significant improvement in relations as the areas of mistrust remained and the subsequent differences over the KIO armed forces retaining their independent existence added to actions that resulted in the ceasefire ending in armed conflict that continues to persist and the various attempts to bring about an agreement have so far failed. An interesting aspect of this conflict is the clear

SPDC regimes. Moreover the ethnic groups did not give up on issues of autonomy and continue to remain suspicious of the Burman majority. Ideally what the ethnic groups want is a federal system that would confine the Union's powers to issues of security, external affairs and finance and customs with a commitment from the central authority on permitting substantial flows of developmental finance to the Frontier Regions. All other powers would be with the states.

They would also prefer that the right to secede be restored, but are aware that with China supporting the authority at Nay Pyi Taw (the Tan Shwe decreed new Capital of Myanmar) they could not force the issue. The ethnic parties in Parliament are small, the largest being the Shan Nationalities Democratic Party (SNDP) and continue to express themselves, whenever the opportunity arises, that they favour a governmental system that would be truly federal in nature and would provide for adequate and meaningful levels of autonomy.

While the ethnic minorities had shown confidence in Aung San and had agreed to display their support for a United and free Burma freed from its colonial yoke, they have over the years seen that all the promises made by Aung San and Tin Tutt have been reversed. They had reposed trust in Suu Kyi, in the hope that the Constitution making that would follow the 1990 elections would help meet most of their demands and safeguards. The subsequent events, once the SLORC refused to accept the verdict of 1990, saw the ethnic group's capacity to bargain for their rights, had to a large extent, been neutralised by the military regime.

It would perhaps be worth mentioning that by most accounts during the period 1948–2010 has seen the rights of the Frontier people being violated. All the initial promises bearing on a federal structure which granted them real autonomy and the right to secede were forcibly reversed and large scale violations of their human rights have taken place. Over the years if anything, they have been confirmed in the view that the Burman majority would not adhere to any promises that granted them what they value in the form of autonomy that would empower

---

violation of the Presidential orders to the Tatmadaw that it should place its ongoing operations on hold have not been implemented by C-in-C Hlaing. The 2008 Constitution does not grant the President of Myanmar the status of the Supreme Commander of the Armed Forces; this remains the prerogative of the C-in-C.

them to manage their domestic affairs while securing resources that would enable them to improve their quality of life.

It now appears that they are no longer willing to accept Suu Kyi's calls for national reconciliation at face value. They would like to see how she and the NLD support them in their demands for autonomy as the Thein Sein government moves towards negotiating and implementing its policy of national reconciliation and national coordination. Given the nature and the extent of the suspicions harboured by the ethnic minority it is hardly surprising that the ethnic groups are openly stating their distrust of all Burmans pointing out that they respect her (Suu Kyi) for fighting for democracy and also as her father's daughter, but they are uncertain of her long-term intentions, pointing out that as a Burman she may be willing to accept a compromise that would deny them true autonomy.

15
Internal Conflict and the Security Issue

The problems that the ethnic groups pose to the Union of Burma because of their strategic geographical location and the large territories that they control provide them also with the opportunity to play the China card depending on the nature of the prevailing Sino-Myanmar relations.[1] This is an element that no one conscious of the future security of the country can ignore and has to provide for. How Suu Kyi comes across in the negotiations on national reconciliation that are on the agenda of the present government shall contribute to the future of Myanmar as a united country. The ethnic minority comprises 32 per cent of the total population of Myanmar. The ethnic groups are located in Frontier Areas of Myanmar with the concerned states bordering Bangladesh on the west, India on the west and north-west, Tibet to the north, Yunnan province of China on the north-east and the east and Thailand on the east and south-east. It is important to also recognise that the British colonial authorities had administered the non-Burman areas as separate

---

[1] China had laid claim to large areas in the north of Burma at the time of the British annexation of monarchical Burma in 1865 'the Chinese Government proposed that the Shwayles (Shweli river), a river which at one part of its course, forms the boundary between Burma and Yunnan, should thence to its confluence with Irrawaddy be taken as forming the frontier between the two countries'. (Dorothy Woodman, *The Making of Burma*, 270). This was proposed by the Marquis Tseng, the Chinese Minister heading the Chinese Legation in London, this claim if it had been acceded to by the British would have brought parts of the North Shan State area and the Kachin State area within China.

'Frontier Areas' as part of their divide and rule policy which has continued to have repercussions on the unity of Burma/Myanmar till today. The geostrategic implications of this combination of Myanmar's frontiers inhabited by ethnic groups—that have been in constant turmoil since 1948—and the involvement of some of its neighbours in supporting insurgencies in the past, has to be dealt with in an environment that grants assurance of equality of treatment to the ethnic minority that would form an essential part of any consensual settlement that the peace movement initiated by Thein Sein concludes, which also ensures that the security and unity of the Union is guaranteed by all parties. The need therefore is for the GOM to find solutions that help meet the demands of the ethnic minority and pacify their innate sense of distrust of their Burman neighbours. In the ultimate analysis, the solution would probably lie in the acceptance of a federal structure that allows for acceptable levels of autonomy that satisfy both the demands of unity and sovereignty. The question remains, can the Burman armed forces largely, if not entirely, accept such a solution in the future and hold out a promise to this effect. After all they had destroyed the rather weak federal structure that the 1947 Constitution had put in place, as they feared that it could lead to the disintegration of the nation particularly as the main ethnic groups continued to rebel against the Union authority and made attempts to utilise the provision that extended to them the right to secede under the 1947 Constitution.

One of the important elements that has driven the move towards national reconciliation is obviously the desire to prevent any future exploitation of differences by any ill-disposed force, including the neighbouring countries. The problems with the Rohingyas for instance involves Bangladesh, the stubborn refusal to consider them as an ethnic minority that is part of the 'Republic' has created a security problem that could lead to the fundamentalists gaining the upper hand and pose a consequential serious threat of terrorist actions. The Burman-dominated armed forces have in the past and also more recently taken positions that are quite openly anti-Muslim in expression and action. In 1991–1992 the armed forces had demolished mosques in Yangon including the desecration of the Muslim scriptures, there was no local protest possible against these actions as the armed forces had openly adopted the position of using brutal force against any opposition. It was also in this period that a large number of Rohingyas were driven out of Myanmar into Bangladesh. The real issue pertaining to the Rohingya minority is the persistently held belief in Myanmar that they constitute an immigrant force that had no citizenship rights and as such could be discriminated against with the intention of driving them out of the country. The persisting problem in the Arakan State revolves around anti-Muslim sentiments harboured and encouraged among the Buddhist community, the Rakhines and the communal riots that have taken place, bringing into play the 2008 Constitution's emergency rule provisions are a clear indication of the enforcement of law that the State could resort to leading to direct rule by the armed forces. It serves as a reminder that the State finds it easier to resort to the armed forces to impose its will rather than use the regular means of restoring order through the legal and administrative machinery at its disposal that should include a utilisation of the security forces under civilian control and management. The problem affecting the Rakhine State could be vitiated by external entities supporting a fundamentalist approach to the problem that could well spill over to adjoining areas. Apart from the Kachin insurgency, and the disruption of the ceasefire process with the different Shan groups, the problem of the Rakhine State pose a set of troubling manifestations that project the varied nature of the problems confronting the national reconciliation process and the wide ranging nature of the sensitivities involved.

The Karen issue is one where Thailand is also involved. It is perhaps the most difficult problem to resolve as it contains within the Karen mind the call for a homeland that is driven by a serious emotional attachment to the establishment of a Karen state that covers all areas that have a major Karen presence which would include territories that are part of the Burman-administered areas. A major development has been the signing of a ceasefire agreement in January 2012 between the government and the KNU. This is in a sense a historic development as the Karens have been in revolt since 1949, albeit there was a truce for a brief period that had been negotiated by Bo Mya the Karen leader leading the Karen military forces and Khin Nyunt. The present ceasefire seems to be one that would last assuming that the national reconciliation talks evolve an acceptable formula to resolve the main differences. The ceasefire permits the conduct by both sides of unarmed patrols; permits the KNU to open liaison offices in 'Government-controlled' areas; they (Karens) are permitted to retain their arms ostensibly for their personal security; there is an assurance that the government was keen to establish an environment of equal rights and there would be ceasefires achieved with all ethnic groups.

Ceasefire agreements have also been secured in the recent past, with a number of ethnic groups which include the Wa State Army, the Shan State Army-South (SSA-S), the Chin National Front and the National Democratic Alliance Army. The main group that continues to fight the government are the Kachins. The Kachin problem is a complex one[2] and has a history including the fact that they have a recognised capability to employ guerrilla tactics that have had a great deal of success in fighting the Myanmar armed forces particularly as the terrain they occupy is mountainous and heavily forested, being well-suited to their military tactics. Another issue that has been at the base of the Kachin problem is that the Kachin are mainly Baptist Christians and form a strong minority that is opposed to any policy that promotes the country officially as a Buddhist nation which is what had led to the initial break down in relations when Prime Minister U Nu, against the original provisions and secular intentions of the 1947 Constitution, declared Burma a Buddhist country in 1961.

The Kachin State has a number of economic advantages, which coupled with its strategic geographical location, confronts many of the projects that the Chinese have an interest in. These include the areas of hydropower and the passage of the gas and oil pipeline from Myanmar to China which is an area that can pose long-term problems to the stability of the country unless the KIO can be pacified and the Kachin interests that it represents can be dealt with within the demands of full autonomy and equality. Currently the demands of the KIO are that the armed forces in the Kachin State area announce a unilateral ceasefire and withdraw to their base areas. The Chinese are directly involved in helping negotiate a

---

[2] Serving as a background to the complexity of the Kachin problem is the fact that not until the British colonial forces were able to deal with the Kachins and bring within the fold of the Burma Frontier Areas they had never been within the sway of the Chinese or Burmese Kingdoms. While it was apparent that the Chinese had during the seventeenth and part of the eighteenth centuries exercised authority 'over a large district in the Irrawaddy Basin, the Kachin communities though at that time comparatively few, still retained their independence' (comment by a Political Officer at Bhamo extracted from the author's readings on the administration in old Burma).

settlement, which so far has proved elusive, the involvement of the Chinese has turned out both as a plus and a negative as any settlement with the KIO shall have their finger print on it that could be exploited whenever China feels it is necessary to safeguard its economic and political interests. The Chinese are sensitive to the fact that the Kachins have been in touch with Washington as their mainly Baptist Christian background is of interest to people in the USA. This factor serves as an additional strategic incentive for China to play a role in bringing about a settlement between the Kachins and Naypidaw.

The sensitivity of this region is brought out by the past history of this region. It was the threat of a Chinese presence that in the past had encouraged the British colonial negotiators to ensure that the Kachin area, with its implications for the security interests of both Burma and British India, was kept firmly within the geographical confines of British Burma. To ensure this they at the time of negotiating the Anglo-Chinese Convention on Burma even proposed that the Shan State could be part of China however as the Chinese were at that time more interested in securing their rights in Tibet they ignored the British suggestion and the Kachin and the Shan areas were both contained as part of the Frontier Areas of British Burma. Of interest are the reasons that motivated London and Calcutta to put forward such a proposal. The intention was that the Chinese not only accept Britain's presence and control in Burma but also that the trading interests that British were developing in China out of India would not in any way be jeopardised. It was again the British trading interests that were kept in the forefront of the policy that they developed over Tibet and the compromises that London negotiated with the Chinese that granted recognition to China's suzerain rights over Tibet.

The KNU in its capacity as a key member of the United Nationalities Federal Council (UNFC) that was formed in February 2011 as a coalition of ethnic armed groups, called on the GOM 'to enter into an inclusive dialogue with all UNFC members to reach a lasting political settlement that addresses ethnic concerns'. The UNFC permitted its individual members to enter into individual ceasefire agreements with the proviso that 'this would lead to political talks with the GOM that would include all the member groups'. These developments do portend that the national reconciliation process has not only to be all inclusive but has to build a consensus that would involve an acceptance of demands like that of real autonomy and visible treatment of equality that are among the main demands of the ethnic minority. The demand for a federal system is a very contentious issue that is generally opposed by the armed forces who are unlikely to accept any political system that they feel could place curbs on their powers including the control that the constitution extends to them. Where Thein Sein and company could be generous is on issues of development which would have to involve social and economic infra-structure development and an improvement in the inputs that would bring about significant quality of life improvements for the people living in the border regions.

There continue to remain serious differences between most of the ethnic groups and the GOM's peace process. At the Union Day meeting in January 2015 between the ethnic groups and President Thein Sein the NCCT refused to sign the GOM's proposed 'Deed of Commitment for Peace and National Reconciliation' claiming it was full of generalisa-tions and said that there was no concrete spelling out by the President on the establishment of the federal union. The NCCT made it clear that unless the GOM moved from generalisations to a clear enunciation of the form that the federal union would take, they were not willing to sign on the dotted line. President Thein Sein had once again followed the approach of suggesting that the ethnic groups sign the 'deed' state-ment as a 'binding promise, not a legal agreement'. President Thein Sein continues to contend that the fact the statement called for the 'building a Union based on democratic and federal principles in the spirit of Pan-glong', should provide the assurance to the ethnic groups that the political negotiations that would follow would put in place the political structure that would meet aspirations. Four groups the KNU, the Democratic Karen Benevolent Army, the Karen factional group the KNLA-Peace Council and the (SSA-S) however signed the statement feeling that the pledge con-tained within it gave them the grounds to do so and that by signing it they had nothing to lose. They also wanted the armed forces to understand that they were committed to securing peace. Not surprisingly the three groups that continue to be involved in armed battles with the Tat-madaw and have not signed ceasefire agreements did not attend the Union Day meeting with President Thein Sein. They were the KIA, the Ta'ang National Liberation Army and the Myanmar National Demo-cratic Alliance Army.

What is central to the reconciliation process is the feeling that Thein Sein, who it is felt has the blessings of the C-in-C of the armed forces, is sincere in his efforts to arrive at an understanding that is acceptable to all parties. His statement in Parliament marking his and his government's first anniversary in power would have helped reaffirm this belief; particularly his references to bringing about 'ethnic peace' which, as he put it, would replace the guns in the hands of the ethnic youth with laptops. The President's assurance that he would like the long-held demand of the right of the ethnic groups to get involved in 'our "all-inclusive political process"' to be fulfilled and went on to suggest that, 'As our country is a Union nation, we must let all ethnic minorities get equally involved in the political process', suggesting that, 'It is necessary that we, the current government, help to end the misunderstanding and mistrust between ethnic groups and the government...We have no trick on the path in the direction of the peace, we conduct peace deals based on the spirit of Panglong Agreement.' The ethnic groups have faith in the spirit of reconciliation that Thein Sein continues to put forward including the position that is reflected in his point of view that 'the armed conflicts will not come to an end if we just blame each other. We have to solve it by political means. For that, it is needed that we must start with cease-fire agreements'. Thein Sein explained that there were three steps in his government's peace process—state-level talks and stopping hostilities, repositioning troops and opening liaison offices in respective regions, and then setting up a timetable for union-level talks.

The GOM has expressed an open commitment to containing the production of opiate drugs in Myanmar, the Shan State region remains the main source for the opium poppy and the production of heroin, most of the heroin that is produced in Myanmar finds a market in China according to UNDOC. The official policy has been to ban the growing of the poppy, focusing on the Kokung and Wa areas where enforcement has involved the use of force. However the effort has not involved the development of alternative crops that would help the farmers to secure themselves and also assure them an income that would grant them food security. The problem is not only a humanitarian one but also poses a continuing area of conflict along the sensitive border area, which has both a Chinese and a Thai involvement. The flow of development funds and the evolving of suitable social and economic programmes is an essential area on which the government has to focus, it does have the involvement of the UN System but it would be useful for a degree of bilateral involvement which would assist by making technology and extension services available to establish the necessary agricultural and alternative job creating factors that would grant the farmers a secure future and ultimately give the people of the area a stake in the peace process. There are also clear indications that some important former army officers, close to the regime, have cornered their home areas for the continuation of the production and distribution of opiate drugs, one such case is that of Kyaw Myint and the Namkhan area that he has cornered for intensive cropping of the opium poppy.

The recent agreement with the 'Restoration Council of the Shan State' and its armed wing the 'SSA' which was announced on 19 May by the parties concerned appears to be a step in the right direction that could help put in place a programme that would assist in eradicating both natural drugs (heroin) and synthetic or chemical drugs like methamphetamines. The Shans have in their discussions with General Soe Win, Myanmar's deputy c-in-c of the army who led the government delegation at the 19 May talks which also included the Railway Minister Aung Min presented a comprehensive plan for drug eradication. The plan includes elements covering development, support and provision of alternative agricultural crops and the adoption of programmes that help create jobs. It includes the involvement of cross border discussions and understandings with the neighbouring countries China and Thailand. This is a positive development as part of the peace process and grants to the ceasefire agreement with the Shans a deeper content. In the peace talks at Kengtung, the SSA reached a 12-point agreement with the government, including co-operation to eradicate narcotics, conducting of joint surveys, promotion of Shan literature and culture, legalisation of the RCSS/SSA, establishment of Shan media and the freeing of all Shan political prisoners. The Shan group was invited by the government negotiators to set up a political party to participate in the next general election in 2015.

What is significant is the understanding that has evolved, at the Kengtung talks and agreement of 19 May 2012 which in effect put in place a process that if followed to its logical conclusion by President Thein Sein and his government could bring the ethnic groups into a negotiated peace that would guarantee Myanmar's sovereignty based on a peace based on granting equality and equal opportunity to the ethnic groups. Thein Sein in his anniversary speech had made a categorical reference to the peace deals being worked out in keeping with the spirit of the Panglong Agreement. That Agreement in its articles V and VII makes clear commitments to the Frontier Areas, on their continuing to enjoy 'autonomy' in internal administration accepting in principle that the Frontier Areas would enjoy 'full autonomy'. Further Article VII clearly states that those areas would 'enjoy' the rights and privileges that which are regarded as 'fundamental in democratic countries'.[3] It would be an acceptable premise that President Thein Sein while making his reference to the Panglong Agreement, within the context of bridging the gaps between the ethnic groups and the government to ensure the removal of misunderstanding and distrust, presumably has the support of the armed forces to grant them autonomy within an acceptable democratic structure. To this have to be added an acceptance of a role for Suu Kyi, as already desired by the Karens and probably also likely to be demanded by the Kachins if a ceasefire with them is established in the near future.

The most important aspect of the national reconciliation process clearly revolves around the issue of 'full autonomy' and how this is to be ensured under a constitutional provision that would bridge the gap between the in principle promise that the Thein Sein Presidency appears to be committed to and the demand of the ethnic groups that this is only achievable under a Republic that is truly federal in nature. This would involve a constitutional amendment that would have to also contain specific provisions that spell out the nature and the extent of the federal system as well as the detailed rights of the autonomous states and the relations with the Union Authority. It would necessarily have to grant full powers to the states as federal entities to deal with subjects that are listed as the responsibility of the states and there would have to be an accepted mechanism that would also deal with issues of socio-economic

---

[3] (V) Though the Governor's Executive Council will be augmented as agreed above, it will not operate in respect of the Frontier Areas in any manner which would deprive any portion of these Areas of the autonomy which it now enjoys in internal administration. Full autonomy in internal administration for the Frontier Areas is accepted in principle.

(VII) Citizens of the Frontier Areas shall enjoy rights and privileges which are regarded as fundamental in democratic countries.

development. The path ahead is a difficult one that shall have to involve a change in the mindset of the armed forces leadership that has so far only felt comfortable with a unitary form of government exercising full control over the entire territory of Myanmar.

For India the resolution of these issues that would bring stability to the entire geo-strategically sensitive frontier areas of Myanmar hold great import as such a stability could assist in denying space to India's insurgent groups that reside in states in the North-East of India and have used Myanmar not only for transit purposes but have installed camps where interests inimical to the stability of India have been involved in granting them material and technical assistance. Another aspect of stability in the region lies with India's efforts to put in place projects that in effect create economic and social development opportunities that serve not only interests in India's North-Eastern states but also Myanmar's adjoining ethnic states' areas. For instance the present unrest in the Rakhine State of Myanmar (Arakan Region) where communal tensions are prevalent between the Buddhist Rakhines and the Muslim Rohingyas who are also largely considered as illegal Bangladeshi immigrants, could have a negative impact for India's involvements in the Sitwe area as well as on the Kaladan Multi-modal Project that grants an alternative route to landlocked Mizoram and would help in furthering the economic development of that state as well as the adjoining Chin State of Myanmar. A resolution of the problems afflicting this area is in the obvious interest of India and to an important extent of the Indo-Myanmar relations.

16

The Bigger Brother: China in Myanmar

The Pre-1948 Period of Sino-Myanmar Relations

Historically China and its emperor loomed large on the horizons of the Burmese monarchy. Here certain factors stand out. The Burmese monarchy did have a close relationship which has been projected as one where it paid tribute to the Chinese Emperor.[1] When Britain made its moves to annex Burma in 1886, the issue of the Chinese reaction and the manner in which China's rights could be defined over Burma and to what extent these should be agreed to by the colonial authority became

[1] Tributary relationship with China appears to have been in operation during the latter part of the Pagan Kingdom it is mentioned in the 'Ta Ming Chi'li (Collected Ceremonies of the Ming Dynasty)' that after the time of Kublai Khan 1260–1294, 'Annam, Champa, Yunnan, Laos Northern Burma…all sent envoys to offer up tribute'. The British Charge d'Affaires in Peking (O'Connor) said 'there is no doubt that traditionally the country is looked upon as a Tributary of China and that a large Burmese Tribute—bearing embassy came to Peking in the year 1875. This is a reference to a decennial tribute arrangement between the Burmese monarchy and Peking. On 1 November 1885 the Chinese Foreign Office (Tsung-Li Yamen) took up with the British the issue of the action that they were contemplating requiring the annexation of Upper Burma, stating that 'Burmah is our tributary State, and sovereignty will compel China to interfere, but England is a friendly Power, and we desire a friendly arrangement'. Subsequently the British and Chinese authorities came to an understanding which accepted the sending of the decennial tribute to China while the British annexed Upper Burma, further the Chinese and the British came to a bargain setting off China's interests in Tibet against the British interests in Burma.

a matter of considerable exchanges between the British Indian authority, the British Cabinet and the Crown. An examination of these exchanges establishes that Britain did recognise that the Chinese had rights even though the documentary evidence created doubts. But the motivation remained that China must not feel alienated over the British moves to invade and take over Upper Burma, this is best brought out in the speech that the British Prime Minister made at the Lord Mayor's banquet on 9 November 1885. He stated that 'any operations which Her majesty's government might conduct against Burma "they would act with the most complete recognition of the rights of China so as to carry with them the assent and the friendship of China"'.[2]

According to the Sino-Burma Convention of 1886 China accepted under Article 2 of the Convention 'that, in all matters whatsoever appertaining to the authority and rule which England is now exercising in Burma, England shall be free to do whatever she deems fit and proper'. Article 3 of the Convention covered the provisions pertaining to a Delimitation Commission marking the frontier between Burma and China including the setting up of a Border Trade Convention with 'both countries agreeing to protect and encourage trade between China and Burma'. The frontier issue, came to the forefront during the annexation of Upper Burma that was carried out by the colonial authorities, the Chinese tried to get the British negotiators to accept the border at the Shweli River, they also tried to claim the areas, east of the Irrawaddy river including all the area that fell under the Kachin State leading up to the river port of Bhamo. The British were able to persuade the Chinese to drop these claims. However an interesting development during the negotiations was the British negotiators, at one stage, placing the offer of the Shan State area—east of the river Salween—on the table with the suggestion that this could go to the Chinese. Interestingly there was the overshadow of the happenings in Tibet at that time with a decision by the British to send a Tibet Mission under the Sino-British Chefoo Convention. To get the British to drop the idea and get their way on Tibet the Chinese dropped their claims to the northern regions including Bhamo. These, thus, came to be part of geographical Burma. They also did not take up the offer on the Shan areas east of the Salween, resulting in the Shan State and areas

[2] Woodman, *Making of Burma*, 252.

adjoining to it also becoming part of British Burma. There have been a number of subsequent critical references to this failure on the part of the Chinese negotiators of that time by Chinese historians.[3] The British were willing to scrap the Tibet Mission to get the agreement of the Chinese on Burma. This is reflected in Article 4 of the Convention that states that, 'In as much as enquiry into the circumstances by the Chinese Government has shown the existence of many obstacles to the Mission to Tibet provided for in the separate article to the Chefoo Agreement, England consents to countermand the Mission forthwith.'

The British efforts to demarcate the frontier between Burma and China were not successful this was only achieved by the U Nu government in 1960. It may be of interest to look at the Chinese approach to negotiating the settlement of the frontier issues with independent Burma and independent India. The British colonial authorities had negotiated the Indo-Tibetan border with Lhasa and the Tibetan authority had accepted the McMohan Line as the border with eastern India. Although the British Indian negotiators had involved the Chinese in the negotiations with the Tibetan negotiators in acknowledgement of the suzerainty of China over Tibet they continued to maintain their position on the border even when the Chinese refused to sign the border agreement. This position on the McMohan Line was maintained in negotiations between Delhi and Beijing even after the independence of India and the establishment of the Mao regime in the PRC. In the case of Burma the British negotiators held border de-limitation talks with the Chinese as provided for within the ambit of the Sino-British Convention on Burma. The negotiations however did not progress to the point of agreement. However once the GOB under U Nu came to the negotiating table adopting the position of not overly projecting its claims as those constituted by Colonial Burma, they were able to secure an agreement that was in keeping with the geographical limits that had been set for British Burma. The only area that remained outside the Sino-Burma Border Agreement of 1960 was the tri-junction between India, Tibet and Burma.

One element of the relations between England and China clearly represented the intent of the British to attach greater strategic importance to

[3] In his book *Sino-Burmese Frontier Problems*, Chang Ch'en Sun mentions that the Chinese Foreign Ministry lacked 'a clear-cut policy vis-à-vis the Burma question'.

Burma in contrast to the relations that they desired with Tibet. As long as the Russian Government accepted that Tibet would remain a buffer between its expansionist ambitions and the British Indian Empire and China remained a suzerain power without a major presence in Tibet, the British were willing to have a lower level presence in Tibet than what had originally been negotiated by Younghusband. Thus we have seen that in the bargain worked out over the frontier of Burma with China the relationship over Tibet was squarely placed within the acceptance of Chinese dominance even though at that time the Tibetans were successfully keeping the Chinese at arm's length. In the case of Burma the recognition was that it provided a land bridge to China to further Britain's trading interests covering trade with China from, India, Burma and of course from the UK itself. Bhamo, the port town close to the end of the navigable route up the Irrawaddy was a key factor in the trading arrangements that the British sought. It was also to ensure the trade routes that the troublesome Kachin used were pacified and subsequently in recognition of their considerable skills in guerrilla warfare Kachin soldiers were taken into the Burma security forces.

17

China–Myanmar
Relations: 1948–1988

Burma was the first country (non-Communist), to recognise the PRC in 1949 thus ignoring the prevailing Cold War imperatives that placed the Chinese revolution in enemy territory by the Western Powers led by the US. But Burma one of the founding members of the Non-Aligned Movement recognised the importance of maintaining good relations with its great neighbour irrespective of the ideology that it had adopted. In the 1950s and the early 1960s the relations between the two countries were good despite the fact that the Burma Communist Party received moral and material support from Mao's China. The relations during this period were defined as fraternal (Pauk Phaw), it was also a period that saw growth in trade relations between the two countries. However, the support that China continued to provide to the CPB and the ethnic groups that were supporting it, leading to an insurgency that challenged Burma's security and sovereignty continued to cause affront to the U Nu administration even leading to U Nu considering joining the USA promoted SEATO. As mentioned earlier he conveyed to Nehru his frustration with the CPB and its being backed by the CPC (Communist Party of China) creating a situation that might compel him to join SEATO; this led to Nehru taking up the matter with Zhou En Lai and a degree of pacification of the situation was secured. For China a friendly Rangoon was of importance as it permitted China to use it freely as a transit state for maintaining its contacts with countries in Asia, Africa and Latin America. These friendly relations continued initially with Ne Win after his take-over of Burma, at the same time the relations between the CPC and the insurgency led by the CPB continued to create tensions and gaps in understanding between the two countries. While this involvement did test the relations, two actions on the part of the Beijing projected a degree of support, that Ne Win could not ignore, as reflective of a friendly attitude on the part of the PRC; first was its endorsement of the nationalisation of the economy by Ne Win and its fallout, that of driving out most of the middle class from Burma even at the price of a large number of 'overseas Chinese' interests being hurt and a large migration of people of Chinese origin from Burma taking place. The second was the warning conveyed to Ne Win that a coup against him was being planned and was imminent enabling him to take counter measures that helped him strengthen and consolidate his position. Zhou En Lai visited Rangoon at this time and offered economic and strategic support to the Ne Win regime.

It was the development surrounding the Cultural Revolution in China and the involvement of the people of Chinese origin, more particularly in the Chinese education and cultural institutions in Burma, that persisted in their efforts to project Maoist ideology that led to differences between the Burmese and the local Chinese, who were seen as an extension of the Chinese Embassy promoted activities in Burma, that led to riots and violence against the people of Chinese origin. These developments led to a breakdown in relations and the violent reactions by the Burmese against the local Chinese population and China's official institutions including the Chinese Embassy in Rangoon being attacked; resulted in Ne Win being described as heading a 'facist dictatorship'.

The relations then took a distinct and sharp downturn with the PRC permitting the CPB leadership including Than Tun to take public positions from platforms within China, opposing the Ne Win government and calling on the people of Burma to work for its removal. At the same time China openly sided with the efforts of the CPB to invade the Shan State, out of its camps in China, with the assistance of the PLA forces. Material support was extended to the CPB and the allied ethnic group forces of the Wa and the Shan by Peking, creating a major hiatus in the relations between the two countries. As Ne Win's Revolutionary Council (RC) increased its 'repression' against the local Chinese and Chinese interests, trade and technical-cum-project assistance between the two countries came almost to a standstill.

The developments of 1967 also indicated that the PRC would take advantage of any opportunity to move away from relations of peace and friendship allegedly in keeping with the five principles of peaceful co-existence, whenever its actions or perceived interests were assumed to be questioned or threatened. At this moment in the relations, China who felt the ground slipping from under its feet as the split with the Soviet Union having surfaced and with the backing that the Soviets were extending to Ne Win and his style of governance, decided to change tack and grant greater tactical and material support to the CPB. To the Chinese the situation indicated that their interests in Burma would best be served by openly playing the CPB support card, especially as the CPB was now closely aligned with the ideology followed by the CPC and was thus opposed to the Soviet line, clearly placing it within the influence of Beijing. The Peking Review issue (no. 35, 5 August 1967) openly carried the claims of the CPB leadership that, 'with the PA base areas and guerrilla zones now established in two-thirds of the country, the CPB's military offensive was about to escalate to "final victory"'.[1] The 'PLA commanders and Red Guards in south-west China were helping the CPB cadres prepare Naw Seng's North-East Command (NEC) soon to launch its dramatic invasion of the Shan State from China on 1 January 1968'.[2]

The period of Chinese involvement with the NEC extended over the period 1967–1973 with the Chinese not only extending material support but also building up infrastructure like roads, bridges and hydel power plants to help the NEC to expand its control over the territory that was under its control. Interesting aspects of these events were the attempts by both Rangoon and Peking to maintain the fig leaf of normalcy by colluding to put across that the actions of violence and challenge to the GOB were internal actions developed by the CPB. Moreover by 1971 the government to government relations were gradually resumed between Peking and Rangoon. The support to the CPB's actions, more particularly those of its NEC command were now operationally confined to the Yunnan provincial administration and the PLA command in that area. Thus, enabling Peking to distance itself, to an extent, over the continuing physical support for the armed actions that the CPB and their allied

---

[1] Smith, Burma, quote by Ba Thein Tin (a CPB Leader), 226–227.
[2] Smith, Burma, 227.

ethnic groups were carrying out against the Tatmadaw. It is worth noting that the China backed operations were better equipped and were able to consistently score victories over the Tatmadaw—a situation that prevailed till China decided to scale down its direct support to the CPB.

The conditions created by the Maoist support for military actions was in keeping with Mao's belief in the use of force to safeguard China's interests irrespective of the military strength of the opponent. This was clearly indicated by China's involvement in the Korean War, and the involvement in the Vietnam War, in both cases Mao took on the might of the US armed forces. Peking also took on Moscow taking aggressive actions on the borders with the Soviet Union. Again the open support extended to the CPB's actions in Burma including the violation of Burma's borders by the PLA operating in support of the CPB were actions that were to put Rangoon on the defensive after the violence committed against overseas Chinese and their Burma-based interests. However in any pragmatic assessment made by Beijing the certainty of a CPB takeover of Rangoon had to be discarded as the CPB's efforts in southern Burma were consistently defeated. An imperative of Beijing's policy has remained that it did not want Rangoon to have a regime in control that would be effectively against China and its overall strategic interests in the region. Evidently China was conscious of the possibility that its actions could lead to the USA gaining a major foothold to work against China. It saw two major pluses in Ne Win, firstly that he was of Chinese origin on one side of his parentage and thus would not inherently be anti-Chinese and secondly that when he took over the reins of power and was able to conclude an agreement with Beijing on the settlement of the Sino-Burmese boundary, he had moved effectively against the KMT forces that had entrenched themselves in the Shan State area on the borders with the PRC. This was an important factor as the KMT forces as long as they were present in strength in Burma would continue to draw American support that posed a problem to the security of the PRC. Ne Win was also seen to be following the neutralist policy of keeping the super powers at bay and by adopting an essentially socialist economic policy and an isolationist policy that maintained that Burma could do very well without foreign influences or involvement in its economic policies, all of which posed no problem to China's strategic or security interests.

To strengthen the point that China has a tendency to assert its position across borders whenever it suits it, at times overtly, but more often covertly is brought out by recently released archival documents, where it is evident that leaders like zhou En Lai and Lin Piao in meetings with the KIO leaders worked openly to persuade them to join the military actions against the central authority in Burma. The whole attempt at this stage was to force Burma into the 'Maoist Chinese mould'. Not surprisingly this close support extended to the CPB, while sustained, led to its many successes posing a threat to the Ne Win regime, also resulted in a degree of dependence that ensured that the withdrawal of material support would lead to the collapse of the CPB's efforts, including a revolt of the ethnic groups that had been a major success element in the armed actions against the Tatmadaw.

The withdrawal of support confirmed that China's main imperative, which still remains as the fulcrum of China's Burma policy, is to prevent any regime that may be hostile to its interests gaining control in Rangoon. It was clear to the Beijing authorities that despite their support to the CPB there was little chance of its overthrowing the Ne Win regime particularly as the open collaboration between the CPB and the Chinese had resulted in a patriotic reaction that had resulted in a significant slow down in new recruits to the CPB. With the end of the Maoist period and its replacement by Deng and his emphasis on building China's economic strength the era of public support for the CPB came to an end (it was not lost on Deng that the CPB leadership had taken Mao's side when Deng was being pilloried) and by 1978 there was a clear two-pronged approach in operation while official relations came to be cordial a balance was created with every official acknowledgement of Rangoon being countered by managed events that continued to show a closeness of relations between the CPC and the CPB at leadership levels. Further Deng did not perceive Ne Win as hostile to China this being proven by the attitude that Ne Win displayed during his 1975 visit to Beijing when he 'expressed the hope that the differences between the two governments could be solved by 'patience, mutual understanding and accommodation'.[3]

Another compelling factor in Beijing's decision to reduce the impact of its support for the CPB was the consequence of the Soviet–PRC split that

---

[3] Working Peoples Daily, 13 November 1975.

led to its critical outburst over the CPB–CPC relationship and the claim that the friendship that Beijing claimed to have towards Rangoon was in direct contrast to its material and military support to the CPB's actions of violence and the violations of Burma's sovereignty by the involvement of the PLA that had sent across mixed nationality units that included ethnic groups of China across the border to fight the Burmese army.

A compelling feature of the warfare and insurgencies that prevailed over the areas east of the Salween covering the areas of the Shan State and the Karenni State was the intensive growth of the opium poppy and the trade in heroin including in the recent years of synthetic drugs and the involvement of not only the insurgent ethnic groups but of drug lords like Khun Sa and the armies that they developed for this purpose with links to the international drug cartels has been a major area of international concern. For the Myanmar Government these have also been areas of national concern as they have been sources of funding the insurgent armies. Eventually the leading drug lord Khun Sa surrendered to Yangon, a direct consequence of the SLORC–PRC relationship strengthening and the limited ceasefires with the ethnic groups surfaced under the efforts of Khin Nyunt. However the drug business continues to remain a powerful element in the eastern frontier states of Myanmar and although there has now been the inclusion of the commitment to the eradication of the drug production and distribution within the recently concluded 10 more comprehensive ceasefire agreements with the ethnic groups, it is still a matter of doubt that this shall happen because of the vested interests involved including the burgeoning presence of the Chinese drug mafia.

The early 1980s saw a change in the official attitude towards Burma by the Chinese Administration moving away from the ambivalent attitude that it had displayed towards Rangoon, with a joint border survey being undertaken and the resumption of more frequent official visits. In 1985 Ne Win was greeted by Deng Xiaoping as an 'old friend' with Ne Win mentioning that there were 'no problems between the two countries'. According to sources the Chinese decided in the early 1980s to pursue a policy that involved a concentrated economic and trade offensive aimed at Rangoon. It was aimed at interlinking the struggling economies of the Yunnan and Szchewan provinces of China to the Burmese economy by making Burma a major trade outlet for the produce of these outlying

Chinese provinces. Exchange of visits by officials from both sides took place to ensure that trade was regularised between the two countries. Not surprisingly it was the Governor of Yunnan who concluded the discussions on a successful basis and the relations between the two countries tended to establish the Yunnan Governor as the main interlocutor between the two countries. One of the aspects of the trade relations was that the Chinese did not distinguish between the legal and the black market trade, this was one way by which they could maintain a viable relationship with ethnic groups like the Kachins and the Shans both of whom had counterpart ethnicities on the Chinese side of the border. One instance of such a relationship was with the Kachin, for instance, who carried on a lucrative trade in jade with Hong Kong via China. The restoration of legal trade, on the Tatmadaw controlled trade routes, saw Yunnan draw up a list of 2000 items mainly from Burma's agricultural, mineral and forestry sectors in exchange for export from it to Burma of manufactured consumer items. According to Martin Smith the Chinese had also set up a 'highly effective economic intelligence gathering system in Burma, with agents in Lashio, Rangoon and Mandalay'. These were useful assets that it could draw upon when the events of 1988 took place with the fall of Ne Win and his BSPP and its replacement by the uniformed military GOM, the SLORC.

18

India–China–Myanmar Matrix: Post 1988

Before we arrive at the present very close and expanded relations between Beijing and Naypidaw it would be useful to contrast the Chinese and Indian approaches to the developments of 1988 leading up to the period concluding in the refusal of the SLORC to handover the reins of government to the elected representatives of the people in 1990. For China the developments of 1988 were responsible for creating an environment that it could exploit to bring Burma/Myanmar firmly within its sphere of influence. China had no hesitation in drawing close to the SLORC and showed a distinct lack of abhorrence for the gross acts of violence committed by it against its own people including rampant violation of human rights, which China itself practiced against its own people in the events of 1989. India on the other hand took an aggressive stance against the SLORC's actions of violence and human rights violations, with an open commitment in support of the students and the voices of democracy that Suu Kyi and her NLD represented. When the SLORC refused to honour its pledge to transfer power to the winners of the elections of 1990, there was a very critical stage that was reached in the relations with Burma/Myanmar, with the GOI refusing to have any meaningful dealings with the SLORC, despite the clear knowledge that the military regime had come to stay at least where the immediate future was concerned. India thus adopted a policy that came to treat the governing regime as a pariah and in the process ignored the gaps that this created in the relationship with an important neighbouring country with which India had sensitive land and maritime frontiers. This only helped China consolidate her position with a Myanmar that had come to be isolated by the international community, thus enabling Beijing to have a free run towards building a close relationship that included not only trade and defence elements but also a political relationship that helped Myanmar to overcome or meet all the criticism and sanctions that came to be practised against it. History shall judge the relevance of the severely negative position that India had practised in the period 1988–1991 in the context of what could have been more beneficial both to Myanmar and India if the former had an alternative to the overwhelming presence that China was building for itself, instead it could have developed a more balanced relationship that would have been positive in the context of both its two large neighbours.

Sino-Myanmar Developments: 1988

It would be important to place the Sino-Myanmar relationship, in the post-1988 period in perspective. China became the principle supporter of the military regime in Myanmar particularly in the period 1988–2010. During this period it helped a beleaguered military to arm itself with upgraded technology and arms equipment that would better enable it to defeat the insurgencies along its borders being carried out by the ethnic groups and also the armed forces of the main drug smuggling syndicates. The knowledge that the Chinese were now in bed with the SLORC/SPDC regime had an impact on the insurgents particularly in the eastern areas bordering China and Thailand (barring the Karen) leading to ceasefire agreements and the establishment of a loose arrangement that assured the ethnic group concerned with a degree of local autonomy and the retention of their arms. It would be relevant to mention that the PRC relationship, in this period, enabled Myanmar to withstand external political and economic pressure and permitted the military regime to carry out the political changes that it desired to bring about via a con-trolled constitution-making process. While the main actors within the international community condemned the process as unrepresentative of the wishes of the people which were clearly reposed in Suu Kyi and her party the NLD, who boycotted the constitution-making process, the military regime succeeded in putting a constitution together modelling it on constitutions that guaranteed a controlling role for the armed forces. The military regime obviously leveraged its relationship with the PRC to withstand international pressure that also to a limited extent included the ASEAN.

Understandably this period also saw the dominance of China both in the trade and investment areas as well in the supply of military hardware and technology. A further aspect of the relationship was the expanding presence in the north-western parts of Myanmar inclusive of Lashio and Mandalay by migrants from China. This important geographical area which has riches of natural resources and business is today almost a part of China and its Yunnan province. In Mandalay Mandarin is widely spoken and the Chinese currency is almost the currency of preference in commercial and consumer transactions.

Given these developments and the permanent need for any ruling authority in Myanmar to keep in mind the mischief potential that China possesses, which it is quite capable of letting loose if it feels that Myanmar is moving in relationship directions that could compromise its interests, the world has to accept the reality that China would continue to play a dominant role in the foreign and regional policy make-up that Naypidaw adopts. For China there is no question that Burma is an important element in its Southeast Asia and South Asia policies and holds an important strategic position in its Asia policy projections. While understandably there have been reservations on the part of Burma watchers, including in India, interestingly ASEAN had also developed reservations over the possibility that China may use Myanmar 'as a staging ground to project military power'. (Albeit that is a view that has come now to be tempered after the adoption of the 2008 Constitution and the subsequent reversion, in 2010–2011 to a nominally civilian rule.) This is culled out of the assessments that were made on Myanmar PM Soe Win's first visit to Beijing in February 2005. In that period among the original ASEAN six there was a feeling in favour of expelling Myanmar from the ASEAN, however, the fear of a strong negative action on the part of China prevented the evolution of a consensus.

It is also important to note that it was during the 2005 visit that Soe Win's Chinese counterpart for the first time expressed the desire that the SPDC government take steps to achieve 'national reconciliation' with Soe Win responding that they were committed to 'developing its (Myanmar's) national economy, maintaining stability and carrying out the seven step road map to build a modern and democratic country'. Than Shwe could not but be aware of the shift in the Chinese position that hitherto had confined itself to suggesting that Myanmar achieve reconciliation with the ethnic groups by now expanding their suggestion to that of stressing that the SPDC now aim for national reconciliation. The Chinese undoubtedly had become aware of the unease over Myanmar that was being felt by the key original members of the ASEAN and though they could not arrive at a consensus over expelling Myanmar the very fact that they were contemplating such a move was a worrying proposition for Beijing. China would have been concerned over any open criticism by the ASEAN states, a consequence of the lack of political progress in Myanmar, as further intensifying the international isolation of that country would also lead to a greater questioning of China's position on Myanmar by the international community.

They would have also have taken into account the moves that had been made to place the India–Myanmar relations on a more pragmatic footing that the Vajpayee-led NDA government in Delhi had already put into motion and which was being carried forward by the Manmohan Singh headed UPA government. Beijing was now, while continuing to maintain the position that the issues of governance and economic development were an internal matter and would be sorted out under the influence of acceptable political progression, also had made the suggestion that the stability and real economic development were in China's strategic interest thus encouraging Tan Shwe to undertake the political steps that could achieve these objectives.

One interesting mention made by Chen Dehai of the Chinese Embassy while briefing the Counsellor of the US Mission in Yangon, after the Soe Win visit to China in 2005 was that 'China does not consider India to be a competitor in Burma or in the region, declared Chen, saying China is actively seeking better relations with India'.[1]

Chen also mentioned that China acknowledged that besides the interest in maintaining stability on its border, China also sees Burma's energy resources and Andaman Sea ports as strategically important. He said

---

[1] One of the WIKILeaked cable.

Burma recognises this as well. According to quotes from the same cable referring to an assessment offered by a senior Singapore Embassy official was that,

> Strategically, China wants access to the ports on the Andaman Sea, not only for trade, but also as a possible staging ground and basing location for aircraft, warships and troops. If a road and railway were built alongside the pipeline it would allow China to base troops along the road and deliver supplies to Chinese naval vessels using Burmese west coast ports. Lim said this potential increase in China's ability to project power in the region is a key concern in Singapore's long-term strategic thinking.

The Strategic and Economic Partnership: Post 1988

The first phase of the partnership between China and Myanmar commenced in the immediate aftermath of the massacres of 1988 in Rangoon and of Tiananmen in 1989 in Beijing with both finding between them a common refrain against student unrest and the international condemnation of the officially sponsored brutalities committed against their own respective people. Myanmar's case was of course much worse as its nominal trade and low levels of assistance for economic and social development came to a halt. China stepped into the breach and there was a doubling of trade between the two countries in the period 1989–1995 rising from US$231 to US$841 by 1995. Parallel to this was the push into Myanmar of Chinese defence supplies at highly concessional rates of sophisticated arms systems valued at US$2.2 billion. This assistance to the armed forces also had a Pakistani content to it under the tutelage of China. In the latter part of the 1990s the Myanmar air force commenced to buy sophisticated aircraft to meet its demand for war craft, transport craft and helicopters, from Russia. It also made some forays into the arms supply markets of Malaysia and Singapore. This diversion of demand to other sources did not compromise the heavy dependence that it had come to maintain on China as Myanmar's main defence equipment supplier.

On the trade and investment areas China has continued to occupy a position of significant strength as a contributor. When the SLORC came to power in 1988 it consciously moved in the direction of adopting policies that laid emphasis on economic growth, however, neither they nor the succeeding SPDC made any effort to rectify the financial infrastructure including the extremely skewed currency that had been in place from the Ne Win period. China along with the ASEAN countries were the ones on which it came to depend to support its efforts at economic growth and investment in the development of infrastructure. China adopted the strategy of expanding its trade in goods and investment in developing capacity in areas of importance to China's interests. The areas of concentrated effort have been in the mining, energy (oil and natural gas) and hydropower sectors and the investment in infrastructure has been largely linked to the areas that have served China's strategic interests. Its main investments have been in developing roads, bridges, ports and communication systems that markedly serve the purpose of linking Myanmar to China's south-western provinces. In the current period the investments are placed at US$18.7 billion in 2010 with US$5 billion in hydropower, US$2.15 billion in the oil and gas sector and US$997 million in the mining sector, this only shows how intense the Chinese presence is in Myanmar's economic development. The current trade figures show that in 2011 the trade between the two countries soared by over 53 per cent reaching US$4.4 billion from US$2.88 billion in 2010. China presently enjoys almost a 40 per cent share of Myanmar's trade where the balance of trade is overwhelmingly in its favour.

In any understanding of the Sino-Myanmar involvement it would be essential to look at the important elements that have come to underscore a relationship that on the surface at least is asymmetrical but is definitely of mutual benefit to both sides. The strategic content revolves around the following basic elements:

- Myanmar's geographical location places it at an important crossroads that covers both South Asia and Southeast Asia with China serving as an apex. This is particularly important to any Chinese moves to establish an alternative strategic arrangement that brings in Myanmar, Thailand, Laos and Cambodia together in an alliance with it that effectively cuts out Vietnam and helps contain it. It also places India firmly within the South Asian region. It does not refuse India its strategic position that would continue to expand in Myanmar as a land bridge with Southeast

Asia and a possible easier land route to Yunnan. It also can become a useful tool in China's hand to control India's presence in Southeast Asia.

- Myanmar serves as an important outlet for China's efforts at promoting the economic position of its landlocked and economically constrained states of Yunnan and Sichuan to the South Asian, the ASEAN region and the Indian Ocean region for their trade items. Myanmar also provides the land link that China is utilising to corner the markets of the states of India's North-East for consumer goods and manufactures from its south-western land-locked states. Its effective policy since 1988–1989 has been to ensure that it established a dominant position as Myanmar's trade partner with the clear intention of exploiting the rich forest and natural resources furthered by the Sino-Myanmar BTA that was signed in 1988 and the payment arrangements for the defence supplies made by China to be set off against the forest and agri-cultural products, minerals and oil and gas deposits.

- Myanmar also serves China's strategic interest by providing it an outlet to the Indian Ocean via the Bay of Bengal thus fitting into its long-term designs of having a two-ocean presence. Further it also serves its overall strategic intent to contain India within the South Asian region. The Chinese presence in Myanmar, Sri Lanka and Pakistan where it has control over ports developed by it pro-vides China with the means to use these areas to not only keep a watch on India's naval foot print but to serve its design to become a global power in the 21st century with capabilities of preserv-ing her trade and supply lines, particularly those in the Indian Ocean Region that also cover its main supply lines for meeting its energy needs. While in the past there were assumptions that the Chinese had set up signals, intelligence posts as part of the control and information gathering on Myanmar's Coco Islands manned by expatriate Chinese. Apparently they set up the lis-tening posts, trained the Myanmar personnel and then moved away from them. This was understandable as they had by then succeeded in placing the requisite systems on board of Myanmar naval vessels that complimented what had been structured on the islands and now also provided them with an information sharing system on mobile platforms that gave them greater insight into all movements in the Bay of Bengal as well as the sensitive area of the Andaman Seas and the Malacca Straits.

- As part of its strategic design covering both the economic and the strategic areas to meet China's immediate and long-term trade and strategic projections the Chinese have taken steps over the years that would help integrate Myanmar, in economic and security terms with Kunming. As part of this design is the 'China Myanmar Transport Corridor' that connects the Yunnan province to ports in Myanmar, as part not only of China's 'Western Development' strategy to bridge the gap of economic disparities between China's eastern and western provinces, but also that helps the landlocked provinces of Yunnan and Sichuan to gain connectivity to the Indian Ocean region as well as make the distribution of goods from these provinces over a spread out market area that comprises of Myanmar, North-East India and the countries of the Mekong Basin. Similarly the oil and gas pipelines are part of the strategic design that concentrates on all infrastructure and trade in natural resources integrating Myanmar into a China-centric arrangement directed to ending up in Yunnan. The aid and loans being extended by China are similarly directed at a concentration on areas like hydropower that are set to the economic benefit of China's western provinces. Perhaps one of the most important strategic developments has been the arrangement that has permitted China to build up the river port infrastructure at Bhamo that is the northernmost port on the navigable part of the Irrawaddy River that also forms part of the network to advance the integration of Myanmar with western China and the overall strategic intent of China's 'two ocean' strategy. Ironically China has succeeded in its designs on Bhamo that were denied to it in the settlement that was arrived at with the British Colonial power in 1866–1867.
- As part of the assessment it is also important to make the point that China does not consider India to be a competitor in Burma or in the region, this has been mentioned in briefings made by Chinese officials and are part of the cables sent out by the US Embassy in Yangon that are part of the collection leaked out by wikileaks.

- China is aware of the changed circumstances that have occurred under President Thein Sein's reforms process that appear to convey a clear message that Myanmar is desirous of widening its economic relationships and in this regard a new foothold has been established by the USA and the EU that does circumscribe China's presence as the main provider of economic and technological expertise to Myanmar. In order to ensure that its strategic interests would not be compromised by the new developments a Comprehensive Strategic partnership that was inked during President Thein Sein's visit to Beijing at the end of May 2011 is now in place. The emphasis during the visit was on the development of a programme to enhance economic co-operation between the two countries on a 'better planned and coordinated' basis. The focus remaining on the 'areas of energy, transport and agriculture'. The Strategic Cooperative Partnership[2] envisages the two countries continuing to maintain the high-level contacts that have become a part of the exchanges particularly since 1989, and the building up of bilateral relations between the 'parliaments, governments, judicial departments and the political parties'. One development of note has been the establishment of co-operative relations between Myanmar's current ruling party the USDP and the CCP that was mentioned during the visit to China by the Secretary General of the USDP in the second half of May this year. The aim of the two parties is 'to make joint efforts for deeper

[2] Comment: The Joint Statement between China and Myanmar reached on 27 May 2011 agreed in principal to maintain high-level contacts between parliaments, governments, legislatures and political parties; to enhance economic and trade exchanges between the two countries to 'create a favorable environment for trade and investment cooperation'; to conduct co-operation in such areas as education, culture, science and technology, health, agriculture and tourism; to strengthen border management co-operation, conduct timely communication on border affairs; to further enhance coordination in the United Nations and other multilateral forums, jointly safeguarding the interests of developing countries. An interesting omission despite the use of the term 'comprehensive' for the partnership is the absence of any reference to the military aspects of the relationship. Considering that the military relationship certainly has a strategic dimension and there is a clear intent on the part of Beijing to utilize its relationship to establish its position in the Indian Ocean. This missing area in the Joint Statement can only be logically explained by the assumption that there is a document that defines the relationship that has been kept confidential and is not in the public domain.

bilateral ties in the coming years'. These developments point to the acceptance by both sides that despite the broadening of Myanmar's ties with the industrialised countries, including Japan (that has in the past been the largest aid giver to Burma/Myanmar), the geographical ties that bind China and Myanmar would not be significantly diluted and that China would continue to enjoy a close relationship that would continue to serve its strategic designs.

Any assessment of Myanmar's place in China's strategic interests in the post 2010–2012 period particularly after the reform process that has shown certain flexibility being adopted by President Thein Sein and his government, on issues of national reconciliation and economic policy that has opened the doors for the removal of sanctions and the arrival of the industrialised countries at the newly opened doors of Myanmar would have to look at the directions that the strategic partnership is likely to take in the changed environment that has now come into play. We need thus to examine the new political environment and what it means in particular for China and India keeping in mind that India has a major opportunity to widen its presence in Myanmar while there is every likelihood that expansive relations that China has enjoyed in the period 1988–2009 are likely to be constrained and a more realistic and balanced relationship is likely to emerge.

Analysis of China's Failure to Take a Changed Myanmar into Account

Any analysis of Sino-Myanmar relations in the wake of the developments post the establishment of the Thein Sein government in 2011 clearly points to China continuing to assume that the elections of 2010 did not forecast any major attitudinal change in the relations between the two countries. Beijing continued to hold to the line that the claim by the USA and the EU that the elections had been flawed and did not represent any change; as the person who symbolised the democratic movement, Suu Kyi, and her party the NLD had been prevented from fighting the elections, accordingly China assumed that the sanctions regime would continue to remain in place and Myanmar's dependence on China to meet her economic, security and international requirements would continue to remain as before. This resulted in a series of policy failures on the part of China arising out of its failure to assess the implications of the political directions that the new government had decided to adopt after its coming to power in March 2011. One interesting aspect was that China who had signed a number of strategic partnership agreements with countries like the USA and Russia and later with India in the 1990s, only came to sign a Comprehensive Strategic Cooperative Partnership Agreement with Myanmar as late as May 2011 when President Thein Sein paid a bilateral visit to China. This suggested that China had till then felt the closeness of her political and economic relationship with the military ruled Myanmar was not an imperative that required such a formal underpinning.

While China was looking at the relations with Myanmar as grounded in the role that it had come to play since 1988–1989, it failed to take account of the consequences to its relationship of the GOM's rapid moves towards political and economic reforms that indicated that there was a political sea change taking place in Myanmar, including the amending of the election law that permitted the NLD and Suu Kyi to enter electoral politics. The stabilising of the currency and the incentives for foreign investment were also steps that came to be recognised as acceptable changes that would permit an easing of the sanctions regime against Myanmar and the resumption of relations with the international community.

The political reforms brought an immediate and positive response from the West that led to an opening of the doors to an expansion of diplomatic and economic relations. Myanmar had arrived and did not have to remain dependent on China as the relations with the international community had turned positive for it. Myanmar had moved away from the pariah status that had limited its options in the past and more particularly since 1990. Beijing appeared to have misread the extent of real goodwill that it had come to enjoy since 1988 and in the process appeared to have come to a number of incorrect decisions and suppositions.

For instance it is worth examining the reasoning that led to the raising the relationship to a strategic partnership just ahead of the political arrangements that brought the West rolling into Myanmar, the first thing to strike was the expectation in China that the strategic partnership would raise the level of the relations to ones of a defining kinship. Chinese President Hu spelt out the four basic characteristics that defined the strategic relations:

1. Elevating bilateral relations and expanding exchanges and co-operation at all levels.
2. Strengthening mutual strategic support.
3. Deepening pragmatic co-operation.
4. Maintaining border stability.

The important new elements were in points 2 and 3 where point 2 seemed to imply a degree of reciprocal behaviour on the part of Myanmar to strategic involvements that further implied that Myanmar would have to accept certain developments that had a strategic component to China's actions aimed at realising its Indian Ocean Region ambitions. It would be reasonable to assume that China expects Myanmar to play its role as an ally, in its ambitious regional foreign policy plans and projections, keeping the ASEAN and more particularly the Mekong sub-region, as the target areas. There was the additional assumption on China's part that Myanmar would endorse China's two oceans policy where Myanmar's geographical location would come to play an important part. This projection could also include the possibility of Myanmar playing a role in China's India policy where it expected India to be contained as a regional power confined largely to South Asia.

Point 3 seems to imply that the economic relationship has to be mutually beneficial, it would thus assume that the incentive for China's involvement in the development of infrastructure has to have a commitment that it also meets China's requirements in keeping with the overall involvement that it has brought about in the linking of Myanmar's economy to the south-western states of China. More importantly it is also a reference to the land corridor arrangement that is planned for linking the Yunnan province to the Bay of Bengal and onwards to South and Southeast Asia.

What China had failed in was to keep a finger on the pulse of the people of the country, the people had come to see China as one that had extended support to the SLORC/SPDC regime, that had brutalised the people and deprived them of their democratic aspirations. Further they also saw that China had come to dominate the economic scene by its concentration on projects that mainly appeared to fit in with China's priorities with not much by way of meeting the economic needs of the common people, particularly the ethnic minority people of Myanmar. It was also apparent that the Chinese did not foresee the rapidity with which the GOM under Thein Sein moved and the immediate response that it got which has now provided them with a flexibility that can be used to broaden the reach of Myanmar's foreign policy and to have alternatives that would reduce the influence and dependence on China bringing it down to more acceptable levels.

Another aspect that has come to the surface was that Myanmar, had, at last moved away from being an embarrassment to the ASEAN and was now perceived as a more contributing partner. It had also placed its relations with India on a footing that made it more comfortable in regional terms and saw advantage for Myanmar's developmental goals by accepting that India was a partner that would not be intrusive in contrast to China's domineering attitude and intrusive demands in the bilateral relationship. The manner in which China had bullied its way on energy issues and the demands that it has come to make on the strategic partnership issues was seen as indicative of the fact that the Chinese leaders did not realise that the defence services had come to feel that their dependence on China was limiting their capability to secure peace and development considered necessary for Myanmar to restore its languishing economy to the competitive levels of its neighbours in keeping with the riches of its agricultural and natural resources and the establishment of a more broad based industry that would benefit from the energy surpluses that could help drive the industry to international competitive levels and attain for Myanmar an economic position of consequence in Asia.

19

President Thein Sein and the Changing Face of Myanmar

While there were great doubts over the direction in which Myanmar would progress under the very restrictive principles of governance which the 2008 Constitution had enshrined within it, ensuring that the mainly Burman Armed Forces would retain control over the future political directions of the country, including the feeling among the people that the new constitution would in all probability continue the brutal and dictatorial rule that the Tatmadaw had exercised since 1962, the reality has been striking, the new dispensation led by Thein Sein has changed the very system of functioning by adopting a policy position that has encouraged the international community to engage itself with the nominally civilian government elected under the aegis of that the 2008 Constitution. Myanmar certainly stands today on the threshold of great change, which if followed to its logical conclusion would bring the people and the country within the global mainstream. However, before arriving at any conclusion it is necessary to take the various factors that presently govern governance into account.

The 2008 Constitution in its present form places severe constraints on Myanmar's road to democracy. Official statements have made the point that the road to democracy is irreversible and perhaps there is a sincerity behind this claim. However the Constitution has barriers that would be difficult to overcome given the provisions that:

- Twenty-fice per cent of the seats in both houses of parliament are reserved for the armed forces; a similar proportion is reserved for them in the State and Regional legislatures. This is a provision that is in confirmation of the Basic Principles of the Constitution that at Article 6 (f) reads, 'enabling the Defence services to be able to participate in the National political leadership role of the State'.
- Under Article 17 (b) it is stated that, 'In the executive of the Union, Regions, States, Union Territory, self-administrated areas and districts, Defence Services personnel, nominated by the C-in-C of the Defence Services to undertake responsibilities of the defence, security, border administration, so forth, shall be included.' This provision is certainly an impediment to any real democratic process being put in place and would have to be deleted.
- Serving armed services personnel can also stand for election from the non-reserved seats. Given the circumstances even a nominal increase in the presence of armed forces personnel via this provision further strengthens the position of the Tatmadaw in controlling the political direction that Myanmar would undertake.
- Amendment to the Constitution requires a majority support that is more than 75 per cent of the votes of the members of both houses of parliament as well as a majority of the votes cast in a nationwide referendum. This provision automatically ensures that nothing can be achieved in this respect without the endorsement of the Tatmadaw, which grants irreversible control to the military hierarchy on any attempt to amend the Constitution.
- The Constitution grants immunity from prosecution to the military on any crimes committed by it. This guarantees immunity to people like Tan Shwe against any claims of their having committed crimes against the state and the people of the country.
- An additional constraining aspect of the system of governance that the 2008 Constitution has put in place lies in the provision establishing an 11 member National Defence and Security Council (NDSC) that is headed by the President and has both the C-in-C

and the Deputy-Commander-in-Chief of the Defence Services as its members, along with the Speakers of both houses of Parliament. Article 201 of the Constitution refers to its formation and makes the point 'led by the President, to enable it to discharge the duties assigned by the Constitution or any law...' The fact that the NDSC is placed within the Executive and for all practical purposes forms a super Cabinet grants it a wide ranging control over not only the decision making process of the Chief Executive but also to exercise control over the legislative process. The fact that the President and the Vice Presidents 'shall not be members of any Hluttaw (Parliament)' makes this body an overarching body.

- Another aspect that places a direct control over the election of the President and the Vice Presidents is that they are not to be elected directly by the people but by an Electoral College which is representative of the three elements in the composition of the legislative system that include those elected to the Parliament and an equal number representing the State and Regional representatives; those elected to the Parliament 'on the basis of township and population' and the group formed by the nominated defence services personnel to the legislative bodies. These three colleges would also be responsible for electing a Vice President by each one of them. Thus the Head of the Executive and his chief deputies while they are possessed of full executive powers are not in themselves members of Parliament and additionally have to take the representatives of the Defence Services along with them to govern the country.

- The Constitution reserves the defence, internal affairs and the border areas portfolios for the Tatmadaw to be headed by those who are nominated for the purpose by the C-in-C who is also designated as the Supreme Commander (covering all security forces including the police and the reserved forces), a post that should normally be the preserve of the President of the country. Furthermore to remove any semblance of active civilian control over the Tatmadaw the C-in-C is autonomous and with full control over promotions and disciplinary actions under the Tatmadaw leadership. The C-in-C has also been given the authority to assign military officers to the leading bodies of the self-administered areas.

Any assessment of what has happened under the reform process that President Thein Sein has put in place cannot ignore the fact that the opening of the door to democratic and economic reform has been made possible because of a dynamic that the defence services after Than Shwe's retirement have put in place. It is not only part of the famous 'seven step' process that the SPDC had adopted to bring in place a new constitution and a change in the power structure for governing the country, but was also apparently based on a 346 page document that evolved within the armed forces themselves. Described as a 'master plan' attributed to Lt Colonel Aung Kyaw Hla—a researcher at the Myanmar Defence Services Academy—it is allegedly the driving force behind the changes that have taken place after the 2008 Constitution was put in place and the Than Shwe-led SPDC ended its hold on power transferring it to the newly elected nominally civilian government headed by Thein Sein, the motivation behind the move being the desire to balance off the domination of China over Myanmar. According to this thesis the intent was not that the opposition led by Suu Kyi be enabled, by a changed approach, to eventually be involved within the governance system, but to utilise concessions to her and the democracy lobby to bring the USA back into a relationship that would help reduce Myanmar's dependence on China in the domestic, security and economic space. The idea behind this being that the US once it re-emerged as a player, having a strategic interest in Myanmar, would result in a more balanced presence of China in Myanmar. It is not an attempt to reduce the importance of China in Myanmar's scheme of things but to make for a more realistic relationship that enabled Myanmar to exercise all options open to it to improve the security and the soci-economic developmental environment.

The other aspect of the apparent return to the barracks, as it were, by the Tatmadaw, that should be taken into account, is the safeguarding of its 'dominant' political position, the overall preservation of its economic and social bases'. Commencing in the 1990s the Tatmadaw has established a strong economic base forming defence services backed corporations and small scale business operations funded by the regimental welfare organisations. It founded the Union of Myanmar Economic Holding Ltd (UMEH) that has managed a large number of enterprises and provided significant financial support to the defence services welfare organisations and funds. Its commercial ventures cover the production and marketing of gems, ownership of garment factories, wood and wood based industries, supermarkets, banking, hotels and tourism. The other large holding is the Myanmar Economic Corporation (MEC) that has within its ambit control over a multitude of economic enterprise areas that include industrial enterprises, trade in goods and services, exploration and extraction of oil and gas, the production and marketing of petroleum products, etc. This only goes to show that the Tatmadaw not only intends to maintain its political tentacles but also to continue to play its part as an economic entity with a commitment to utilise its economic resources to aid the social requirements of both the serving and the retired armed services personnel. This enables it to retain its position as an exclusive elite that because of its increasing economic and business clout ensures the continuing loyalty of armed services personnel, both retired and serving, and their families; all of whom form an expanding support and influence base in the governance of the country as an extremely significant stakeholder that could control all present and future actions by the governing polity of Myanmar.

The fact that in recent times Myanmar has given a head to the moderate approach adopted by President Thein Sein, that significantly amended the rules to permit the registration of the NLD as a political party under the 2008 Constitution, followed by the permission to Suu Kyi and her party to participate in a free and fair bye-election for 45 seats of which 43 were won by her and her representatives enabling her to become a participant in the governance process, was a development that granted substance to the political reform process that was launched by Thein Sein. These developments resulted in the international community viewing these developments as positive in intent, leading to the assumption that eventually a more flexible political approach would be adopted by the armed forces. These were also seen as an indication that Myanmar was taking steps to towards the eventual establishment of a democratic Myanmar, that would come to look at its relations with the rest of the world not only out of the prism held out to it by China. To this had to be added the entire agenda that Thein Sein adopted to meet the requirements of national reconciliation, the attempt to bring the ethnic groups into the security and political mainstream based on equality and the adherence, within acceptable limits, to the Panglong Spirit. Further the advances on the economic and social developmental fronts attracted positive support for Myanmar not only from the USA, the EU and Japan but also from its other neighbours particularly India and the ASEAN; it also resulted in attracting back the involvement of the international financial institutions.

While all these political and economic policy changes should be seen as favourable developments we have to also keep in mind that the aspect of the 'master plan' to 'crush the opposition' has not disappeared, the Constitution makes it clear that anyone who 'shall himself, one of the parents, the spouse, one of the legitimate children or their spouses owe allegiance to a foreign power or a citizen of a foreign country', cannot be qualified to become either the President or a Vice President of the country. This is a provision that is clearly directed at Aung San Suu Kyi who was married to a foreign national, and has two children who are foreign citizens. This provision in Article 59(f) of the Constitution prevents her from becoming the chief executive of the country, even if she and her party win the elections that are to be held in 2015. The military, for all practical purposes placed a seal on how the country was to be run and managed by ensuring that the military has the upper hand and through the emergency provisions that the C-in-C can exercise, under the Constitution, it can take over the country at any time that it feels its interests that it equates as the interests of the country, are likely to be compromised.

The other compelling factor and imperative that faces those looking at the new openings in Myanmar is the sustainability of the reforms process. It is apparent that for the present at least the moderates are holding the proverbial upper hand. The fact that the Tatmadaw appointed Vice President, General Tin Aung Myint Oo, a recognised hardliner 'resigned' on 1 July 2012 because of his differences over the political reforms is evidence that the C-in-C Hlaing has gone along with the reforms set out by Thein Sein. That it took over a month for the Tatmadaw to put in place his replacement was seen as indicative of the negotiations to allay the fears of the hardliners that had to be undertaken for them to agree on the nomination of the Navy Chief Admiral Nyan Tun, an alleged moderate, as the Vice President. This was obviously seen as a victory of the moderates, which would help the continuation of the reforms and the national reconciliation process. Another open secret is that both General Hlaing and the Speaker of the Parliament Shwe Man hold the ambition of replacing Thein Sein as the President. In any contest between them in the future, the armed forces Parliamentarians nominated by the C-in-C would play an important role in the nomination and selection of the next President assuming that the fight lies within the ambitions of these two important personalities. The main hurdles, confronting the political moves towards realising a functioning and preferably liberal democracy remain constitutional in nature and also the role that the defence services and their leaders would remain insistent on retaining, and the amount of control that they would be willing to resign from, to help dilute the present levels of control that the constitution extends to them.

Any examination or assessment of where the immediate future lies has to take into account that the defence services have to accept that the very logic that lies behind the moves that have been made so far to reform the political process in the direction of establishing a momentum in favour of a liberalising democracy and the move towards national reconciliation makes it desirable that the momentum continues. The co-operation of the defence services with the reform process is an imperative as while safe-guarding their individual and collective interests that has been achieved by the Constitution the military has to accept that deep amendments to the Constitution would have to be undertaken to remove the barriers to both national reconciliation and the achievement of a democratic polity that is free to govern the State once it wins an election. In many ways the true test of the sincerity of the moderate group and their capacity to deliver on democracy and a solution to the issues that continue to dog true peace and stability to the nation based on reconciling with the ethnic groups would come to a head in 2015 when fresh elections are scheduled to take place. The overwhelming support that the NLD and Suu Kyi secured in the by-elections is a pointer to the fact that if the elections in 2015 are free and fair, as was the case when the by-elections took place, then it is quite likely that she and her party would end up as the majority party in the next Parliament. What happens then; the present constitutional provisions, as we have mentioned earlier, would prevent her from being even considered as a Presidential or Vice Presidential candidate. The other fact being that the third of the electoral college could vote for a candidate that is acceptable to the C-in-C that could in itself create a confrontational situation. Another factor is the role of the NDSC which has powers granted to it under the constitution that appear to make it a supra governmental and decision making body outside the control of Parliament; that could, given the sensitivity that continues to prevail on issues of unity and governance, would in all probability continue to assert the primacy of the top positions in government being held only by a nominally civilian personality having direct links to the military and acceptable to it. Such an approach would set the cat among the pigeons that could result in the down scaling of the relations that have now been secured by Thein Sein with the USA, the EU and Japan. It would also belie the claim made by President Thein Sein and his political adviser Nay Zin Latt that the move to democracy is irreversible.

On the issue of the ethnic groups the situation remains volatile, the ceasefire arrangements with the 10 seem to be holding but the Shan State Army has gone on the offensive after entering into a ceasefire agreement, the battles with the Kachins also continue and what is most revealing is the open defiance of the President's orders to the army leadership that the armed offensive against the Kachins be placed on hold. Then there is the other aspect pertaining to the issue of the spirit of Panglong governing the national reconciliation process that has been indicated as a factor where the President has suggested a stepped approach to arriving at reconciliation. There are enough suggestions, that were endorsed also by an outgoing Myanmar Ambassador to New Delhi, that the Panglong spirit and the ensuing Agreement represented understandings with a limited number of ethnic groups, albeit important ones, implying that the 'spirit' was not representative and the process that they intended following would be more inclusive and would lead to a more realistic settlement. This is an approach that in itself could vitiate the atmosphere and lead to a strengthening of the distrust with which the ethnic groups view the attitude of the Burman majority.

Another issue that remains to be resolved is the suggestion that the armed forces of the ethnic groups be merged into the Border Guard Force that would be entirely under the command of the Myanmar military, this for obvious reasons is not acceptable to the ethnic groups. In fact this is in a sense a reversal of the position that had been adopted when the first four ceasefire agreements had been signed in 1989 with the four groups that formed the breakaway ethnic groups from the CPB after rebelling against it. The real advantage that accrued to these four groups was the provision that permitted them to retain fully armed forces that helped them in securing their position. Just as an example take the case of the Wa and the area that they control under the United Wa State armed force. The area is stable, has little or no interference from the side of the Burman military or administration. It has established a very lucrative drugs production and trading system. They are not just producing heroin but also have become a major manufacturer and distributor of methamphetamines and have developed close commercial arrangements with the Chinese mafia. A feature of the commercial activity of the Wa (incidentally the area that they control is on the border with China that they cross at will) is the arms trade that they have been conducting for instance with the ULFA, Naga and Manipuri insurgents on the Indian side. Considering the encouragement that they continue to receive from the Chinese side their dealings with Indian insurgents by providing equipment out of the war industry that they had been enabled to set up with the help of the PLA during the heyday of the support that was being extended by the latter to the CPB, is an indication of the closeness of the relations with the Chinese and an indication of the potential for mischief that remains inherent to the border areas which can be utilised by the Chinese whenever it suits their interests. It is also an indicator to the potential that this provides to the Chinese to keep an option open on their India policy to create further difficulties for India in the North-Eastern states, not only directly but through proxies. Apart from the Wa the other fully armed and supported ethnic group based in the Northern Shan State alongside the borders with China are the Kokang, who are now once again in revolt against the Myanmar Government and have taken up arms against the Myanmar Army, are also involved, with Chinese backing, in providing arms and ammunition to Indian insurgent groups that are largely based in the Naga areas of the Sagaing Division of Myanmar. Added to this activity are reports of arms released by China's PLA also finding their way into the areas in Myanmar where the Indian insurgent groups are based.

One area where the reform process launched by Thein Sein could proove successful and over time help moderate the problems facing Myanmar, on the political front, is the concentration on the opening up of the economy with the aim of 'tripling' the GDP and the steps that have been put in place to set the Myanmar economy to help set it on the road to achieving this goal. The opening up of the economy to make it more attractive to foreign and domestic investment is squarely placed on a developmental goal that concentrates efforts on socio-economic development. The direction of the concentration involves goals that help accelerate in job creation and opportunities that would benefit all ethnic groups and not just the Burman majority. This is part of the 'master plan' that in a sense augments the approach that the SLORC had tried to put in place as part of its attempt to unravel the damage to the economy that the Ne Win period (1962–1988) had brought about by its socialist and isolationist policies that had moved the country from a promising economic future to the UN mandated Least Developed Country Status.

The SLORC/SPDC economic policies however were severely hampered by the closing of doors to Myanmar by the international community, reducing its international contacts to the ASEAN, India and on a more dominant basis China. The factor of internal instability, the increasing isolation imposed by the Western Sanctions that also prevented a positive role on the economy being played by Japan, despite the interest that a number of entities including important western energy players like Total continued to display in exploiting Myanmar's oil and gas riches, prevented any real or major change on the economic and more importantly on the developmental side. The reforms policy that came to be adopted was linked to the political reforms that were put in place helped widen the investment basket and also brought greater focus of the relevant players in the international community to the areas of socio-economic development essential to the future of Myanmar as a part of the expanding Asian economies and their role as drivers of the global economy.

20

The Economic Future of Myanmar

In the scheme of things that place the present regime as serious contributor to developing the economy has been the reform of the financial space by aligning the currency to its real market values and the announcement that the State would no longer be hostage to Ne Win's penchant to demonetise the currency at will. To this were added the first step financial reforms permitting the establishment of banks including branches of foreign banks. These steps placed before the people of the country, incentives to increase savings to meet the needs of an expanding economy and as the economic opportunities create a larger and more affluent middle class this should also result in more investible capital becoming available for development.

One element of Thein Sein's approach to the domestic policy scene and his moves on both political and economic reforms was put forth by him as a continuation of the flow that Than Shwe and the SPDC had commenced, this appears to suggest that the steps are not unilateral to the so called 'moderates' but in reality part of the road that had been advocated by the 'Aung Kyaw Hla's master plan' which at its core suggests that economic development, that would have the involvement of the international community, would help stabilise the country and would help reduce the animus of the ethnic groups as their youth gain from the economic growth that would create jobs and investment opportunities.

Apparently even in the more limited opportunity base that the SLORC/SPDC had been able to put in place had led to the positive of a large number of the ethnic youth concentrating on moving ahead and placing greater emphasis on issues of education and economic opportunity keeping the political issues of reconciliation to be resolved on a long term goal basis. This led the military hierarchy recognising the importance of and as an essential part of the ceasefire process to concentrate on economic development and quality of life improvements.

It is evident that for all practical purposes the political system that has been established under the 2008 Constitution would require a substantial change to bring an acceptable degree of democracy that also satisfies all the main parties that effectively form the Presidential electoral college namely the ethnic groups, the defence services and the mainline electorate that represents to a very large extent the ethnic Burman majority. This would obviously have to involve the Karens who presently fall outside all of the above three categories as their territorial area has yet to be conceded on the ground.

It shall also mean that the defence services leadership would have to accept that the demands for a federal system and autonomy for the ethnic states does not pose a threat to the unity and sovereignty of Myanmar. Granting these demands of the ethnic groups would help reduce the long standing distrust that has governed relations with them, in fact progress in these areas would help bring the ethnic groups within the political, and socio-economic mainstream granting equality of opportunity and quality of life improvements leading to the stability of the country and by developing a secure environment attract the kind of investments that the country needs from domestic and external sources that would help Myanmar reach the kind of balance in her international relations that it now appears to desire, seeking to contain the dominance that China has achieved over the country's strategic, security and socio-economic environment.

All the steps that have been taken require the underpinnings of an extensive technical backstopping that Myanmar at present lacks and as such there is much that has been adopted that is difficult to implement as the institutional depth that this requires needs a considerable degree of capacity building. To clarify, the people of Myanmar, in the majority are subject to large scale impoverishment and vulnerability, the loosening of the authoritarian rule to which they have been subjected between 1962 and 2010, has created a new set of expectations, any failure to deliver, which seems likely because of serious institutional gaps, could lead to unrest and a possible reversal of the present moves towards liberalisation working in favour of policy prescriptions that the hardliners prefer.

The reforms that have been put in place, have been largely driven by internal considerations, but have also had behind them the desire to open up Myanmar to the Western countries, Japan and the international financial institutions that could have a stake in the future development of the country. The involvement of the international community, including a greater presence of ASEAN, Japan and India, in the socio-economic future that Myanmar has prepared for itself, has to be directed by a distinct commitment, both financial and institutional to assist in Myanmar's comprehensive socio-economic development.

A brief listing of the economic reforms measures that have been adopted by the Thein Sein regime that favour the opening up to the international community certainly suggest that the GOM is creating opportunities that would attract the kind of investment that would be greatly beneficial to the people of the country. The list contains the following important steps:

- The adoption of legislation permitting the formation of independent trade unions, the right to strike and a legislated provision for dispute settlement. The ILO convention on the Right to Association has thus been incorporated within the legal system.
- Acts that amend the commercial and tax laws have been adopted to make business more attractive including the granting of incentives that would attract investment in key developmental areas.
- The adoption of measures that cover areas relating to land management.
- Measures relating to the conservation of the environment.
- Measures that move the currency into a market related currency value system aligning it to market forces. The currency reform and the reform of the regulatory framework for investment have effectively removed some of the major barriers in the way of foreign investment including the flow of investments to the extremely important infrastructure sector of the economy. It has to be recognised that the present status of the socio-economic infrastructure area is in an exceptionally sorry state. The currency

at present follows a managed float system that places its value, for the present, at Kyat 820 to the dollar within a trading range of plus/minus 2 per cent. This float has been adopted in consultation with the International Monetary Fund.

What is also of significance is the fact that for the first time since 1962 the government is actually sincere in consulting with the people and has taken their will into account in two major foreign aided projects, the Mytisone Hydro-power project being built by a Chinese Company and a Thermal Power plant being built by a Thai company at Dawei, both of them having a considerable financial outlay, having their permission to build being withdrawn to meet the concerns of the local people allegedly on environmental grounds. This was an indication that GOM was willing to abide by the concerns of the people in making public and political policies that have the benefit to the people as their aim. It would here be worth pointing out that the Dam project had a largely Kachin negative on it who felt that they are not beneficiaries in the given scheme of things even where the projects being invested in were on their territory; however there is also the need that the Thein Sein government felt that it was essential at this stage that its actions should convey to Beijing that they could not take Myanmar for granted any longer and that the commercial benefits on investments had to be seen to be benefitting Myanmar to an extent had to be in the context of meeting the principals of equity and mutual benefit.

21

Of Burma's Past and Myanmar's Future

Myanmar has reached a stage that has the potential for it to attain its rightful place as a regional power of substance. It is worth recalling that Myanmar has the second largest population in the ASEAN and has largely unexploited riches in natural resources that makes it attractive both as a market and as an investment destination to major global economies. However the problems in the way of this being achieved, within a reasonable period of time require a complex of actions related to a substantive change to the fundamental provisions of the 2008 Constitution that would require large scale amendments amounting to its being rewritten; a pragmatic solution to meeting the demands and aspirations of the ethnic minorities, their empowerment and equality of treatment thus removing their distrust of the Bamar majority; an even handed approach to meeting the strategic and security needs of both China and India and a continuation of the open door economic policies.

The present situation where the progress towards democracy is one that continues to create doubts over the extent to which the Tatmadaw shall permit a liberal approach. As we have noted earlier there are important impediments in the way of real democracy coming to function under the present constitution. There are also major elements that come in the way of the persisting demands for real autonomy under federal arrangements that the ethnic majority feels absolutely necessary as that is the only way they feel that they can safeguard their rights. Under the present provisions of the constitution, as already illustrated, Aung San

Suu Kyi despite being the most popular leader and with a good chance of securing a majority of seats in the 2015 election cannot be appointed as President, or for that matter even a Vice President. This has already created tensions and her request to President Thein Sein that all parties concerned be invited to work out amendments to the 2008 Constitution did not receive a positive response. The 26 March 2014 speech to Parliament by Thein Sein however spelt out an in principal acknowledgement of the need for Constitutional reforms by stating that 'in order to meet democratic standards, the current content of the charter must be amended'. He went on to suggest that, 'I would urge you to do it softly and gently, depending on the experience, long sightedness and sincerity of all stake holders involved.' He made the point that if the amendments were based on such an approach 'it will not lead to deadlock'. On the subject of the present role and position assigned to the military under the Constitution the President stated that the 'army will retain a role in politics, making this point clear he said that 'the army still needs to be present at the political round table talks where political problems are solved by political means'. Commenting further he made the point that 'reducing the army's role gradually depends on internal peace and development as well as the maturity of the democracy'.

Keeping in mind that President Thein Sein is the moderate and liberal face of the armed forces and has carried out significant reforms to open the country and grant it a liberal projection has won him and Myanmar a degree of international endorsement, the steps that he has taken cannot be ignored in any assessment that is made on the future of Myanmar as a full democracy where the people and not the armed forces call the shots. It is worth recalling at this point that the 2015 elections shall be of great moment to the future of Myanmar. The four personalities who in a sense form and lead the political dialogue are President Thein Sein who may not be in contention, the Speaker of Parliament and Chairman of the ruling party the USDP Shwe Mann who has definite ambitions to replace Thein Sein as the next President, then there is Aung San Suu Kyi the leader of the NLD who is the most popular civilian leader who has an established position with the Bamar majority while retaining to a limited extent the trust of the ethnic minority and has the support of the West and in a practical way of India, and lastly there is the C-in-C of the Army Minh Aung Hlaing who retires next year and also has the ambition to move into the top executive job of Myanmar. These four between them hold the key to what should transpire between now and the elections of 2015 on the changes in the rules under the 2008 Constitution that would enable the people's wishes to prevail. What has been of interest has been that both Suu Kyi and Shwe Mann have jointly shown themselves as favouring the relevant changes to the constitution though they do not necessarily agree on the extent to which the changes should take place. They have held meetings at which they have arrived at a degree of understanding. However Suu Kyi has a much more advanced position on the constitutional changes. Suu Kyi has established a working arrangement with the 88 Generation Students Group's on the issues covering the amendment to the constitution where in a statement that she made in February 2014 she stated that she would work with them to demand reforms through 'people's power' demonstrations. The dog in the manger however remains the USDP that despite the understandings that have come to exist between Shwe mann and Suu Kyi appear to be reluctant to support far reaching changes to the constitution.

More important has been the position on constitutional amendments that have been reflected in a speech that Senior General Hlaing made on 27 March 2014 at the Armed Forces Day Parade at Ni Pyi Taw where he defined the role of the armed forces in safeguarding the constitution that he emphasised had been adopted by 92.48 per cent of the voters 'who cast their ballot in favour of the constitution during a referendum in 2008'. He in particular drew attention to the fact that the constitution could only be amended under Chapter 12 that required 'the prior approval of more that seventy-five per cent of the representatives of the Union Parliament'. This speech is an important reflection on the fact that the 25 per cent nominated armed forces members of the Union Parliament hold the key to any amendments taking place, thus placing a premium on the agreement of the armed forces and obviously of the Senior General on any amendments, or proposals to that effect, being adopted.

Reading Senior General Hlaing's comments along with those of President Thein Sein on the subject it is clear that Suu Kyi's bids for changes to Article 59(f) that in its current wording would prevent her from holding the highest office of State, is unlikely to be achieved under the present dispensation. The Myanmar Constitutional Review Committee, a 109 member parliamentary group, given the composition of the Parliament was dominated by the official ruling party—the USDP, tasked to examining potential amendments and changes to the 2008 Constitution, in its report suggested only one serious recommendation relating to 'greater devolution of authority to states and regions'. This is an effort, in principal, to meet a major and persistent demand of the ethnic groups for autonomy and a federal structure. Thie Committee, not surprisingly, suggested that no changes take place to Article 59(f). The implication being starkly clear, that the present Parliament where 80 per cent of the Members are from the USDP, does favour any amendment to Article 59(f). This also means that the growing unease with which Washington and the EU have come to feel over the stalling of further progress on the political reform process shall result in the remaining sanctions being persisted with. However the practical aspects of keeping engaged with Myanmar continue to prevail including the emphasis on the strategic aspects of the US policies towards China and the important geo-strategic presence of Myanmar in that context. There is therefore a muting of the West's concerns over the progressing of democracy in Myanmar and the need in that context for substantial amendments to the Constitution.

Interestingly there has been little thought that appears to have been given to the possibility that the forthcoming elections of 2015 may result in a decision where the NLD may attain the overall majority that would require a decision on who would take over as the President of the country. As the electoral college may still result in the job either going to the nominee of the armed forces or the possibility that there would be stalemate that would have to be resolved through understanding between the armed forces and the NLD that would leave Suu Kyi out and have instead a candidate who would have the endorsement of the armed forces. What could not be ruled out is the possibility that a hung political process could once again see the emergence of the army taking control of the country.

Understandably the two contenders who stand to gain from the present situation and its reflection on the 2015 elections could be Shwe Mann who has made known his intention of replacing Thein Sein as President in 2015 and the other is the unannounced contender the present Senior General Hlaing who on his retirement is said to have ambitions of becoming the next President. For both of them and for that matter for Thein Sein, who has so far not ruled himself out, having Suu Kyi as the winner of the 2015 elections but disqualified to be appointed President, is a beneficial factor that may only to an extent be questioned by the pro-Suu Kyi West who cannot prevent one of the above three from taking over the position of President. The assumption for 2015 is that Suu Kyi and her party shall do well and secure at least a working majority in the elections however even under the best case scenario this only grants her a simple majority that is not enough for her to carry out significant amendments under the new Parliament without the assistance of the representatives of the states controlled by the ethnic groups and of course the armed forces representatives. There is however one element that could play an important role in the whole issue of Suu Kyi and the Presidency, this is the somewhat remote possibility that the armed forces would bring the same pragmatism into play that they had shown when they had permitted her and her party to participate in the by-elections. Considering that the driving force behind this approach was undoubtedly the need to win the trust of the Western countries led by the Obama administration and the pragmatism that it had shown in the discussions that commenced quietly in 2009 with the SPDC and followed up on with the Thein Sein dispensation, the possibility that a via media shall be settled on that would in pragmatic terms remove the disqualification obstacle, cannot be entirely ruled out. A via media to this effect could be found by the group of 31 MPs who are considering the report of the 109 and could come up with a solution. The armed forces could take into account that the involvement of Washington in Myanmar is of strategic importance to Myanmar's interest in keeping a balance in its relationship with the PRC as they do not want China again to attain an overwhelming presence in Myanmar. They would also have to take into account that the removal of the remaining sanctions by the USA and the EU was dependent on the reform process continuing in the direction of removing the existing barriers in the way of full democracy. The 2015 elections in this sense have become a testing ground for the future reactions of the Western countries to Myanmar and its potential as a strategic partner in the Asia Pacific Game. One possibility that cannot be ruled out is for the military leadership taking into account the problems that the elections in 2015 could create may plug for postponing the elections for some time.

However, one fall out of the electoral victory of Suu Kyi and the NLD was the negative feelings that evolved within the USDP over the present system of Parliamentary elections of first by the post. Both the USDP, which reflected the views of the armed forces elite and surprisingly the ethnic groups, came to feel that it would be better to amend the electoral system by replacing it with proportionate representation. The feeling among these two being that proportionate representation would place a degree of restraint on a purely popular vote leading to an overwhelming mandate to a single party. The fear being that this could reduce the opposition to irrelevance. However one positive to emerge out of the negotiations over amending the provisions relating to the amendment of the constitution was the understanding among the Parliamentary panel of reducing the qualification for the amending of the constitution from the present 75 per cent to a lower figure that would help reduce to an extent the existing dominance of the armed forces over the amendment process. However, it should be pointed out that the present Parliament has an overwhelming presence of members belonging to the USDP and as such they would continue to control a dilution of the present provisions of the Constitution which grants them full control over what could be adopted in terms of Constitutional amendments. It is apparent that the armed forces would prefer the debate on amendments to remain within the confines of the present Parliament and that agreement is reached in such a way that the primacy of the armed forces is not diluted or changed in a manner that would reduce their hold on the future political, security and strategic directions that the country would pursue. This only goes to confirm the position adopted by many within the USDP that favour the postponement of the 2015 elections.

The thinking within the USDP and the military appears to be that with the move to proportionate representation there would be a balancing presence of the armed forces and the regional representatives within the ruling executive even if an amended Constitution results in Suu Kyi becoming the next President of the country with a Parliament that grants the NLD a majority control over the legislative processes. Taking such thinking into account that reflects the desire to contain or restrain the people's desire to extend Suu Kyi and the NLD its unstinting support; it is hardly a surprise that the Electoral Commission has postponed indefinitely the by-elections for the existing 35 vacancies in Parliament that were to go to the polls in December 2014.

It would also be appropriate to point that in November 2014, coinciding with the presence of global leaders, including the President of the

USA and the head of the EU Japan, China and India on account of the ASEAN Summit chaired by President Thein Sein with Myanmar playing host, there was renewed pressure in favour of political reforms that would remove the constraints on the people's will being fully expressed in a liberal and open democracy. There was a significant indication of this with the President of the USA endorsing the signature campaign organised by Suu Kyi conveying overwhelming popular support for the political reforms being carried out to their logical end. The fact that Thein Sein has also come out more positively on amending the offending provisions of the constitution, is a clear sign that the GOM and more particularly the armed forces feel that some compromise was essential to keep the West interested and more actively involved in the economic progress of Myanmar.

The other area that needs to be addressed urgently is reconciliation with the ethnic groups where the issue of the universal ceasefire still remains outside reach as differences remain, including over issues relating to the integration and control of the ethnic groups armed forces whom they would like to retain for their own protection. The federalism and autonomy issues also remain a major stumbling block as far as the peace process is concerned. Other issues that continue to dog the national reconciliation process are even basic elements like the failure to agree on the 'military code of conduct' and on the formation of a 'joint monitoring team' all of this being attributed by the ethnic negotiators to the reluctance on the part of the Union Peacekeeping Work Committee (UPWC) to discuss these issues, by placing the cart before the horse, by maintaining that all these vital issues, that are political in nature, be discussed after the universal ceasefire is in place.

The ethnic groups also have major issues over the insistence of the armed forces on the six points put forward by the C-in-C General Min Aung Hlaing that he insists the ethnic groups must commit themselves, to adhere to, for the national reconciliation to become a reality, these have been spelt out by General Hlaing as:

1. Genuine desire to achieve eternal peace.
2. To adhere to the signed agreement.
3. Not to take advantage of the peace agreement.
4. Not to be a burden to the people.

5. Adhere to the existing current laws.
6. Adhere to the 2008 Constitution and co-operate to drive for democracy.

While the first four principles, as outlined above are like motherhood and are probably acceptable the last two create problems as they fly in the face of the primary demands of the ethnic groups that require adherence to the original agreement, enshrined in the Panglong Agreement, of full autonomy and the functioning of a true federal system.

The reality is that the process of national reconciliation remains at a difficult cross roads and needs to be overcome on the basis of mutuality that is the only way to achieve peace. There is no doubt that while the peace process is underway, some of the ethnic armed forces have continued to build up their strength, a claim put forward by General Hlaing. He has also claimed that these forces are receiving material help from not only domestic forces but also external forces. As has been spelt out earlier the threat to the security of Myanmar, posed by the possibility of the differences between the ethnic groups and the Union of Myanmar, could and have been exploited, by external forces, remains a live issue and is one that can impact negatively on both the strategic stability of the region and the sovereignty of Myanmar. We have also shown the negative impact that this has on the security environment of India the problem created by the Indian insurgency forces has been exploited by the Pakistani ISI via Bangladesh in the recent past and continues to be exploited by the Chinese. It is therefore in the interest of the region as a whole that the national reconciliation process is successful enabling the establishment of complete control by the GOM over a vast and strategically important geographical area, along Myanmar's borders, that is the domain of the many estranged ethnic groups, but also helps to bring under effective control and reform the drug situation that continues to flourish in the ethnic group controlled areas.

As for the ethnic minority where there still remain problems of establishing a universal and effective ceasefire between their armed forces and the Tatmadaw enabling the pursuit of a political dialogue that while preserving the unity and the integrity of the country would grant a mutually acceptable degree of autonomy to the ethnic minority in governing of their own areas. The Thein Sein government is insistent on a comprehensive ceasefire that would then enable the national reconciliation process to go forward. It also means that in this sensitive area the present constitution shall have to be extensively amended to remove the overwhelming controls that the armed forces at present retain on the ethnic states. The complexity of the situation is projected by the prevailing situation where even after having signed a ceasefire the Southern Shan State Army, the Kokang Myanmar National Democratic Allaiance Army (MNDAA) and the Ta'ang National Liberation Army allegedly supported by the KIA continue to conduct operations as they feel that the agreements are being violated on the issue of autonomy and the right of the ethnics to retain their armed forces to safeguard their rights. All of this is a reflection of the fact that the trust deficit continues to prevail. The fact that the armed forces have continued to disregard the Thein Sein government's orders in the Kachin State has also contributed to the lack of trust in the word of the GOM.

While the ethnic groups might see some promise over their main demands on control over the governance of the states that the Myanmar Constitutional Joint Committee has proposed on the greater devolution of authority to the states and regions, they have still to gain an acceptable commitment over the issues of federalism and greater autonomy, as such the peace process as part of the national Reconciliation process remains contentious where the demands of the ethnic groups are still to be negotiated through a political dialogue. While any expectation that the peace process shall be a renewal of the original Panglong spirit in its absolute sense is impractical it is likely, however, once the consolidated political talks do commence, there may be substantial give on the part of Nay Pyi Daw on autonomy. However given the persistent opposition to a real federal system being maintained by the armed forces, who continue to feel that this would set the road to the unity of Myanmar being destroyed, this issue remains a festering sore in the relations with the ethnic groups.

Another issue that has to be taken into account is the increasing communal disharmony that has surfaced in the Myanmar of today. In the case of the Rakhine State that borders on Bangladesh there is the presence of the Rohingya community a 800,000 strong Muslim group considered by Myanmar to be illegal Bengali migrants and as such having no citizenship rights. The Rohingyas were taken note of in earlier British recordings where it was noted that the influx of 'Chittagonians' could well result in the original inhabitants of the Arakan being overtaken by them. However nothing was done to prevent the settling of the Bengalis in this area of Myanmar and it has over a period of time resulted in strong communal feelings with the Budhist Rakhines ensuring that they would not gain recognition as citizens of Myanmar. In the early nineties the SLORC in support of local sentiments forced out a large number of Rohingyas into Bangladesh leading to tensions among the neighbouring countries. Today it is pertinent to point out that the Rakhine have demonstrated their antagonism to the extent that in the current census undertaking the word Rohingya to describe the Arakan Muslim community is not included in the census questionnaire or in the ultimate conclusion of Myanmar citizenship. The Rakhine State has been a centre of communal disharmony leading to law and order issues where there has been resort to military actions and controls to keep a lid on the situation. However there is little doubt that the Rohingyas shall continue to be discriminated against and there shall be unrest in the sensitive Rakhine State where the intention is to drive the Rohingyas out of Myanmar. This is why there is persistence in describing them as Bengalis and to point them out as Bangladeshi migrants who as such cannot expect to have any rights in Myanmar.

The situation of the Rohingya Muslims where human rights issues have resulted in the involvement of the UNHCR and that of the international community and bilaterally of Bangladesh also, in pressurising the GOM to take appropriate actions to safeguard the interests of the Rohigyas by granting them the status of a minority ethnic community of Myanmar. This pressure has not resulted in the solution of the Rohingya problem and there is little sympathy shown by the GOM towards resolving the livelihood and human rights problems faced by the Rohingya.

The Buddhist antagonism against the Myanmar Muslims who are of Bamar origin has also been on the rise. The assumption among the more radical Burmans including some of the more militant monks, forming what has come to be known as the 969 campaign, remains that the Myanmar Muslims are expanding at an aggressive rate and could well come to attain a majority status overcoming the Buddhist numbers. One of the issues on this account has been the demand for marriage laws that would prevent marriages between Buddhist and non-Buddhists taking place without a prior permission being sought and given for that purpose.

There has also been violent action by the more militant Buddhists against the Muslim community that has been accused of practising large scale conversions including through the marriage route. One has to conclude that the disruptions in society that have led to such ethnic and religious discord can also be laid at the doors of socio-economic problems arising out of the prevailing gross poverty and restricted opportunities that face the people of Myanmar in general. The issues of ethnic and religious disharmony can only be resolved by the reforms in both the political and the economic areas leading to growth, the creation of jobs and business opportunities.

The Muslim issue now has reached a position that could well lead to overall security problems not only for Myanmar itself, but has the potential of spreading violence that poses a threat to the security of vital economic areas that cover projects within Myanmar undertaken by China and India. The issue is also of concern to the whole of Southeast Asia as pointed out by a former Secretary General of ASEAN (Surin Pitsuwan) who stated that these developments 'would have wider strategic and security implications for the region'. The problem has been complicated further by the fact that the Myanmar Parliament has before it four bills that in effect are an attack on religious freedom and women's rights. These laws are projected by the Organisation for the Protection of Race and Religion (Ma Ba Tha) as essential to protect Buddhism against the threat from Islam. The four proposed laws pertain to 'Buddhist Women's Marriage Bill; Religious Conversion Bill; Population Control Bill and a Monogamy Bill'. Of these four bills the more controversial are the Buddhist Women's Marriage Bill and the Population Control Bill. The first is the subject of great criticism among women and the second for its political and social implications as it is set to largely target the Muslim population of Myanmar who are considered to be growing at rates that are far in excess of the majority population. Another factor that without giving way to any exaggeration is that vested political interests are positioning themselves to exploit the growing anti-Muslim feelings, among the majority Burman population, for political gain driven by the desire to place barriers in the way of further democratisation of Myanmar. The possibility that cannot be ruled out is suggestive of the possibility that the contemplated religious and marriage laws could be utilised to develop further pressure in favour of preventing any amendment or dilution of the intent of Article 59(f) on the grounds of maintaining the primacy of the civilisational purity of Buddhism and its majority status within Myanmar.

It is worth pointing out that the anti-ethno sentiments directed against the Muslims and Islam have their roots in the colonial period. It was during this period that large scale immigration had taken place creating the feeling among the Burmans that their national identity was at stake. As mentioned earlier the nationalist sentiments that came in conflict with the colonial system and the movement to secure independence had also seen violent actions against Muslim and Hindu migrants. However, a factor that was also present in the thinking of the Burmans was that they were set against the domination of the Hindu business and land owning entities who were not not considered however as a pernicious group that was out to destroy the Burman's national identity, whereas the attitude towards the Muslims was severely antagonistic and has only come to gather greater resonance against the threat from Islam since independence. There is an obvious fallout of the anti-Muslim developments in Myanmar in countries like Malaysia and Indonesia where tensions have risen among Buddhists and Muslims including clashes between Myanmar Muslim and Buddhists in Malaysia. There have been similar events that have also taken place in Indonesia where a threat to the Myanmar Embassy was also reported. Even in India there have been repercussions of the Myanmar tensions reflected in an attack in Bodh Gaya by fundamentalist Muslims. There is substance to the apprehensions that violent reactions linked to the Muslim bashing in Myanmar could take place in Southeast Asia leading to negative pressures on the unity of ASEAN itself.

In many ways the external relations of Myanmar shall continue to rest on the poles of China and India as its great and immediate neighbouring powers that hold a significant capacity to contribute to the economy and institutional development of the country. They could also be the contributors to the unity and security of Myanmar by assisting it in securing a greater degree of involvement of the ethnic groups in the social and economic developmental processes that would bring them on par with their Burman counterparts. In the process both China and India could also ensure that the economic progress of their own frontier people along areas that border on Myanmar. The other important poles are the US and Japan that would grant greater economic and strategic depth to Myanmar and help it to overcome the present dominance of China both in the security and the economic areas. The fourth pole is ASEAN of which Myanmar is not only a member but is strategically located to act as a land bridge between South Asia and more particularly for India with the ASEAN region creating a much larger economic base that would enrich the region as a whole. The communications network that this development implies would cover both road and rail connectivity that would further also link India's North-East not only to the ASEAN region as a whole but also to the western and north-western regions of China. Keeping in mind its strong relationship, despite some of the current hiccups, China has worked on Myanmar to seek its co-operation on influencing ASEAN on China's thinking on regional multilateral issues and on the territorial disputes pertaining to the South China Sea area.

Both for India and China, Myanmar represents a strategic opportunity. For India the development of infrastructure and economic links for its north-eastern region with Myanmar and through Myanmar are of great strategic importance. The development and operationalisation of the Sitwe Port industrial development complex along with the operationalisation of the Kaladan Multi-modal Project would be of great significance to the development of India's north-east region as a whole. This and the adjoining areas of Myanmar, rich in hydrocarbons, add to the strategic interest that India has in Myanmar and the establishment of the requisite infrastructure would make an important contribution to meeting India's vast and growing energy needs.

China has similar interests in developing Myanmar as its strategic land link providing it with a corridor to its ambitions in the Indian Ocean region. To this has to be added the development in Yunnan of what is described as its 'bridgehead' interest, which is focused on developing further linkages between Yunnan and Myanmar as part of Beijing's long term interest of establishing itself in the Indian Ocean region. Further the oil and gas pipeline projects that not only deal with gas supplies from Myanmar but also provide China with the alternative of having energy supplies from the Gulf countries transit through the Myanmar pipeline reducing its dependence on the Malacca and Sunda Straits supply routes. For China the continuation of friendly and co-operative relations with Myanmar is thus of considerable strategic interest. Equally China would utilise its position to prevent the expanding Myanmar relations with the

USA to gain a strategic content that would contain China's regional and great power ambitions within the ambit of Washington's Asia-Pacific policy gambit.

One area that China has up its sleeves is the hold that it has on some of Myanmar's ethnic groups, in particular the Wa and the Kokang, that could lead to its creating problems for Myanmar's security whenever China felt that Nay Pyi Daw was working against its strategic, security or business interests. At the same time it has to be recognised that China has recognised, to some extent, that it had made serious mistakes in its relations with Myanmar. In the post-1988 period till the coming to power of the Thein Sein regime, China had taken full advantage of the exclusivity that both the SLORC and the SPDC governments had granted to China as they faced the isolation and multilateral actions that the Western powers had subjected Burma to. However China's mistake was to perceive that the USDP government would be a continuation of the armed forces rule, they did not expect that the opening of the doors to the democratic process and the positive reactions to the election of Suu Kyi and her party to Parliament, of the Western countries would present to Thein Sein and company an alternative to China's overwhelming presence, permitting the lowering of relations with China to a more realistic level. It also meant that China would have to move away from conducting its relations, particularly its economic and commercial relations with the ruling military elite to a broader range or people including the local people where it was carrying out infrastructure or investment activities. Further that it had to be more transparent and accountable in its business dealings including in the areas where it was exploiting Myanmar's natural resources. People's concerns and environmental issues also soon came to the fore and Beijing was unable to change course to meet the surfacing aspirations that the GOM was willing to accept as important considerations that would require amending or denying China its pursuit of important projects in Myanmar. This led to gaps in understanding and China has had to carry out a degree of course correction. All this however does not mean that Myanmar has reduced its overall dependence on China or that it could afford to ignore China's strategic interests.

Conclusion

To conclude it is clear that Myanmar and India have now reached a level of relationship which is realistic and pragmatic and keeps the mutual demands and requirements in mind. The exchanges between the President of Myanmar and the Prime Minister of India have covered all areas that would provide the necessary content to the relations where mutual benefit is a visible plus and enables Myanmar to draw on India's developmental achievements that fit into Myanmar's socio-economic developmental plans. Whatever may have been the hang ups of the events of 1988 and of the reversal of the election results of 1990 have now been subsumed into a relationship that is based on a sound foundation of bilateral understandings. The relations with Suu Kyi and the attempts at arriving at national reconciliation that would to an extent meet the demands of the ethnic groups is another positive that India is happy with. The understanding that Myanmar can draw on India's democratic institutions and experiences is another area that helps strengthen the relations between the two countries. The meeting between the Indian PM and Suu Kyi at the end of May 2012 has helped place India's democratic credentials in place and the reference to support for democracy in the Joint Statement should help close the chapter of a flawed relationship with the forces of democracy in Myanmar. One positive that should emerge out of the closer relations is the establishment of an informal understanding that officials and the political leadership on both sides should feel free to visit and engage each other without having to follow the rigidity of protocol. In a sense it would be desirable for the relations to revert to the easy informality that had governed the Nehru–U Nu relations in the 1948–1962 period not excluding the aberration of the two years interregnum when Ne Win headed a caretaker government in Rangoon.

China shall of course remain a major force in Myanmar's foreign and regional policy, but it shall have to accept that the relations would be moderated by the relations with other countries and the international community. The removal of sanctions and the return of the international financial institutions provide Myanmar with a new flexibility based on choices that a wider international presence provides. It also means that the isolation of Myanmar is at an end and implies that the security that China had provided to Myanmar in the face of international hostility that Myanmar had been subjected to in the post 1988 period, is no longer a requirement and Myanmar does not have to depend on its support for support to meet its international obligations.

Myanmar's geo-strategic position with China as a neighbour with its strategic ambitions could also see a new balance with the involvement of relations that are rapidly developing with the US. Myanmar would now have the ability to set off what China demands of it with what it can strive for with a US that has a clearly defined Asia Strategy. It is apparent that there is now a new dimension that has been added to Myanmar's role—both bilateral and regional—that places Myanmar in a position to evaluate its relations with China placing them away from dependence to a more pragmatic and realistic level.

Today's Myanmar remains a complex of issues that require careful handling and India as well as the international community has to give it time to adjust to the expectation levels on the issues of democracy, the reducing of the role to an appropriate level of the armed forces, the establishment of peace and understanding with the ethnic groups so that peace is established and the institutional backup that would bring social and economic development would enable security to the frontiers of Myanmar and would reduce the possibilities of external exploitation of the type that China threatens would be reduced to manageable levels.

Annexures

Annexure I

Ministry of External Affairs Annual Reports

Reference to bilateral relations with Myanmar subsequent to the events of 1988 and the 1999 elections.

The selected Annual Reports of the Ministry of External Affairs provide a clear idea of the manner in which relations between New Delhi and Yangon shifted from a position of opposition to co-operation. The period 1988–1992 was one of criticism and expressed concern; by the end of 1992 the Narasimha Rao government had commenced the move towards co-operation, but with a degree of support still being extended to the forces of democracy. With the coming of the NDA government and subsequent to that, it has been a move towards normal relations, leaving it to the international community and the ASEAN to deal with issues of human rights, democracy, etc.

Annual Report 1988–1989

Developments in Burma were a cause of concern. It was hoped that the situation will be resolved soon in accordance with the wishes of the people of Burma.

Annual Report 1989–1990

While maintaining a policy of strict non-interference in the internal affairs of Myanmar, India continued its principled support to the democratic aspirations of the people of Myanmar.

Annual Report 1990–1991

The first genuine elections held in Myanmar after almost 28 years resulted in an over-whelming verdict in favour of democratic forces. Despite this clear verdict, power has not been transferred to the elected representatives of her people. We hope this will be done soon, so that normalcy can return to the country facilitating the revival and strengthening of our bi-lateral relations with Myanmar and enabling her to play her rightful role in the comity of nations.

Annual Report 1991–1992

India views with regret that political power still remains to be transferred to the people's representatives after the general elections in Myanmar in May 1990. India is equally distressed at the continued house detention of Ms Aung San Suu Kyi. Despite its policy of non-interference in the affairs of other countries, India cannot ignore the democratic aspirations of the people of Myanmar and has, therefore, expressed her strong apprehensions about the lack of progress towards democracy and infringement of human rights in Myanmar. India hopes that the ruling government would release Ms Aung San Suu Kyi and pave the way for the introduction of the democratic processes of governance.

[India, both on her own through public statements and in concert with other like-minded nations through a resolution adopted at the Third Committee of the UN expressed concern about the absence of democracy and widespread infringement of human rights in Myanmar.]

[The President of India, while accepting the credentials of the new Myanmar Ambassador to India 'also praised the non-violent, Gandhian leadership of Ms Aung San Suu Kyi'. He went on to say that, 'India sincerely hopes that SLORC would take necessary steps, enabling the country to take up its rightful place among the community of nations.']

Annual Report 1992–1993

Despite some tentative steps taken by the Myanmar Government recently towards addressing the issue, Myanmar's suppression of the democratic movement continued to be a factor in India's relations with that country...India extended support to a UN Resolution on Myanmar calling for an early restoration of democracy and human rights and the immediate and unconditional release of all political prisoners, including Aung San Suu Kyi.

India watched with close attention the changes introduced by Gen Than Shwe...including the decision to convene a National Convention... to formulate a new Constitution for Myanmar.

With a view to move towards a better working relationship with the Myanmar Government, India received a delegation from Yangon, led by the Director General of the Myanmar Foreign Office in August 1992. Discussions held during the visit identified concrete areas for bilateral co-operation including border trade, prevention of narcotic trafficking and contacts between civilian and military authorities to prevent illegal activities, etc.

Comment: The nature and tone of India's approach to relations with the SLORC/SPDC governed Myanmar shows a distinct change from 1992 onwards. It is now a moving towards 'realpolitik' in which India follows a two track approach in which issues of world concern related to the people's democratic aspirations and the release of Suu Kyi is being left to actions being taken at the level of the UN system, while at the bilateral level, the public denunciation is slowly becoming muted, so as to smoothen the path to a relationship based on a pragmatic recognition of the ground realities.

Annual Report 1998–1999

Visits were also exchanged with Myanmar which enabled us to identify the directions of co-operation.

The Commerce Secretary led an inter-ministerial delegation... accompanied by a business delegation to Yangon to explore ways and means of expanding trade and economic linkages, by promoting cross border [trade and collaborative] projects in areas such as power, mining and oil & gas...

The sectoral level dialogue took place in January 1999, to discuss issues related to border management.

Annual Report 2000–2001

India continued to intensify co-operation with Myanmar, with focus on development of human resources and infrastructure.

India's bilateral relationship with Myanmar has come to be character-ised by frequent interaction at both at the political and the official levels. This trend continued with exchange of visits which served to provide direction and impetus to the relationship…

Annual Report 2008–2009

Relations with Myanmar continued to develop further during the period and became truly multifaceted…PM of Myanmar Thein Sein visited India for the BIMSTEC Summit in November 2008 and Vice President Hamid Ansari visited Myanmar from 5–8 February 2009.

Source: Taken from the Ministry of External Affairs official website: http://www. mea.gov.in

Annexure II

Trade and Project Assistance

Assistance both financial and project-related was extended to Burma/ Myanmar from the time it gained independence in 1948. Some of the key commitments are as follows:

1. The Commonwealth extended a loan of Sterling 6 million of which India's contribution was Sterling 1 million.
2. India extended defence assistance to Burma at Prime Minister U Nu's request and the arms so supplied helped beat back the insur-gents. This is referred to in U Nu's memoir *Saturday's Son*.
3. In 1950, India sold on concessional terms six Dakota Aircraft to help meet Burma's immediate transportation needs including in the area of defence.
4. In April 1954 India waived 50 per cent of Burma's outstanding liabilities that arose from the separation of Burma from India in 1937. Statement of the Finance Minister in the Indian Parliament.
5. March 1954: Indo-Burma Rice Agreement covering the period 1954–1956 during which 900,000 tonnes of rice was to be bought by India.
6. 1956: India extended a loan of ₹5 million to be set off against supply of Burmese rice to India. India continued to purchase rice

from Burma even when its needs were being met by American food assistance under PL 480.

7. 1957: India extended a loan of ₹300 million repayable in 24 half yearly instalments at a special interest rate of 4.1 per cent to help Burma tide over its economic difficulties.

8. 1969: India extended a credit of ₹4 crore with a balance of ₹11 crore to be secured through bank credits.[1] Based on credits extended by India, Burma had imported ₹5 crore worth of cotton textiles and yarn from India. The Burmese Government had taken the decision that, all things being equal, preference would be given to purchase of goods from India.

9. 1970: Ne Win during his visit to India concluded an Economic and Trade Agreement and a rice contract in which India agreed to buy 100,000 tonnes of rice that year. Again, it was not required, but it was done to help Burma out of its financial constraints.

10. 1974: India expanded its credit line to Burma to ₹7.5 crore, covering the purchase from India of cotton textiles and yarn, pharmaceuticals, chemicals and dyes and engineering goods. India was to buy rice products, pulses, fertilisers, animal feed, minerals, ores, hides and skins.

11. 1979: India extended financial assistance of ₹2.17 crore to enable the setting up of 21 small scale industries to help boost Myanmar/ Burma's manufacturing capacities.

12. Indo-Myanmar Border Trade Agreement signed in 1994 and came into operation in 1995.

13. 1995: First Indian Trade Exhibition.

[1] India being a capital shy state was in no position to match the terms, conditions or the extent of credits and loans that industrialised countries like Japan and West Germany were in a position to offer. It is worth noting that Ne Win's Myanmar/Burma had taken steps to curb its outside contacts and to reduce the level of its trade and economic contact, within this overall limitation the countries that had a degree of preference were Japan, West Germany and to a logically lower extent India. In this period India made it clear that it would like to have a close economic and trade relationship and was not overly concerned over balanced trade between the two countries, only in its overall expansion. In 1969 the Burma Government wanted India to extend a credit/loan of ₹15 crores at favourable terms. India was only able to offer ₹4 crores and suggested that the balance of ₹11 crores could be from specialized bank credit. In contrast, Japan had in the same year signed an investment agreement of US$80 million and with Bonn a US$35 million investment agreement was signed. The terms of these loans were very favourable for Burma: project capital at 3.5 per cent interest with a 25 year no-repayment clause and thereafter repayment also spread over 25 years.

14. November 1997: Second Indian Trade Exhibition where fifty Indian business entities participated displaying engineering goods, transport sector products, pharmaceuticals and chemicals, white goods etc. The Indian Minister of State for Commerce announced a US$10 million line of credit aimed at promoting Indian trade and economic co-operation with Myanmar.

15. 1999: US$2 million loan for setting up small-scale manufacturing units in areas that would boost industrial development. Industries set up under this loan covered an oxygen plant, an acetylene plant and an aluminium conductor plant.

16. 2000: Loan Agreement under which India extended US$15 million, part of which was utilised to set up a plant for the manufacture of cables, another to manufacture electric cables and a plant for the manufacture of sub-stations for power distribution.

17. A loan of US$25 million which was utilised in part to set up manufacturing units for the manufacture of bicycles, sewing machines and electric motors.

Source: Author's compilation.

Annexure III

Indo-Myanmar Trad e Relations

Table A3.1

Indo-Myanmar Trade Relations between 1997–1998 and 2008–2009

Date	(in US$ millions)		
	Exports	Imports	Total
1997–98	49.31	224.01	273.32
1998–99	30.12	173.76	203.88
1999–2000	34.10	171.59	205.69
2000–01	52.71	181.69	234.40
2001–02	60.89	374.43	435.32
2002–03	75.07	336.04	411.11
2003–04	89.64	409.01	498.65

Table A3.1 Continued

Table A3.1 Continued

Date	(in US$ millions)		
	Exports	Imports	Total
2004–05	113.19	405.91	519.11
2005–06	110.70	525.96	636.66
2006–07	139.95	781.93	921.87
2007–08	185.43	809.94	995.37
2008–09	221.64	928.97	1150.61
2009–10 (Apr–Jun)	44.50	254.62	

Source: Trade figures are based on official statistics of the Department of Commerce Export–Import Data Bank.

Imports from Myanmar mainly comprise of pulses, teak, other timber and maize. Exports to Myanmar comprise steel, pharmaceuticals, cement and fertiliser.

Indo-Myanmar border trade pact was launched on 12 April 1995 by India's Commerce Minister P. Chidambaram and Trade Minister of Myanmar Lt Gen Tun Kyi. The two countries have now decided to convert border trade into normal trade.

Source: Based on archives on trade statistics of the Ministry of Commerce http://www.commerce.nic.in.

Annexure IV

Indo-Myanmar Economic Co-operation

Aided Projects

To strengthen economic ties, India has taken steps to improve India's air, road and sea links with Myanmar. It is also worth mentioning that while government to government ties have grown and can be described as maintaining an upward trend in various project areas, investments from the private sector are yet to reach acceptable levels.

More recently, a number of positive developments have taken place in the areas of trade, investments, power, oil and gas, manufacturing and vocational training/education.

The two Indo-Myanmar Associations based in Yangon are:

- Indo-Myanmar Association (this is basically a cultural association);
- The Myanmar–India Chamber of Commerce (this has a large number of Indian Companies registered with it).

The signing of the following bilateral and multilateral arrangements should help expand India's trade and economic ties with Myanmar:

- 1999: Agreement on Science and Technology.
- 2003: Setting up of a joint trading committee (JTC).
- 2003: Agreement on the extension of a credit line of US$25 million with the intention of boosting India's exports.
- Agreement between the two Foreign Offices for regular consultations; visa agreement on visa exemption for Diplomatic and Official Passport holders.
- MOU on co-operation in Education.
- 2004: MOU on co-operation in the area of Railways.
- MOU on co-operation on the Tamanthi Hydro Electric Power Project.
- In 2005 and later in 2006 two MOUs were signed covering co-operation in the area of hydro-carbons/petroleum and energy.
- 2006: MOU on co-operation in Buddhist Studies.
- 2006 Framework agreement on mutual co-operation in the area of Remote Sensing.
- 2007: MOU to enhance IT skills in Myanmar and the setting up of a centre for this purpose.
- 2008: During the visit of the then Indian Minister of State for Commerce and Power Jairam Ramesh a number of important agreements/arrangements were signed between the two countries:

  1. Double Taxation Avoidance Treaty
  2. Bilateral Investment Promotion Agreement
  3. Agreement on banking services to be provided by the United Bank of India on the Indian side and by Myanmar Economic Bank to help facilitate border trade. The services extended by the two banks would help implement the Border Trade Agreement, such as by expanding the list of tradable items at

all the existing border trade crossing points, besides the ones to be added. Subsequently, in the meeting of the JTC it was agreed to convert border trade into 'normal trade' at all the crossings points, including the one to be added, Avankhu in Nagaland; the list of commodities were expanded from 22 to 40.

4. Agreement for the extension of a credit line worth US$64 million by the EXIM Bank of India to the Myanmar Foreign Trade Bank for the construction of three 230 kv transmission lines for power distribution in Myanmar.

5. A second agreement between these two banks for the extension of a fresh credit line worth US$20 million for setting up a manufacturing unit for aluminium conductors.

6. MOU: The National Hydroelectric POWER Corporation Ltd of India and Myanmar's Hydroelectric Power Department for the construction of the 1200 MW Tamanthi Hydro Power Project and the 600 MW Shwezaye Hydro Power Project.

7. Agreement between ONGC/GAIL and the Myanmar Oil and Gas Enterprise for three offshore blocks [costing] US$150 million. This was subsequent to the agreement signed by the visiting Indian Petroleum Minister for Exploration of Oil and Gas in Myanmar.

8. ESSAR Oil has signed two production-sharing contracts. This is the first private sector Indian company to enter the energy area in Myanmar. The Adani Group, which is a leading Indian infrastructure entity, is also reportedly negotiating an arrangement in the area for the distribution of gas at the consumption level.

Among the most important trade and projects areas where India is fully engaged are:

• Bay of Bengal Initiative for Multi-Sectoral, Technical and Economic Co-operation (BIMSTEC) (1997)
• Mekong–Ganga Co-operation (2000)
• India–Myanmar–Thailand Trilateral Highway Project
• Trans-Asian Railway

Annexures 213

Major Indian Projects in Myanmar

A number of projects were undertaken by India post 1992, once the relations were put on the road to a degree of normalcy. Given below is a representative list of these projects:

1. 160 km Tamu–Kalewa Road (completed);
2. Construction and upgradation of the Rhi to Tidim and Rhi to Falam Roads;
3. Grant of US$57 million for the upgrading the Yangon–Mandalay Railway Line and the Myanmar railway network;
4. US$20 million assistance for the renovation of the Thanlyin Refinery and;
5. Tha Htay Chaung Hydropower Project US$60 million.

Areas where Myanmar would like Indian Private Sector to Invest

- Pharmaceuticals
- Cement
- Steel
- Fertiliser
- Information Technology
- Food Processing
- Transportation: In this area India's largest indigenous automobile manufacturer TATA Motors has signed an agreement for the development of a truck manufacturing entity at Magwe to initially produce 1,000 trucks a year and eventually 5,000 trucks per annum; this is a joint venture with the Myanmar Automobile and Diesel Industries.
- Textile
- Mines based industry

Kaladan Multi-modal Transit Transport Project

This $110 million project was agreed upon during the visit of General Maung Aye to India in April 2008 and involves the re-construction of the Sitwe Port in the Rakhine province of Myanmar, the dredging of the Kaladan River from Sitwe to Setpyitpyin in the Chin State and the construction of a 65 km road from Setpyitpyin to the border district of Lawngtlai in the Indian State of Mizoram. On completion, it would provide a significant alternative route to India's North-East and lessen the headache of getting Bangladesh to grant transit facilities via Chittagong to India's North-East states.

The development of the Sitwe port is of vital importance to any Indian plan for the economic and social development of the Myanmar regions west of the Irrawaddy and the North-Eastern states of India; it would thus be in India's interest to extend incentives to Indian entrepreneurs who set up industries in this region and take advantage of its natural resources, as well as of the infrastructure being developed by India, which includes not only the Kaladan project but also other roads, a possible oil/gas pipeline, water transport and hydro-power [plant].

Source: Compilation based on official report on relations with Myanmar, http://www.mea.gov.in

Annexure V

Panglong Agreement

A conference having been held at Panglong, attended by certain Members of the Executive Council of the Governor of Burma, all Saohpas and representatives of the Shan States, the Kachin Hills and the Chin Hills, the members of the conference, believing that freedom will be more speedily achieved by the Shans, the Kachins and the Chins by their immediate co-operation with the Interim Burmese Government, have accordingly, and without dissentients, agreed as follows:

(I) A representative of the Hill peoples, selected by the Governor on the recommendation of representatives of the Supreme Council of the United Hill Peoples, shall be appointed a Counsellor to the Governor to deal with the Frontier Areas.

(II) The said Counsellor shall also be appointed a member of the Governor's Executive Council without portfolio, and the subject of Frontier Areas brought within the purview of the Executive Council by constitutional convention as in the case of Defence and External Affairs. The Counsellor for Frontier Areas shall be given executive authority by similar means.

(III)   The said Counsellor shall be assisted by two Deputy Counsellors representing races of which he is not a member. While the two Deputy Counsellors should deal in the first instance with the affairs of the respective areas and the Counsellor with all the remaining parts of the Frontier Areas, they should by Constitutional Convention act on the principle of joint responsibility.

(IV)   While the Counsellor in his capacity of Member of the Executive Council will be the only representative of the Frontier Areas on the Council, the Deputy Counsellor(s) shall be entitled to attend meetings of the Council when subjects pertaining to the Frontier Areas are discussed.

(V)   Though the Governor's Executive Council will be augmented as agreed above, it will not operate in respect of the Frontier Areas in any manner which would deprive any portion of these Areas of the autonomy which it now enjoys in internal administration. Full autonomy in internal administration for the Frontier Areas is accepted in principle.

(VI)   Though the question of demarcating and establishing a separate Kachin State within a Unified Burma is one which must be relegated for decision by the Constituent Assembly, it is agreed that such a State is desirable. As first step towards this end, the Counsellor for Frontier Areas and the Deputy Counsellors shall be consulted in the administration of such areas in the Myitkyina and the Bhamo District as are Part 2 Scheduled Areas under the Government of Burma Act of 1935.

(VII)   Citizens of the Frontier Areas shall enjoy rights and privileges which are regarded as fundamental in democratic countries.

(VIII)   The arrangements accepted in this Agreement are without prejudice to the financial autonomy now vested in the Federated Shan States.

(IX)   The arrangements accepted in this Agreement are without prejudice to the financial assistance which the Kachin Hills and the Chin Hills are entitled to receive from the revenues of Burma and the Executive Council will examine with the Frontier Areas Counsellor and Deputy Counsellor(s) the feasibility of adopting for the Kachin Hills and the Chin Hills financial arrangements similar to those between Burma and the Federated Shan States.

Signatories

Burmese Government:
Aung San

Kachin Committee:
Sinwa Naw, Myitkyina
Zaurip, Myitkyina
Dinra Tang, Myitkyina
Zau La, Bhamo
Zau Lawn, Bhamo
Labang Grong, Bhamo

Chin Committee:
Pu Hlur Hmung, Falam
Pu Thawng Za Khup, Tiddim
Pu Kio Mang, Haka

Shan Committee:
Saohpalong of Tawngpeng State.
Saohpalong of Yawnghwe State.
Saohpalong of North Hsenwi State.
Saohpalong of Laihka State.
Saohpalong of Mong Pawn State.
Saohpalong of Hsamonghkam State
Representative of Hsahtung Saohpalong. Hkun Pung
U Tin E
U Htun Myint
U Kya Bu
Hkun Saw
Sao Yape Hpa
Hkun Htee

Source: The Panglong Agreement has been taken from an image of the Agreement
    available at http://www.freekachin.org

Annexure VI

China in Myanmar: Hydropower Sector

China has developed a very strong presence in the hydropower sector in
Myanmar with this benefitting the two countries, as it helps narrow the
power deficit in Myanmar and also in terms of revenue derived from the

large scale evacuation of surplus power to Western China. The following are the investments being made by China:

1. There are 45 Chinese companies involved in 63 hydropower projects in Myanmar covering construction, generation and distribution of electric power.
2. The Tsang Dam on the Salween, which is projected to generate 7100 MW of power and to be linked to the Greater Mekong Power Grid.
3. The Hat Gyi Dam also on the Salween along the Thai border to generate 1200 MW of power.
4. MOUs have been signed with various Chinese companies for further hydropower development along the upper reaches of the Salween River for the generation of an additional 2400 MW, most of the power being generated would be exported to Thailand.
5. Hydropower generation projects on the Shweli river, they are three in number to generate 1420 MW power. The location is in the Shan State on the border with China.
6. In the Kachin State, the Chinese are involved in a number of dams, which are projected to generate 13360 MW of power, the bulk of the power generated would be exported to China. Of course as we are aware the largest of these, the Myitsone project, the permission to construct this has now been withdrawn.

The official Chinese position is that its investment in Myanmar's infrastructure is not only to mutual benefit but it ensures for it a continuing importance in Myanmar's present and future political, economic and foreign policy framework.

There were fairly serious demonstrations against power outages by people in the larger cities like Yangon, subsequently the Interior Ministry, reported that Myanmar plans to build more power plants in the country with companies from the US, Japan and South Korea. It was mentioned that the companies with which 'Myanmar's ministry of electric power will co-operate in building power plants are General Electric Co. and Caterpillar Co. of the US, J Power Co. of Japan and BKB Co. of South Korea.'

The report said a 600 MW coal-fired power plant near Yangon will be built on a joint venture with the Japanese firm, while another

500 MW gas-fired power plant shall be built in collaboration with the South Korean company. Currently, there are 18 hydropower, one coal-fired and 10 gas-fired power stations in Myanmar, which generate a maximum of 1,610 MW in the monsoon season and 1,340 MW in summer.

China and Myanmar: Oil and Natural Gas

Some 16 Chinese are reportedly involved in the exploitation of 21 onshore and offshore petroleum projects; of these the most significant are the Arakan blocs that include also the sale of the Shwe gas to China at highly favourable prices to China. The other major development has been the agreement between the two countries permitting China to construct two parallel pipelines for the transport of oil and gas traversing over 2000 kilometres across Myanmar from the Arakan State. The first is the gas pipeline that is to transport the Shwe gas to Kunming the capital of the Yunnan Province of China. The second would transport crude oil. The location is of considerable strategic importance for China as these pipelines would enable China not only to transport oil and gas to locations in China that it may secure in Myanmar itself, but also permit it to utilise a secure and alternative route to convey gas and oil supplies that it imports from the Gulf, and other locations. The setting up of the requisite terminal in the Arakan region is therefore a major security and strategic achievement.

Source: Author's compilation from various sources.

Annexure VII

Joint Statement on the occasion of the visit of Prime Minister of India Dr. Manmohan Singh to Myanmar

1. The Prime Minister of the Republic of India, Dr Manmohan Singh, is paying a State visit to the Republic of the Union of Myanmar from May 27 to 29, 2012 at the invitation of the President of the Republic of the Union of Myanmar, U Thein Sein. He is accompanied by his wife Shrimati Gursharan Kaur.

2. The Prime Minister was accorded a ceremonial welcome in Nay Pyi Taw and the President of Myanmar hosted a Banquet in his honour.

3. The visit of the Prime Minister the first after 25 years is a historic milestone in the relations between India and Myanmar.

4. The two leaders held a restricted meeting, followed by delegation level talks on bilateral, regional and international issues of mutual interest. The talks were held in a warm, cordial and constructive atmosphere reflecting the close and friendly relations between the two neighbouring countries and peoples.

5. During the official talks, the Prime Minister of India was assisted by the External Affairs Minister Shri S.M. Krishna, National Security Adviser Shri S. Menon, Principal Secretary to the Prime Minister Shri Pulok Chatterji, Foreign Secretary Shri Ranjan Mathai, Ambassador of India to Myanmar Dr V.S. Seshadri and other senior officials.

6. The President of Myanmar was assisted by U Wunna Maung Lwin, Union Minister for Foreign Affairs and other Union Ministers and the Myanmar Ambassador to India U Zin Zaw and Senior Government Officials.

7. The Prime Minister of India and the President of Myanmar comprehensively reviewed the multifaceted bilateral relationship and took stock of developments since the very successful State visit of President U Thein Sein to India in October 2011. They expressed satisfaction at the ongoing official exchanges and the growing economic, trade and cultural ties, as well as people-to-people exchanges.

8. The two leaders agreed on a vision for the future in the pursuit of the common good—bilaterally, regionally and globally. They agreed to co-operate in the areas such as border area development, transportation, connectivity, agriculture, trade and investment, promotion of friendly exchanges and human resource development. They recognized that peace and stability in the region is necessary for development and well-being of the people of their respective countries. In this context, they emphasized the importance of close co-operation between India and Myanmar and the need to effectively harness their respective resources for the good of the peoples of the two countries.

9. The Prime Minister of India congratulated the President of Myanmar on the path breaking reform measures taken by the Government of Myanmar towards greater democratisation and national reconciliation. He commended the on-going efforts at political, economic and social reform, which included negotiation of preliminary peace agreements with several ethnic groups as well as dialogue with various democratic political parties including the National League for Democracy led by Daw Aung San Suu Kyi. He also expressed appreciation for the free, fair and peaceful conduct of the recent by-elections.

10. The Prime Minister of India reiterated India's readiness to extend all necessary assistance in accelerating the country's democratic transition and developing the capacity of democratic institutions such as the Parliament, National Human Rights Commission and the Media. Recalling the very successful visit of a Parliamentary delegation led by Thura U Shwe Mann, Speaker of Pyithu Hluttaw, to India in December 2011, the Prime Minister conveyed India's readiness to undertake training programmes for Myanmar Parliamentarians and staff.

11. The following instruments for enhancing bilateral co-operation were signed during the visit:

    (i)   Memorandum of Understanding regarding US$500 million Line of Credit.
    (ii)   Air Services Agreement between India and Myanmar.
    (iii) Memorandum of Understanding on the India-Myanmar Border Area Development.
    (iv)   Memorandum of Understanding on Establishment of Joint Trade and Investment Forum.
    (v)   Memorandum of Understanding on the Establishment of the Advance Centre for Agriculture Research and Education (ACARE).
    (vi)   Memorandum of Understanding on Establishment of Rice Bio Park at the Department of Agricultural Research in Nay Pyi Taw.
    (vii) Memorandum of Understanding towards setting up of Myanmar Institute of Information Technology.
    (viii) Memorandum of Understanding on Cooperation between Dagon University and Calcutta University.

(ix) Memorandum of Understanding on Cooperation between Myanmar Institute of Strategic and International Studies and Indian Council of World Affairs.

(x) Agreement on Cooperation between Myanmar Institute of Strategic and International Studies and Institute for Defence Studies and Analysis.

(xi) Cultural Exchange Programme (2012–2015).

(xii) Memorandum of Understanding on establishing of Border Haats across the border between Myanmar and India.

12. The two leaders underscored that bilateral relations between India and Myanmar are rooted in shared history and geography, culture and civilization. Welcoming that the range and frequency of engagement between the two countries had intensified significantly since Myanmar's transition towards a more democratic form of Government in March 2011, they committed to further enhancing these exchanges so as to take bilateral co-operation to a higher level. The two leaders expressed satisfaction at the recent successful visits from Myanmar including that of the Foreign Minister of Myanmar U Wunna Maung Lwin in January 2012; the Minister of Construction of Myanmar U Khin Maung Myint in February 2012; and from India including the visit of the Minister for Water Resources and Parliamentary Affairs of India Mr P.K. Bansal to Myanmar in February 2012. The two sides agreed to continue with the frequent exchanges of visits at the leadership level.

13. Both leaders reaffirmed their shared commitment to fight the scourge of terrorism and insurgent activity in all its forms and manifestations. Both of them emphasized the need for enhanced co-operation between security forces and border guarding agencies for securing peace, security and stability in the border areas, which was crucial for overall development. In this context, the two leaders welcomed the holding of the first meeting of the bilateral Regional Border Committee whose deliberations were useful in promoting such co-operation and understanding for better border management. Both leaders reiterated the assurance that territories of either country would not be allowed to be used for activities inimical to the other, including for training, sanctuary

and other operations by terrorist and insurgent organisations and their operatives.

14. Both leaders also alluded to the importance of sound border management as an intrinsic part of maintaining border security. In this context, they directed that the respective Survey Departments should inspect and maintain boundary pillars in a systematic manner. They also directed the respective Heads of Survey Department to finalise dates for an early joint inspection of the sectors jointly identified at the 17th National Level Meeting.

Connectivity

15. The two leaders emphasised the importance of enhancing connectivity between the two countries as a means of promoting commercial, cultural, touristic and other exchanges between the peoples of the two countries. They expressed satisfaction at the steady progress being made on the Kaladan Multi-modal Transit Transport Project. They welcomed the finalisation of the site of the Land Customs Station at Zorinpui (Mizoram) following joint inspection by Indian and Myanmar delegations in April 2012. It was noted that the project would enhance bilateral trade, people to people contact and contribute to the development and prosperity of the people living in the 'land locked' North Eastern region of India.

16. The Prime Minister of India announced that India would undertake the task of repair/upgradation of 71 bridges on the Tamu-Kalewa friendship Road. The two leaders decided that India would undertake the upgradation of the Kalewa-Yargyi road segment to highway standard while Myanmar would undertake that of upgradation of the Yargyi-Monywa stretch to highway standard by 2016. This project would help in establishing trilateral connectivity from Moreh in India to Mae Sot in Thailand via Myanmar. The two leaders welcomed the revival of the Joint Task Force on the Trilateral Highway between India-Myanmar –Thailand. It was agreed that efforts would be made to establish seamless trilateral connectivity by 2016.

17. Taking into account the importance of enabling people-to-people contacts, the two sides agreed to launch a trans-border bus service from Imphal, India to Mandalay. The two leaders directed

the concerned officials from both sides to finalise all modalities to enable its early operationalisation.

18. They also welcomed the signing of the new Air Service agreement which would enhance direct air connectivity and facilitate easy business interaction, tourism and people-to people exchanges.

19. The two leaders decided to constitute a Joint Working Group to determine the technical and commercial feasibility of cross-border rail links and the commercial feasibility of direct shipping links between the two countries.

20. The two sides also discussed the possibility of Indian participation in development of key infrastructure projects, like Dawei port in Myanmar.

Development Co-operation

21. The two leaders expressed satisfaction at the growing dimension of development co-operation between the two countries which is being financed under grants and concessional loans amounting to US$ 1.2 billion till date. Taking stock of ongoing projects in the areas of infrastructure, agriculture, human resource development, industrial development, power, health etc., the two leaders agreed to identify more projects of benefit to the people of Myanmar in future.

22. Both leaders welcomed the signing of the MoU on the US$ 500 million Line of Credit extended by India to the Government of Myanmar which would pave the way for its early operationalisation. The Line of Credit will be utilised in the infrastructure development projects, including in the fields of Agriculture and Irrigation, Rail Transportation, and Electric Power in Myanmar.

23. Identifying the need for special focus on the development and prosperity of the people in bordering areas, the two leaders agreed to co-operate to bring about overall socio-economic development in the border areas by undertaking both infrastructure development and micro-economic projects, including upgradation of roads and construction of schools, health centres, bridges, agriculture and related training activities in the area in accordance with the MoU on India-Myanmar Border Area Development that was signed during the visit. The President of Myanmar also welcomed India's offer of assistance in production of large Cardamom in the Naga Self Administered zone.

24. Expressing their commitment to enhance co-operation in Science & Technology, the two leaders noted with satisfaction that the first meeting of the India-Myanmar Joint Working Group on Science and Technology was held on April 3, 2012. The Joint Working Group has identified some priority areas for future co-operation in the fields of agricultural biotechnology, post harvest technology, medical biotechnology, medical research and renewable energy. The two leaders welcomed these decisions and agreed that Myanmar would prepare specific proposals on some of its priority projects so that they can be taken forward for implementation.

25. Under a MoU signed during the visit, the two leaders decided to set up the Myanmar Institute of Information Technology with financial and technical assistance from India. The Indian Prime Minister announced continued technical and financial support for the India-Myanmar Centre for Enhancement of IT Skills in Yangon for a further 5 year period when it will also undergo a technology upgrade. The Indian Prime Minister announced a Fellowship for Myanmar Researchers to work in Indian Universities and Research Institutions, under which 10 slots would be allocated every year. Each Fellowship would be for 4–6 months duration in the areas of Atmospheric and Earth Sciences, Chemical Sciences, Engineering Sciences, Life Sciences, Medical Sciences, Mathematical and Computational Sciences and Physical Sciences.

26. The Prime Minister of India announced that in keeping with India's commitment to developing human resource capacity in Myanmar, the existing number of training slots for Myanmar, including under the Indian Technical and Economic Cooperation (ITEC) Programme, would be doubled from the current 250 to 500. The President of Myanmar welcomed this significant gesture.

27. The Myanmar President thanked the Indian side for its offer to train Myanmar diplomats in conference management and for the assistance in setting up language laboratories and conference rooms in Nay Pyi Taw and Yangon and e-research centre in Nay Pyi Taw for the Ministry of Foreign affairs.

28. The two sides also expressed their commitment to enhance co-operation in the area of Agriculture. The President of Myanmar

thanked India for the agricultural machinery that had been gifted to Myanmar under a grant of US$ 10 million and conveyed that the machinery had been distributed to various locations of Myanmar and is being used for the benefit of Myanmar's farming community. Under the MoU signed during the visit, the two leaders decided to establish the Advanced Centre for Agricultural Research and Education as a Centre for Excellence using cutting edge technology along with traditional knowledge and ecological conservation with financial and technical assistance from India. They also agreed to set up a Rice Bio Park within the Department of Agricultural Research, Yezin in Nay Pyi Taw in order to demonstrate available techniques of sustainable rice biomass utilisation. These two institutions together will provide technological and research inputs to the Myanmar farming, academic and business communities. The President of Myanmar also thanked the Prime Minister for India's support to the construction of a modern cyclone-proof rice silo within the Model Integrated Farm at Nay Pyi Taw.

29. The Myanmar side requested for India's assistance in arranging training programmes/fellowships in the areas of dairy development, cattle breeding, vaccine technology and assistance in setting up a milk and milk product factory in Shan State. The Indian side agreed to consider the proposal favourably.

Trade and Investment

30. Alluding to the mutually agreed target of doubling the bilateral trade by 2015, both leaders emphasized that there is considerable untapped potential for greater trade and urged the business community to capitalize on this potential. Investments by Indian companies in areas like ports, highways, oil & gas, plantation, manufacturing, hospitality and ICT would be specifically encouraged. In this context, the two leaders underscored the importance of the newly created Trade and Investment Forum in enabling timely and accurate exchange of information and ideas.

31. They assured that both Governments would work to identify and remove various impediments to bilateral trade. In this context, they welcomed the establishment of a representative office of the United Bank of India in Yangon as a first step in facilitating

business-friendly banking transactions between the two countries. The Myanmar side welcomed the proposals for the training of Myanmar officials in the Banking sector by Indian banks and for co-operation in the Agriculture Banking sector. Considering the vast potential for promoting trade between the two countries, both sides agreed that the Reserve Bank of India would sign an MoU with the Central Bank of Myanmar on currency arrangements between India and Myanmar in the near future. Further, the Reserve Bank of India would also conclude an MoU with the Central Bank of Myanmar to serve as a platform for an exchange of views on issues of mutual interest. The two sides agreed upon sharing of banking experiences and technical know-how from State Bank of India or any other bank as mutually agreed.

32. Both leaders urged the business community to enthusiastically participate in each other's trade fairs and also to share information on the prevailing trade and investment policies through organization of seminars and business related events in specific sectors of mutual interest. In this context, they welcomed the organization of the first Enterprise India Show in Yangon in November 2011 by CII and UMFCCI and the decision taken to make it an annual event.

33. Taking into account the needs of communities residing near the border, the two leaders welcomed the decision to set up border haats along the border and the MOU agreed for this purpose. They also noted that the decision to upgrade banking infrastructure at border trade points would also facilitate greater trade between people living in these areas.

34. The two leaders directed that a bilateral Border Trade Committee should be set up to implement the earlier decision that meetings would be held regularly between the border trade officials and businesspersons in Tamu-Moreh and Rhi-Zowkhathar.

Power and Energy

35. The two leaders emphasised the need for closer co-operation to further energy security. In this context, they welcomed the signing of the Production Sharing Contract between the Government of Myanmar and the Jubilant Energy of India. They encouraged investment by Indian companies in Myanmar oil and gas sector, including in available blocks that are being offered for investment which

have good prospects. They also agreed to encourage investment by Indian companies in downstream projects in the petroleum industry.

36. The Myanmar President expressed his appreciation to India for undertaking the preparation of Detailed Project Reports of the Tamanthi and Shwezaye hydropower projects. Both leaders directed their respective officials to study the contents of the DPRs and finalise the future course of action, taking into account technical, commercial and socio-environmental considerations.

Culture and People to People Exchanges

37. The two leaders emphasized the centrality of culture in further deepening the close bonds between the peoples of India and Myanmar and expressed satisfaction with the signature of the Cultural Exchange Programme (CEP) for the period 2012–2015. It was noted that the CEP would also promote cultural exchanges between the North Eastern States of India and the bordering areas of Myanmar.

38. They also welcomed the preparations that have been made towards organizing the International Conference on Buddhist Heritage in Myanmar in December 2012 with the co-operation of the Indian Council for Cultural Relations, Ministry of Religious Affairs of Myanmar and the Sitagu World Buddhist Association.

39. The Myanmar side thanked India for its decision to gift a 16 feet sand stone replica of the Sarnath Buddha later in the year that will be installed in the precincts of the Shwedagon Pagoda. A smaller replica will be unveiled by the Prime Minister during his visit. The Myanmar side also conveyed its appreciation to India for the facilities and courtesies being extended to Myanmar pilgrims visiting India.

40. The two leaders expressed satisfaction at the ongoing pace of work on the project for conservation and restoration of the Ananda Temple in Bagan, Myanmar by the Archaeological Survey of India which is expected to be completed over the next 2 years.

41. The two leaders also welcomed the formalization of contacts between Indian and Myanmar think tanks and academic institutions and urged scholars to participate actively and exchange views in academic events being held in either country.

42. The President of Myanmar welcomed the announcement made by the Prime Minister regarding the Government of India's support for setting up a school with technical assistance from India.

Regional and Multilateral

43. The two leaders discussed a broad range of regional and international issues of mutual interest. They agreed to continue their coordination on issues of common interest on the international agenda.

44. The two leaders emphasized the importance of close coordination towards the cause of regional co-operation. The Prime Minister of India extended his good wishes to Myanmar for a successful term as BIMSTEC Chair, including its proposal to host the next BIMSTEC Summit meeting. The two leaders looked forward to further intensification of ASEAN-India co-operation under Myanmar's chairmanship of ASEAN in 2014. The Prime Minister of India emphasised that Myanmar holds a significant place both in India's Look East Policy and in its collaboration with ASEAN countries under the Initiative for ASEAN Integration (IAI). The two leaders agreed to co-operate closely on activities related to the forthcoming ASEAN-India Commemorative Summit.

45. The Prime Minister of India thanked the President of Myanmar for the warm and gracious hospitality extended to him and the members of his delegation during their stay in Myanmar.

46. The Prime Minister invited the President of Myanmar to visit India on mutually convenient dates which will be decided through diplomatic channels. The President of Myanmar accepted the invitation

Source: Text is available at http://www.mea.gov.in, under bilateral statements.

Bibliography

Appadorai, A., *A Select Documents of India's Foreign Policy and Relations 1947–1972*. Vol. I. OUP, 1982.

————, *Select Documents on India's Foreign Policy and Relations, 1947–1972*, Vol. II. OUP, 1984.

————, *Domestic Roots of India's Foreign Policy*. OUP, 1971.

Appadorai, A. and M.S. Rajan, *India's Foreign Policy and Relations*. South Asian Publishers Private Ltd, 1985.

Asian News Digest, 1955–1999. Press Enclave, Saket, New Delhi.

Asian Recorder, 1950–1955. India International Library, New Delhi.

Aung Myoe, Maung, 'Building the Tatmadaw: The Organisational Development of the Armed Forces in Myanmar 1948–1998', Working Paper No. 327, Australian National University, 1998.

Aung-Thwin, Michael, 'Hierarchy and Order in Pre-Colonial Burma', *Journal of South East Asian Studies*, 16, no. 2 (1984): 224–232.

————, *Pagan: The Origin of Modern Burma*. Honolulu University Press, 1985.

Becka, Jan, *The National Liberation Movement in Burma during the Japanese Occupation (1941–1945)*. Vol. 42 of Dissertationes Orientales. Academia, 1983.

Bertil, Lintner, *Burma in Revolt Opium and Insurgency since 1948*. White Lotus, 1994.

Boucaud, Andre and Louis Boucaud, *Burma's Golden Triangle*. Asia 2000, 1992.

British Burma Gazetteer (Vol I and II), Government Printing Press. Rangoon, 1810.

Cady, John F., *A History of Modern Burma*. Cornell University Press, 1958.

Carey, Peter (ed.), *Burma: The Challenge of Change in a Divided Society*. Palgrave Macmillan, 1997.

Clifford, Hugh, *Further India*. White Lotus, 1990.

Crosthwaite, Charles, *The Pacification of Burma*. London, 1912.

Dixit, J.N., *My South Block Years: Memoirs of a Foreign Secretary*. UBS Publishers, 1996.

Donnison, F.S.V., *Burma*. Praeger, 1970.

Dutt, V.P., *India's Foreign Policy*. Vikas Publishing House, 1984.

Grare, Frederic and Amitabh Mattoo (ed.), *India and ASEAN: The Politics of India's Look East Policy*. Centre de Sciences Humaines, 1991.

Gravers, Mikael, *Nationalism as Political Paranoia in Burma: An Essay of the Historical Practice of Power*. Curzon Press, 1999.

Greenwood, Nicholas, *Shades of Gold and Green—Anecdotes of Colonial Burmah 1885–1948*. Asian Educational Services, 1998.

Gupta, S. *India and Regional Integration in Asia*. Asia, 1964.

Harrison, S.S., 'Troubled India and Her Neighbours', *Foreign Affairs*, January 1973.

Harvey, G.E., *British Rule in Burma 1824–1942*. Faber & Faber, 1946.

————, *History of Burma From the Earliest Times to March 10, 1824: The Beginning of the English Conquest*. Longman's Green and Co., 1925.

Heesterman, J.C. 'The "Hindu Frontier"', in *India and Indonesia*, ed. J.C. Heesterman et al. (pp. 1–16). University of Leyden, 1989.

J.S. Furnivall, *An Introduction to the Political Economy of Burma Peoples*, 3rd ed. Literature Committee and House, 1957.

————, *Colonial Policy and Practice: A Comparative Study of Burma and Netherlands and India*. Cambridge UP, 1948.

Karunakaran, K.P. (ed.), *Outside the Contest: A Study of Non-alignment and the Foreign Policies of Some Non-aligned Countries*. People's Publishing House, 1963.

Lintner, Bertil, *Blood Brothers: Crime, Business and Politics in Asia*. Silkworm Books, 2002.

————, *Land of Jade: A Journey through Insurgent Burma*. White Lotus, 1990.

————, *Outrage: Burma's Struggle for Democracy*. Hong Kong Review Publishing Co., 1994.

Longer, V., *The Defence and Foreign Policies of India*. Sterling Publishers, 1988.

Mahajani, Usha, *The Role of the Indian Minorities in Burma and Malaya*. Vora, 1950.

Malcom, Howard (Reverend), *Travels in Burmah, Chittagong and Arracan*. Fleet Street, 1839.

Mansingh, Surjit, *India's Search for Power: Indira Gandhi's Foreign Policy 1966–1982*. SAGE, 1984.

Maung, Maung U., *Burmese Nationalist Movements 1940–1948*. Kiscadale, 1989.

————, *From Sangha to Laity: Nationalist Movements in Burma 1920–1940*. Manohar, 1980.

Maung, Mya, *The Burma Road to Capitalism: Economic Growth Versus Democracy*. Praeger, 1998.

MEA Recorder and discussions.

Myint, Ni Ni, *Burma's Struggle Against British Imperialism*. The Universities Press, 1983.

Myint-U., Thant, *The Making of Modern Burma*. Cambridge, 2001.

————, Thant, *The River of Lost Footsteps: Histories of Burma*. Farrar, Straus and Giroux, 2006.

Nanda, B.R., *Indian Foreign Policy: The Nehru Years*. Vikas, 1976.

Nehru Archives Nehru Memorial

Nu, U Nu, *Saturday's Son*. Yale University Press, 1975.

Panikkar, K.M., *Future of South East Asia: An Indian View*. Macmillan, 1943.

————, *India and the Indian Ocean*. George Allen and Unwin, 1951.

Rajan, M.S. (ed.), *India's Foreign Relations during the Nehru Era: Some Studies*. Asia Publication House, 1976.

Rao, A. Narayan, *Indian Labour in Burma*. Keshari Press, 1944.

Ray, Nihar-Ranjan, *Sanskrit Buddhism in Burma*. Volume 9 of *Bibliotheca Orientalis: Burma*. Orchid Press, 1936.

Renard, Ronald D., *The Burmese Connection: Illegal Drugs & the Making of the Golden Triangle*. Lynne Rienner Publishers, 1996.

Sen, N.C., *A Peep into Burma Politics 1917–1941*. Kitabistan, 1945.

Silverstein, Josef, 'The Political Legacy of Aung San', Cornell Data Paper no. 86, 1972.

————, *Independent Burma at Forty Years: Six Assessments*. Cornell, 1989.

Singh, V.S., 'Recent Trends in Indo-Burmese Relations', *IDSA Journal*, October 1972.

————, *Burma and India 1948–1962: A Study in the Foreign Policies of Burma and India and Burma's Foreign Policy towards India*. Oxford and BH, 1979.

Smith, Martin. *Burma—Insurgency and the Politics of Ethnicity*, Zed Books Ltd., 1991.

Soe, Myint. *Burma File: A Question of Democracy.* India Research Press, 2003.

South, Ashley Mon, *Nationalism and Civil War in Burma.* Routledge, 2003.

Stienberg, David I., *The Future of Burma: Crisis and Choice in Myanmar.* University Press of America, 1990.

Sulistiyanto, P., *Thailand, Indonesia and Burma in Comparative Perspective.* Ashgate Publishing Ltd., 2002.

Sun, Chang Ch'en, *Sino-Burmese Frontier Problems.* Peking, 1937.

Suu Kyi, Aung San, *Freedom from Fear.* Penguin Books, 1991.

———, *Letters from Burma.* Penguin, 1995.

———, Aung San, *The Voice of Hope.* Penguin, 1997.

———, Aung San. *Burma and India: Some Aspects of Intellectual Life under Colonialism.* Allied Publishers, 1990.

Swe, Ba, *The Burmese Revolution.* Rangoon, 1952.

Taylor, Robert H., *Foreign and Domestic Consequences of the KMT Intervention in Burma.* Cornell, 1973.

———, *The State in Myanmar.* Foundation Books, 2009.

Turnell, Sean, 'The Chettiars in Burma'. http://www.econ.mq.edu.au/Econ_docs/research_papers2/2005_research_papers/chettiar.pdf

Tucker, Shelby, *Burma: The Curse of Independence.* Pluto Press, 2001.

Vohra, D.C., *India's Aid Diplomacy in the Third World.* Vikas, 1970.

Wintle, Justin, *The Perfect Hostage: A Life of Aung San Suu Kyi.* Hutchinson, 2007.

Woodman, Dorothy, *The Making of Burma.* Cresset Press, 1962.

Yang, Bo, *Golden Triangle Frontier and Wilderness.* Joint Publishing Co., 1987.

Index

About the Author

Preet Malik, a career diplomat, had served as the ambassador to Bahrain, Cuba and Myanmar and was the high commissioner to Singapore, Tanzania, Seychelles, Malaysia and Brunei.

In a career spanning decades, Preet Malik has held various national and global positions. He has served as the director, Ministry of Commerce, Government of India, and the Deputy Permanent Representative and Minister Extraordinary and Plenipotentiary to the Permanent Mission of India to the UN, New York. He was the Vice President of United Nations Economic and Social Council (ECOSOC). From 1992 to 1995, he was initially the Additional Secretary and then the Special Secretary (Economic Relations) in the Ministry of External Affairs, Government of India, where he headed the relations with SAARC and was involved in the definition and initiation of South Asian Free Trade Area (SAFTA).

Preet Malik has written extensively on Indian Foreign Policy and economic diplomacy in the *Financial Express* during the period 1995–2000. He has also contributed to the publication *Indian Foreign Policy Agenda for the 21st Century*.